Mono Record Collector's Handbook

By

Phil Rees, BSc BA PhD

Cumbria
England

Cranmore Publications

Reading
England

Copyright © 1999-2012 by Phil Rees

All rights reserved. This book, or parts thereof, may not
be reproduced in any form without permission.

A catalogue record for this book is available from the British Library

First Edition November 1999

Second Edition January 2002

Reprinted with minor amendments November 2003, January 2012

ISBN: 978-1-907962-59-2

Please note that this book is a companion to the original guide to stereo LPs
which has been in print for 20 years. It is called:

Audiophile Record Collector's Handbook

Table of Contents

Preface and Acknowledgements 2

Abbreviations 4

Columbia 33CX 7

Columbia 33C (10") 22

HMV ALP 25

HMV BLP (10") 40

HMV CLP 42

HMV DLP (10") 45

HMV COLH 47

HMV RLS 50

HMV XLP 51

HMV CSLP 54

Parlophone 55

Decca LXT 59

Decca LX (10") 76

Decca LW (10") 79

Decca BR (10") 85

Decca ACL 88

Decca Brunswick 95

Ace of Diamonds Grand Opera Series (GOM) 99

Lyrita 101

About the Author

I have a BSc degree (1st class) in mathematics from Manchester University and worked as a designer in the computer industry until the early 1990s.

I have been a record collector and/or dealer for many years. I became aware of the great sound quality of some of the early Deccas and RCA "shaded dogs" during the mid 80s. I then formed a collection including practically every worthwhile RCA shaded dog, Mercury, Decca SXL, Lyrita, EMI, etc. This collection was acquired by a process of swapping records with many internationally based fellow collectors.

Around 1989 I started selling records in my spare time, and in 1993 this became a full time activity. The business was joined by my wife, Jan, in 1994 and has since supplied many thousands of audiophile records to collectors all over the world, being generally regarded as the premier international source of quality English vinyl.

To keep my brain active I have been studying philosophy part time and was recently awarded a PhD from Reading University.

Preface and Acknowledgements

The Audiophile Record Collector's Handbook (ARCH) has been in print since 1991. It is aimed mainly at collectors of fine sounding analogue stereo LP records. In this sense it was responding to a worldwide interest in vinyl LPs from the standpoint of their great sound quality.

During the latter part of the 1990s the enormous interest in stereo records began to reduce from its almost obsessive levels and people began to take more interest in the mono recordings of the 1950s.

I am not ashamed to include myself in this. In a way it has been like returning to one's musical roots, replacing the concerns of audiophile stereo (image placement, depth, dynamic levels, etc) with the deeper concerns of true music making (artistic sincerity, emotional immediacy, etc).

It seems obvious that the same demand that made ARCH so popular also exists for the mono LPs. The basic requirement for any collector is to have full details of what there is to collect. I daresay that errors and omissions will be found, but the ALP, BLP, CLP, DLP, 33CX, 33C, and LX lists herein are pretty-well complete. I regard the LXT list as complete in the LXT2nnn series, but not complete for the LXT5nnn series. The ACL list is very comprehensive and close to complete.

With any list of monos there is always the problem of the transition to stereo that occurred for the most part around 1959-1961. The policy I have generally adopted is to avoid listing mono LPs where there is a stereo equivalent.

A word about photographs of record labels. ARCH included black and white photographs, but I no longer feel this is appropriate. To do full justice to the number of different labels and variations thereof one needs scores, if not hundreds, of photos, and they really do need to be in colour. This would greatly increase the price of this modest book.

I would like to thank my friend Tony Kind for his great help in producing these lists. Without his constant enthusiasm and encouragement most of these lists would have been seriously incomplete. I must also thank my friend Takashi Sakuma for his great help with the LXT list.

In the 1991 preface to the original issue of ARCH I wrote these words, and they remain appropriate now: As the 1990s unfold, LP production has come to a halt. It is fairly safe to say that no more worthwhile classical recordings will ever again be released on vinyl. Consequently, all the great analogue records are now **history**. Getting to know that history can be a most rewarding pastime and I commend it to all.

Phil Rees

Wiltshire, 1999

Preface to the second edition

The above is the preface to the original and first edition of this book which then had the different title: "Audiophile Record Collector's Handbook, Mono supplement". This second edition has grown so much that I no longer see it as a supplement but as a book in its own right, hence the change of title.

In the first edition I acknowledged the help of my friend Tony Kind. I here reiterate those thanks for the extraordinary amount of help he has given me. Without his work this new edition would not have appeared and he is, in effect, the joint author.

In addition to the correction of various errors, this edition aims to extend existing lists so that they may be as complete as possible, and also to include new series from the major companies already represented. I have also added extensive listings for the Parlophone, Brunswick, and Lyrita companies.

Introductory information has been added for each list, attempting to place each series in its historical context.

The coverage of the HMV catalogue is extended to include RLS, XLP, and CSLP.

Similarly the Decca catalogue is greatly improved by the enlarged listings of LXT, LW, LX, ACL as well as the inclusion of BR and GOM series.

I believe that the LXT series is now substantially complete and its usefulness has been enhanced by the addition of cross reference to corresponding SXL stereo issues.

The improvements made in this edition have resulted in complete or near complete listings for virtually all the labels included, though for good reason there is no claim for completeness for CLP, DLP, PMC, PMD listings.

With cross references to previous issues in the case of XLP and ACL being included for the first time, I believe this booklet is a very significant tool for the mono collector.

Phil Rees

Wiltshire, 2002

Abbreviations

AdSC	Accademia di Santa Cecilia Rome
ARCH	Audiophile Record Collector's Handbook (companion to this book)
BamSO	Bamberg Symphony Orchestra
BavSO	Bavarian Radio Symphony Orchestra
BBCSO	BBC Symphony Orchestra
BFCO	Bath Festival Chamber Orchestra
BNSO	Bournemouth Sinfonietta
Bolshoi	Bolshoi Theatre Orchestra
BPO	Berlin Philharmonic Orchestra
BRSO	Bavarian Radio Symphony Orchestra
BSO	Berlin Symphony Orchestra
CBSO	City of Birmingham Symphony Orchestra
Ccgbw	Amsterdam Concertgebouw Orchestra
CKC	Choir of Kings College Cambridge
Clvlnd	Cleveland Orchestra
CMI	Collegium Musicum Italicum
CSO	Chicago Symphony Orchestra
DSRO	Danish State Radio Orchestra
DrSt	Dresden Staatskapelle
EMCL	Early Music Consort of London
ENOC	English National Opera Company
FNRO	French National Radio Orchestra
Glynd	Glyndebourne
GSOpB	German State Opera Berlin
HO	Halle Orchestra
IPO	Israel Philharmonic Orchestra
LACO	Los Angeles Chamber Orchestra
LAPO	Los Angeles Philharmonic Orchestra
LBE	London Baroque Ensemble
LGO	Leipzig Gewandhaus Orchestra
LenPO	Leningrad Philharmonic Orch
LenSO	Leningrad Symphony Orch
LMP	London Mozart Players
LPO	London Philharmonic Orchestra
LSO	London Symphony Orchestra
LWS	London Wind Soloists

MCO	Moscow Chamber Orchestra
MFO	Menuhin Festival Orchestra
MMF	Maggio Musicale Fiorentino
MPO	Moscow Philharmonic Orchestra
MRSO	Moscow Radio Symphony Orchestra
NOS	National Orchestra of Spain
NSOL	New Symphony Orchestra of London
NYPO	New York Philharmonic Orchestra
NYPSO	Philharmonic Symphony Orchestra of New York
ONDF	Orchestre National de France
ODP	Orchestre de Paris
ONB	Orchestre National de Belgique
OROH	Orchestra of Rome Opera House
OSR	Orchestre de la Suisse Romande
OTNO	Orchestra of the Theatre National de l'Opera
PCO	Paris Conservatoire Orchestra
PO	Paris Opera
Phild	Philadelphia Orchestra
Philh	Philharmonia Orchestra (including New Philharmonia)
PJBE	Philip Jones Brass Ensemble
PTSO	Pittsburgh Symphony Orchestra
RCASO	RCA Victor Symphony Orchestra
RCAVO	RCA Victor Symphony Orchestra
RLPO	Royal Liverpool Philharmonic Orchestra
ROHCG	Orchestra of the Royal Opera House Covent Garden
RPO	Royal Philharmonic Orchestra
SCA	Salzburg Camerata Academica
SM	Salzburg Mozarteum
SOL	Sinfonia of London
StCO	Stuttgart Chamber Orchestra
StPh	Stuttgart Philharmonic Orchestra
USSR	USSR Symphony Orchestra
VdiR	Virtuosi di Roma
VME	Vienna Mozart Ensemble
VPO	Vienna Philharmonic Orchestra
WarPh	Warsaw Philharmonic Orchestra
WarSO	Warsaw Symphony Orchestra
WSO	Würtemberg Symphony Orchestra
ZIM	Zimbler Sinfonietta

Columbia 33CX

Columbia LP records were first released in October 1952 at the same time as their HMV ALP counterparts.

The early labels are dark blue with gold lettering with the word "COLUMBIA" in bold letters just above the spindle hole.

Later labels in the series are red and black with black lettering, similar in style to the second SAX label. The last number used was CX5279 in mid 1967 by which time stereo and mono editions were numbered in parallel in the SAX and CX series.

CX1001	Strauss,R: Don Juan Till Eulenspiegel	Philh	Karajan
CX1002	Balakirev: Symphony	Philh	Karajan
CX1003	Berlioz: Overtures Corsaire, Benvenuto, Beatrice, Francs Juges	Philh	Kletzki
CX1004	Beethoven: Symphony 5	VPO	Karajan
CX1005-6	Wagner: Die Walkure Act 3	Bayreuth	Karajan Varnay Rysanek etc
CX1007-9	Mozart: Marriage of Figaro	VPO	Karajan Schwarzkopf
CX1010	Beethoven: Piano Concerto 5	Philh	Karajan Gieseking
CX1011	Beethoven: Violin Concerto	Phild	Ormandy Francescatti
CX1012	Brahms: Piano Quartet in Gmin	Busch, Hermann Busch, Gottesmann, Serkin	
CX1013-5	Mozart: The Magic Flute	VPO	Karajan Seefried Dermota
CX1016-18	Bizet: Carmen	L'Opera Comique Cluytens Michel/Jobin	
CX1019	Berlioz: Harold in Italy	RPO	Beecham Primrose
CX1020	Castelnuovo-Tedesco: Guitar Concerto	New London Orch Sherman Segovia	
CX1021-5	Wagner: Die Meistersinger	Bayreuth 1951 Karajan	
CX1026	Tchaikovsky: Symphony 6	VPO	Karajan
CX1027	Brahms: Piano Concerto 2	Phild	Ormandy Serkin
CX1028	Haydn: Symphony 92	Clvlnd	Szell
	Symphony 101	Phild	Ormandy
CX1029	Ravel: Scheherazade, Mussorgsky: Songs & Dances of Death	Columbia SO Bernstein Jennie Tourel	
CX1030	Tchaikovsky: Romeo & Juliet, Francesca da Rimini	NYPO	Stokowski
CX1031	Mozart: Quintet in Dmaj, Quintet in Cmin	Budapest Quartet	
CX1032	Chopin: Waltzes		Lipatti
CX1033	Handel: Water Music, Tchaikovsky: Nutcracker	Philh	Karajan
CX1034	Mahler: Symphony 4	NYPO	Walter Halban
CX1035	Beethoven: Symphony 7	Philh	Karajan
CX1036	Dvorak: Symphony 8	NYPSO	Walter
CX1037	Tchaikovsky: Capriccio Italien, Bizet: Carmen Suite	Columbia SO Beecham	
CX1038	Mozart: Symphony 31, Haydn: Symphony 93	RPO	Beecham
CX1039	Schubert: Symphony 8, Beethoven: Symphony 8	RPO	Beecham
CX1040	Schubert: Songs (An die Musik,Gretchen am Spinnrade,etc)	Schwarzkopf Edwin Fischer	
CX1043	Beethoven: Trio Op 70/1, Fantasia Op 77, Piano Sonata Op 78	Adolf Busch, Hermann Busch, Serkin	
CX1044	Recital (Mozart, Schumann, Strauss, Schubert)	Schwarzkopf Moore	
CX1045	Schumann: Symphony 3	NYPO	Walter
CX1046	Beethoven: Symphony 3	Philh	Karajan
CX1047	Sibelius: Symphony 5, Finlandia	Philh	Karajan
CX1048	Brahms: Piano Concerto 1	Philh	Rieger Malcuzynski
CX1049	Prokofiev: Symphony 1, Falla: 3 Cornered Hat, Ravel Dukas	Philh	Markevitch
CX1050	Schumann: Quintet Op 44	Budapest Quartet Curzon	
CX1051-2	Lehar: The Merry Widow	Philh	Ackermann Schwarzkopf Gedda
CX1053	Brahms: Symphony 1	Philh	Karajan
CX1054	Bartok: Concerto for Orchestra	Philh	Karajan
CX1055	Beethoven: "Waldstein" and "Appassionata" Sonatas		Gieseking

CX1056-7	T.S. Eliot: Murder in the Cathedral		Robert Donat & Old Vic Company
CX1058-0	Bellini: I Puritani	La Scala	Serafin Callas Di Stefano
CX1061	Haydn: "Lark" and "Sunrise" Quartets		Budapest Quartet
CX1062	Beethoven: Symphony 6	RPO	Beecham
CX1063	A Garland for the Queen, Songs for mixed Voices		Cambridge Univ Madrigal Soc
CX1064	Franck: Symphony	ONDF	Cluytens
CX1065	Tchaikovsky: Sleeping Beauty, Swan Lake	Philh	Karajan [SAX2306]
CX1066	Chopin: Piano Concerto 2	Philh	Kletzki Malcuzynski
CX1067	Goldmark: Rustic Wedding Symphony	RPO	Beecham
CX1068	Mahler: Symphony 1	MIN	Mitropoulos
CX1069	Mozart: Operatic Arias	Philh	Pritchard Schwarzkopf
CX1070	Beethoven: Piano Concerto 5	Phild	Ormandy Serkin
CX1071	Mozart Violin Con K 216, Mendelssohn Violin Conc op 64	Phild	Ormandy Stern
CX1072	Brahms: Paganini Variations, Schumann: Etudes Symphoniques		Anda
CX1073	Beethoven: Pathetique & Moonlight sonatas		Gieseking
CX1074	Bach,J.S: Organ Music vol 1 (Cmaj, Amin, Gmin)		Schweitzer
CX1075	Cherubini: Requiem Mass	AdSC	Giulini
CX1076	Ravel: L'Heure Espagnole		L'Opera Comique Cluytens
CX1077	Beethoven: Symphony 5	NYPO	Walter
CX1078-9	Delius: A Mass of Life	RPO	Beecham
CX1080	Beethoven: Piano Concerto 3	Phild	Ormandy Arrau
CX1081	Bach: Chorale Preludes		Schweitzer
CX1082	Schubert: Symphony 8, Mozart: Symphony 41	NYPSO	Walter
CX1083	Stravinsky: Le Sacre du Printemps	NYPSO	Stravinsky
CX1084	Bach: Organ Music vol 3 (Cmaj, Dmaj, Dmin, Mendelssohn)		Schweitzer
CX1085	Sibelius: Symphony 1	RPO	Beecham
CX1086	Beethoven: Symphony 3	RPO	Beecham
CX1087	Rimsky-Korsakov: Le Coq D'Or, Franck: Le Chasseur Maudit	RPO	Beecham
CX1088	Mozart: Symphony 29, Eine Kleine Nachtmusik	Perpignan	Casals
CX1089	Mozart: Sinfonia Concertante	Perpignan	Casals Stern Primrose
CX1090	Mozart: Divertimento K251	Perpignan	Casals
CX1091	Mozart: Piano Concerto K271	Perpignan	Casals Hess
CX1092	Mozart: Piano Concerto K482	Perpignan	Casals Serkin
CX1093	Beethoven: Piano Sonata Op 5/2, 7 Variations, 12 Variations	Casals	Serkin
CX1094-5	Puccini: Tosca	La Scala	De Sabata Callas Gobbi
CX1096-7	Humperdinck: Hansel & Gretel	Philh	Karajan Schwarzkopf
CX1098	Debussy: Preludes book 1		Gieseking
CX1099	Ravel: Rapsodie Espagnole, Debussy: La Mer	Philh	Karajan
CX1100	Stravinsky: Circus Polka, Ebony Concerto, Fireworks, etc	NYPSO	Stravinsky Szigeti
CX1101	Boccherini: String Quartets Op 39/3, Op 58/3		Italian Quartet
CX1102	Mozart: String Quartets K387, K421		Italian Quartet
CX1103	Beethoven: String Quartet Op 130		Italian Quartet
CX1104	Haydn: Symphonies 94, 103	RPO	Beecham
CX1105	Mozart: Symphony 38, Handel: Faithful Shepherd Suite	RPO	Beecham
CX1106	Liszt: Piano Concerto 2, Piano Sonata	Philh	Susskind Malcuzynski
CX1107	Strauss,R: 4 Last Songs, Capriccio (Closing Scene)	Philh	Ackermann Schwarzkopf
CX1108	Bach,JS: Suites 1,2	Prades	Casals
CX1109	Bach,JS: Piano Concerto in Fmin	Prades	Casals Haskil
CX1110	Bach,J.S: Sonata 3 for Clavier & Viola Da Gamba, Chromatic Fantasia and Fugue, Italian Comcerto	Casals	Serkin
CX1111	Franck: Violin Sonata, Debussy: Violin Sonata	Francescatti	Casadesus
CX1112	Delius: Appalachia	RPO	Beecham
CX1113	Bach,J.S: Violin Concerto in Dmin Concerto for Clavier, Flute, Violin in Amin	Prades Prades	Casals Szigeti Casals Schneider Horszowski
CX1114-5	Lehar: The Land of Smiles	Philh	Ackermann Schwarzkopf
CX1116	Saint-Saens: Symphony 3	NYPO	Munch

CX1117	Beethoven: Symphony 3	NYPO	Walter
CX1118	Franck: Variations Symphoniques, D'Indy: Symphony on a French Mt Air	NYPO	Munch Casadesus
CX1119	Songs by Ravel and Poulenc	Pierre Bernac	
CX1120	Beethoven: Symphony 7	NYPO	Walter
CX1121-3	Bach,J.S: B Minor Mass	Karajan Schwarzkopf Gedda etc	
CX1124	Beethoven: Symphony 6	Philh	Karajan
CX1125	Sibelius: Symphony 4, Tapiola	Philh	Karajan
CX1126-7	Oscar Wilde: The Importance of Being Earnest	Gielgud Evans etc	
CX1128	Mozart: Piano Works Vol 1		Gieseking
CX1129	Wagner: Tannhauser Ov & Venusberg Music, Tristan & Isolde	Philh	Kletzki
CX1130	Recital of Operatic Arias by Nicolai Gedda	Philh	Galliera Gedda
CX1131-2	Donizetti: Lucia di Lammermoor	Florence	Serafin Callas Di Stefano Gobbi
CX1133	Tchaikovsky: Symphony 5	Philh	Karajan
CX1134	Ravel: Alborada del Gracioso, Daphnis & Chloe Suites 1&2	ONDF	Cluytens
CX1135	Prokofiev: Piano Concerto 3, Visions Fugitives, etc	ONDF	Cluytens Francois
CX1136	Beethoven: Symphony 1, Overtures Egmont, Leonora 3	Philh	Karajan
CX1137	Debussy: Images, Estampes Pour le Piano		Gieseking
CX1138	Chopin: Mazurkas 7, 15, 17, 20, 27, 32, 41 Polonaises 2,5,6		Malcuzynski
CX1139	Tchaikovsky: Symphony 4	Philh	Karajan
CX1140	Mozart: Horn Concertos 1-4	Philh	Karajan Brain
CX1141	Khachaturian: Violin Concerto	Philh	Goossens Igor Oistrakh
CX1142	Mozart: Piano Works Vol 2		Gieseking
CX1143	Rachmaninov: Piano Concerto 2, Preludes	Philh	Galliera Anda
CX1144	Beethoven: Piano Sonata 23, Brahms: Intermezzo Op 118/6, Bach, J.S: Chromatic Fantasia & Fugue		Malcuzynski
CX1145	Fauré: Requiem Mass	St Eustache Cluytens Duruflé (organ)	
CX1146-8	Handel: Messiah	RLPO	Sargent
CX1149	Debussy: "Shorter Piano Works"		Gieseking
CX1150-2	Offenbach: Tales of Hoffmann	Opera-Comique Cluytens	
CX1153	Bizet L'Arlesienne Sts 1, 2, La Jolie Fille de Perth Suite	ONRF	Cluytens
CX1154	Song recital (Schubert:,Faure,Chausson,etc)	Mattiwilda Dobbs Moore	
CX1155	Debussy: String Quartet, Milhaud: String Quartet 12	Italian Quartet	
CX1156	Tchaikovsky: Piano Concerto 1, Delibes: Coppelia	Philh	Galliera Anda
CX1157	Schubert: Rosamunde Ballet Excerpts	Philh	Kletzki
CX1158	St-Saens: Sym Poems Trials of Hercules, Danse Macabre, etc	Orch Des Concerts Colonne Forestier	
CX1159	Britten: Vns on Theme of Frank Bridge, V-Williams: Tallis	Philh	Karajan
CX1160	Mozart: Piano Sonatas K310, K280		Gieseking
CX1161	Rachmaninov: Piano Concerto 3	Philh	Kletzki Malcuzynski
CX1162	Wolf: Lieder Recital	Hotter	Moore
CX1163	Albinoni: Violin Concerto in D, Gabrieli, Marcello, Vivaldi	I Musici	
CX1164	Tchaikovsky: Serenade for Strings, Smetana: Bartered Bride	Philh	Kletzki
CX1165	Brahms: Violin Concerto	Philh	Kletzki Martzy
CX1166	Menotti: Amelia Al Ballo	La Scala	Sanzogno Panerai Carosio
CX1167	Borodin: Symphony 2, Ippolitov-Ivanov: Caucasian Sketches	Philh	Kletzki
CX1168	Beethoven: String Quartets Op 18/1, Op 18/2	Hungarian Quartet	
CX1170	Vivaldi: Concertos	I Musici	
CX1171	Cimarosa: 2 Flute Concertos, Paisello: Overture La Scuffiara, Scarlatti: Symphony 5, Concerto 3	Alessandro Scarlatti Orch	
CX1172	Beethoven: String Quartets op 18/3-4	Hungarian Quartet	
CX1173	Bizet: Symphony in C, Overture "Patrie"	ONDF	Cluytens
CX1174	Mendelssohn: Midsummer Nights Dream	Philh	Kletzki
CX1175	St-Saens: Carnival of the Animals,Britten: Young Person's Guide	Philh	Markevitch Anda Siki
CX1176	Bartok: For Children, Sonatina		Anda
CX1178	Mozart: Eine Kleine Nachtmusik, Sinfonia Concertante K297B	Philh	Karajan
CX1179-81	Bellini: Norma	La Scala	Serafin Callas

CX1182-3	Mascagni: Cavalleria Rusticana	La Scala	Serafin Callas Di Stefano
CX1185	Beethoven: Piano Sonatas 31, 32		Siki
CX1186-7	Strauss,J: Vienna Blood	Philh	Ackermann Schwarzkopf Loose
CX1188	Beethoven: Piano Concerto 3	PCO	Cluytens Gilels
CX1189	Tchaikovsky: Manfred Symphony	Philh	Kletzki
CX1190	D'Indy: Symphony on a French Mt Air, Franck: Symphonic Vns	OdeP	Cluytens Ciccolini
CX1191	Beethoven: String Quartets Op 18/5, Op 18/6	Hungarian Quartet	
CX1192	Concertos by Rossini, Galuppi, Tartini, Marcello	I Musici	
CX1193	Christmas Carols and Sacred Music	St Pauls Cathedral Choir Bower	
CX1194	Beethoven: Violin Concerto	Stockholm SO Ehrling Oistrakh	
CX1195-6	Verdi: Requiem Mass	La Scala	De Sabata Schwarzkopf
CX1197-9	Homage to Diaghilev (Satie, Debussy, Ravel, Tchaikovsky, etc)	Philh	Markevitch
CX1201	Franck: Sonata in Amaj, Szymanowski: Sonata Op 9	Oistrakh	Yampolski
CX1202	Liszt: Sonata, Mephisto Waltz, Etude de Concert La Campanella		Anda
CX1203	Beethoven: Quartet 59/1 ("Rasoumovsky")	Hungarian Quartet	
CX1204	Operatic Arias by Puccini (Manon Lescaut, La boheme, Butterfly, Suor Angelica, Gianni Schicchi, Turandot)	ORTF	Markevitch Callas
CX1205	Bliss: Miracle in the Gorbals, Music for Strings	Philh	Bliss
CX1206	Berlioz: Symphonie Fantastique	Philh	Karajan
CX1207	Mahler: Symphony 1	IPO	Kletzki
CX1208	Tchaikovsky: Romeo&Juliet Borodin: Polovtsian Dances, Moussorgsky: Night on Bare Mt	ORTF	Markevitch
CX1211-2	Leoncavallo: Pagliacci	La Scala	Serafin Callas Gobbi Di Stefano
CX1213	Recital of French Songs (Debussy, Faure, Chausson, Duparc, etc)	Merriman	Moore
CX1215-6	Rossini: Italian in Algiers	La Scala	Giulini Petri Sciutti Valletti
CX1217	St-Saens: Piano Concerto 2, Mozart: Piano Sonata K570	ONDF	Cluytens Gilels
CX1218	Poulenc: Les Mamelles de Tiresias	L'Opera Comique Cluytens	
CX1219	Mendelssohn: Symphony 3, Ov Calm Sea & Prosperous Voyage	IPO	Kletzki
CX1220	Mozart: Piano Works Vol 4		Gieseking
CX1221	Falla: Nights in the Gardens of Spain, Homenajes	ONDF	Halffter Ciccolini
CX1222-3	Schubert: Winterreise	Hotter	Moore
CX1224-5	Strauss,J: A Night In Venice	Philh	Ackermann Schwarzkopf
CX1226	Strauss,R: Arabella (hlts)	Philh	Matacic Schwarzkopf
CX1227	Beethoven: Symphony 2, Coriolan Ov	Philh	Karajan
CX1228	Stravinsky: Pulcinella, Baiser de la Fee	ONDF	Markevitch
CX1229	Debussy: Nocturnes, L'Apre Midi D'un Faune, Marche Ecossaise	FNRO	Inghelbrecht
CX1230	Haydn: String Quartets 17, 76	Italian Quartet	
CX1231	Arias from Mefistofele, Sicilian Vespers, Andrea Chenier, etc	Philh	Serafin Callas
CX1232-3	Bizet Les Pecheurs de Perles	L'Opera Comique Cluytens Angelici	
CX1235	Mozart: Piano Concertos K466, K503	Philh	Rosbaud Gieseking
CX1236	Beethoven: String Quartets Op 59/2, Op 95	Hungarian Quartet	
CX1237	Madrigals and Scared Music	St Pauls Cathedral Choir Bower	
CX1238	Chopin: Piano Concerto 1, Liszt: Piano Concerto 1	PCO	Tzipine Francois
CX1239-40	Bach,J.S: 4 Orchestral Suites	Philh	Klemperer
CX1241	Brahms: Haydn Variations, Hindemith: "Nobilissima Visione"	Philh	Klemperer
CX1242	Mozart: Piano Works Vol 5 (Piano Sonatas K279, K311, etc)		Gieseking
CX1243	Spanish Song Recital (Falla, Mompou, Montsalvage, Turina, etc)	Merriman	Moore
CX1244	Brahms: Quartet Op 67	Italian Quartet	
CX1245	Bartok: String Quartets 1 & 2	Vegh Quartet	
CX1246	Lalo: Symphonie Espagnol	Philh	Martinon Oistrakh
CX1247-8	Elgar: Dream of Gerontius	RLPO	Sargent
CX1249	Bach,J.S: Chorale Preludes		Schweitzer
CX1250-1	Mahler: Symphony 9, Schönberg: Verklarte Nacht	IPO	Kletzki
CX1252-3	"Le Groupe Des Six"	PCO	Tzipine
CX1254	Beethoven: String Quartets 9, 10	Hungarian Quartet	
CX1255	Brahms: Klavierstucke Op 76, Fantasia Op 116		Gieseking

CX1256	Brahms: Klavierstucken op 118-119, Rhapsodien op 79		Gieseking
CX1257	Mozart: Symphonies 29, 41	Philh	Klemperer
CX1258-60	Verdi: The Force of Destiny	La Scala	Serafin Callas
CX1261	Debussy: Etudes Book1 Nos 1-6 & Book 2 Nos 7-12		Gieseking
CX1262-4	Mozart: Cosi fan Tutte	Philh	Karajan Schwarzkopf
CX1265	"Opera Intermezzi" (Carmen, Thais, Traviata, Cav&Pag, etc)	Philh	Karajan
CX1266	Beethoven: Symphony 5, Fidelio highlights	Philh	Karajan Schwarzkopf
CX1267	Bartok: String Quartets 3 & 4	Vegh Quartet	
CX1268	Bruch: Violin Concerto 1, Prokofiev: Violin Concerto 1	LSO	Matacic Oistrakh
CX1269	Schubert: Schwanengesang	Hotter	Moore
CX1270	Beethoven: Overtures Fidelio, Leonora 1,2,3	Philh	Klemperer
CX1271	Mozart: Piano Works Vol 6 (Sonatas K284,K401,K533, etc)		Gieseking
CX1272	Beethoven: Quartets Op 127, Op 135	Hungarian Quartet	
CX1273	"Portrait of the Waltz" (Mozart, Liszt, Berlioz, St-Saens, Sibelius, Chabrier, etc)	Philh	Markevitch
CX1274-5	Bruckner: Symphony 4	Philh	Von Matacic
CX1276	Vivaldi: Concerti, Leo: Concerto, Sacchini: Overture	Alessandro Scarlatti Orch	
CX1277	Cimarosa: Oboe Concerto, Lully: Ballet Suite, Tartini: Concerto	Alessandro Scarlatti Orch	
CX1278	Beethoven: Symphony 4, Ah Perfido!	Philh	Karajan Schwarzkopf
CX1279	Tchaikovsky: String Quartet Op 22	Armenian String Quartet	
CX1280	Balakirev: Symphonic Poems Thamar & Russia, Oriental Fantasy Islamey	Philh	Matacic
CX1281	Glazunov: Violin Concerto, Paganini: Violin Concerto 1	Philh	Matacic Rabin
CX1282	Debussy: La Boite a Joujoux, Children's Corner Suite	ONDF	Cluytens
CX1283	Schumann: Kreisleriana, Carnaval		Anda
CX1284	Schubert: String Quartet 14	Armenian State String Quartet	
CX1285	Bartok: String Quartets 5 & 6	Vegh Quartet	
CX1286	Bach,J.S: Violin Sonatas 1, 2		Martzy
CX1287	Bach,J.S: Violin Sonatas 3, 4		Martzy
CX1288	Bach,J.S: Violin Sonatas 5, 6		Martzy
CX1289-91	Rossini: Il Turco in Italia	La Scala	Gavazzeni Callas
CX1292-4	Strauss,R: Ariadne Auf Naxos	Philh	Karajan Schwarzkopf Streich
CX1295	Prokofiev: String Quartet 2, Malipiero: String Quartet 4	Italian Quartet	
CX1296-8	Puccini: Madame Butterfly	La Scala	Karajan Callas
CX1299-1301	Gounod: Mireille	1954 Aix en Provence Festival Cluytens	
CX1302	Beethoven: Piano Concerto 1, "Moonlight" Sonata	Philh	Galliera Anda
CX1303	Khachaturian: Violin Concerto	Philh	Khachaturian Oistrakh
CX1304	Debussy: Preludes book 2		Gieseking
CX1305	Opera recital (Rigoletto, Golden Cockerel, Sonnambula, etc)	Philh	Galliera Mattiwilda Dobbs
CX1306	Pergolesi: Concertinos 1, 2, 3	I Musici	
CX1307	Pergolesi: Concertinos 5, 6, Sonata, Sinfonia	I Musici	
CX1308	"Spanish Classical and Traditional Music"	Capilla Clasica Polifonica Enrique Ribó	
CX1309-10	Strauss,J: Die Fledermaus	Philh	Karajan Schwarzkopf
CX1311	Sibelius: Symphony 1	Philh	Kletzki
CX1313	Walton: Scenes from Troilus and Cressida	Philh	Walton Schwarzkopf
CX1315	Mozart: Piano Works Vol 7 (Sonatas K281, K547a, 9 Vns K573, Rondo K511, 6 Vns K398		Gieseking
CX1316	Bartok For Children Volume 2		Anda
CX1317	An Evening with Robert Burns	Saltire Music Group	
CX1318-20	Verdi: Aida	La Scala	Serafin Callas
CX1321	"A Mozart Song Recital"	Schwarzkopf Gieseking	
CX1322	Mozart: Quintet K452, Beethoven: Quintet Op 16	Gieseking	Brain etc
CX1323	Rachmaninov: Piano Concerto 3	PCO	Cluytens Gilels
CX1324-6	Verdi: Rigoletto	La Scala	Serafin Gobbi Callas
CX1327	"Ballet Music from the Operas"	Philh	Karajan

CX1328	Tchaikovsky: Romeo and Juliet,		
	Strauss,R: Death and Transfiguration	Philh	Galliera
CX1329-30	Strauss,J: The Gypsy Baron	Philh	Ackermann Schwarzkopf
CX1331	Recital of Duets (Monteverdi, Dvorak, Carissimi)	Schwarzkopf Seefried Moore	
CX1332	Sibelius: Symphony 2	Philh	Kletzki [SAX2280]
CX1333	Beethoven: Piano Concerto 4	Philh	Galliera Arrau
CX1334	Borodin: String Quartet 2, Shostakovich: String Quartet Op 49	Armenian String Quartet	
CX1335	Philharmonia Prom Concert (Strauss, Chabrier, Weinberger, etc)	Philh	Karajan
CX1337	Chopin: Piano Sonata 3, Enesco: Piano Sonata 3		Lipatti
CX1338	Chopin: Recital		Malcuzynski
CX1339	Respighi: Brazilian Impressions, Fountains of Rome	Philh	Galliera
CX1340	Pergolesi: La Serva Padrona	La Scala	Giulini Carteri
CX1341	Sibelius: Symphonies 6, 7	Philh	Karajan
CX1342	Khachaturian: Sonata for Violin and Piano Op 1,		
	Prokofiev: Violin Sonata 2	Oistrakh	Yampolsky
CX1343	Beethoven: Piano Sonata Op 53 (Waldstein),		
	Prokofiev: Piano Sonata Op 29, Scriabin		Eugene Malinin
CX1344	Piano Recital (Chopin, Debussy, Paderewski, Prokofiev, etc)		Malcuzynski
CX1345	Mozart: Piano Works Vol 8		Gieseking
CX1346	Beethoven: Symphony 3	Philh	Klemperer
CX1347-8	Handel: Israel in Egypt	Liverpool Philh	Sargent
CX1349	Schubert: Symphony 8, Brahms: Haydn Vns	Philh	Karajan
CX1350-2	Ravel: The Complete Piano Works		Gieseking
CX1353	Dallapiccola: Canti di Prigonia, 4 Poemes Hindous, Berceuse Phoque,	AdSC	Markevitch
	Guarnieri: String Quartet 2	Pascal Quartet	
CX1354	Respighi: The Birds, Botticelli Triptych	Alessandro Scarlatti Orch	
CX1355	Brahms: Symphony 2	Philh	Karajan
CX1356	Borodin: Symphony 1, Rimsky-Korsakov: Capriccio Espagnol	Philh	Galliera
CX1357	Concertos by Vivaldi, Corelli, Martini	I Musici	
CX1358	Mozart: Piano Works Vol 9		Gieseking
CX1359	Schubert: Sonatinas D384, D385	Martzy	Antonietti
CX1361	Mozart: Symphony 39, Clarinet Concerto	Philh	Karajan Walton
CX1362	Brahms: Symphony 4	Philh	Karajan
CX1363	Schubert: Symphony 6, Grieg: Norwegian Romance	RPO	Beecham
CX1364	Chopin: Piano Sonata 2, Shostakovich: 3 Preludes & Fugues		Gilels
CX1365	Vivaldi: The 4 Seasons	Philh	Giulini Parikian
CX1366	Liszt: Piano Concerto 1, Hungarian Fantasia	Philh	Ackermann Anda
CX1367	Mozart: String Qt K458, Schubert: String Qt in Cmaj D32	Italian Quartet	
CX1368	Recital (Mozart, Schubert, Debussy, Chopin, Granados, Lazar)		Iturbi
CX1369	Rachmaninov: Piano Concerto 2	Philh	Ackermann Malinin
CX1370-1	Verdi: La Traviata	La Scala	Serafin Gobbi Stella
CX1372	Schubert: Rondeau Brillant D895, Fantaisie D934	Martzy	Antonietti
CX1373	Bach,J.S: Double Violin Concerto,		
	Violin Concerto in Emaj, Sarabande	Philh	Ackermann Kogan
CX1374	Beethoven: Piano Sonatas Op 109, Op 110		Gieseking
CX1375	Shakespeare: As You Like It excerpts, Sonnets	Evans	Redgrave
CX1376	Verdi: Opera Choruses (Nabucco, Lombardi, Ernani, Traviata, etc)	La Scala	Serafin
CX1377	Tchaikovsky: Symphony 6	Philh	Karajan
CX1378	Haydn: Symphonies 86, 92	Scarlatti Orch Caracciolo	
CX1379	Beethoven: Symphony 7	Philh	Klemperer
CX1380	Mozart: Piano Sonatas K331, K332, Beethoven: Monlight Sonata		Iturbi
CX1381	Brahms: Violin Sonatas 1, 2	Kogan	Mitnik (piano)
CX1382	Brahms: Handel Vns, Intermezzo Op118/6, Rhapsody Op 79/2		Malcuzynki
CX1383	Haydn: Quartets Op 33/3, Op 39	Italian Quartet	
CX1384	Eighteenth Century Comedy Album	Evans	Gielgud
CX1385	"Callas sings Lucia" (hlts)	MMF	Serafin Callas Gobbi

CX1386	Piano Recital (Bach, Scarlatti, Chopin, Ravel)		Lipatti	
CX1387-9	Sheridan: The School for Scandal	Parker	Andrews Bloom Evans	
CX1390	Taneiev: Concert Suite for Violin and Orch Op 28	Philh	Malko Oistrakh	
CX1391-2	Beethoven: Symphony 9	Philh	Karajan Schwarzkopf	
CX1393	Strauss,R: "Irresistible Strauss" (Waltzes and Polkas)	Philh	Karajan	
CX1394	Mendelssohn: Italian Symphony, Schubert: Symphony 8	ONDF	Markevitch	
CX1395	Mozart: Violin Concerto K216, Prokofiev: Violin Concerto 2	Philh	Ackermann Kogan	
CX1396	Beethoven: String Quartet Op 74	Italian Quartet		
CX1397-8	Handel: Solomon	RPO	Beecham	[SAX2499-2500]
CX1399	Schubert: Sonatina D408, Sonata D574	Martzy	Antonietti	
CX1400-1	Cornelius: Der Barbier von Baghdad	Philh	Leinsdorf Schwarzkopf	
CX1402	Mascagni: Cavalleria Rusticana (hlts)	La Scala	Callas Di Stefano	
CX1403	Mozart: Concerto for 2 Pianos K365, Bach: Concerto in Cmaj for 2 Pianos	Philh	Galliera Haskil Anda	
CX1404	"Songs You Love"	Schwarzkopf Moore		[SAX2265]
CX1405	Beethoven: Quartets Op 130, Op 133	Hungarian Quartet		
CX1406	Hoffnung: Musical Festival Concert	Royal Fest Hall 13th Nov 1956		
CX1407	Schumann: Cello Concerto, Tchaikovsky: Rococo Variations	Philh	Sargent Fournier	[SAX2282]
CX1408	Galuppi: String Quartet in Gmin, Boccherini: La Tiranna Spagnola, Gambini: Quartet in Gmin	Italian Quartet		
CX1409	Recital of Songs by Grieg and Richard Strauss	Aase Nordmo Lovberg Moore		
CX1410-2	Verdi: Falstaff	Philh	Karajan	[SAX2254-6]
CX1413	St-Saens: Symphony 3	OdeP	Cluytens	
CX1414	Malipiero: Symphony 6, Petrassi: Portrait of Don Quixote	Scarlatti Orch Caracciolo		
CX1415	Mozart: Violin Sonata K454, Tartini: "Devil's Trill" Sonata	Oistrakh	Yampolski	
CX1416	Liszt: Petrarch Sonnets 47, 104, 123, Apres une Lecture du Dante		Bela Siki	
CX1417	Beethoven: Piano Sonatas Op 31/2, Op 31/3		Gieseking	
CX1418	Ceremonial Music of the Synagogue	Kacmann		
CX1419	Schumann: Symphonies 1, 4	IPO	Kletzki	
CX1420	Tchaikovsky: Hamlet Ov, Balakirev: Ov on Russian Themes	Philh	Von Matacic	
CX1421	Moussorgsky-Ravel: Pictures at an Exhibition	Philh	Karajan	[SAX2261]
CX1422	Tchaikovsky: Violin Concerto, St-Saens: Intro & Rondo Capriccioso	Philh	Galliera Rabin	
CX1423	Schubert: Octet	Oistrakh	Knushevitsky Oborin etc	
CX1424	Mozart: String Quartets K421, K428	Smetana Quartet		
CX1425	Prokofiev: Cello Concerto Op 58, Milhaud: Cello Concerto 1	Philh	Susskind Starker	
CX1427	Beethoven: Piano Sonatas Op 10/3, Op101		Anda	
CX1428	Mozart: Piano Works Vol 10 (Sonata K330, Sonata K309, Rondo K485, etc)		Gieseking	
CX1429	Liszt: Psalm 13, Brahms: Song of Destiny	RPO	Beecham	
CX1430	"Italian String Qt in the 17th Century" (Gabrielli,Marini,Scarlatti,Neri,etc)	Italian Quartet		
CX1431-3	Mendelssohn: Elijah	RLPO	Sargent	
CX1434-6	Cimarosa: Il Matrimonio Segreto	La Scala	Sanzogno	
CX1437	Stravinsky: The Nightingale	ONDF	Cluytens	
CX1438	Mozart: Serenata Notturna, Adagio & Fugue, Beethoven: Grosse Fuge	Philh	Klemperer	
CX1439	Berlioz: Symphonie Fantastique	FNRO	Cluytens	
CX1440	Shostakovich: Symphony 1, Prokofiev: Scythian Suite	ONDF	Markevitch	
CX1442	Beethoven: Quartet Op 131	Hungarian Quartet		
CX1443-4	Chopin: Etudes Op 40, Etudes Op 25, Allegro de Concert Op 46		Arrau	
CX1445	Schubert: Piano Sonata Op 120, 4 Impromptus Op 142		Bela Siki	
CX1446-7	Orff: Die Kluge	Philh	Sawallisch	[SAX2257-8]
CX1448	Brahms: Lieder Recital	Hotter	Moore	
CX1449	Schumann: Symphony 2, Overture Scherzo & Finale	IPO	Kletzki	
CX1450	Balakirev: Symphony 1	RPO	Beecham	

CX1451	Salieri: Overtures Axur, Re d' Ormus, Vivaldi: Concerto	Alessandro Scarlatti Orch	Schippers	
CX1453	Mozart Piano Works vol 11			
	(8 Minuets, Allegro, Sonata K498a, 6 German Dances K509)		Gieseking	
CX1456	Bartok: Bluebeard's Castle	Budapest Opera	Ferencsik	
CX1457	Mozart: Symphonies 25, 40	Philh	Klemperer	[SAX2278]
CX1458	Haydn Symphonies 101, 102	FNRO	Markevitch	
CX1459	Chopin: Etudes Op 25, Ballade No 1		Anda	
CX1460	Beethoven: String Quartet in Op 132	Hungarian Quartet		
CX1462-3	Mozart: Die Entfuhrung Auf Dem Serail	RPO	Beecham	[SAX2427-9]
	(Note: the mono occupied 4 sides but the stereo required 5 sides)			
CX1464-5	Puccini: La Boheme	La Scala	Votto Callas Moffo	
CX1466	Violin Recital (Debussy, Falla, Ysaye, Tchaikovsky, Suk, etc)	Oistrakh	Yampolsky	[SAX2253]
CX1467-8	Grieg: Lyric Pieces		Gieseking	
CX1469-71	Bellini: La Sonnambula	La Scala	Votto Callas	
CX1472-4	Verdi: Un Ballo in Maschera	La Scala	Votto Callas Gobbi	
CX1475	Schumann: Symphony 3, Manfred Overture	IPO	Kletzki	
CX1476	Boccherini: Symphony in Amaj, Symphony in Cmin	Alessandro Scarlatti Orch		
CX1477	Dvorak: Cello Concerto, Faure: Elegie for Cello & Orch	Philh	Susskind Starker	[SAX2263]
CX1478	Bach,J.S: Toccata & Fugue, Fantasia, Chorale Preludes, etc		Commette	
CX1479	Mendelssohn: Songs without Words		Gieseking	
CX1480	Orff: Carmina Burana	Cologne RSO	Sawallisch	
CX1481	Tchaikovsky: Piano Concerto 1	FNRO	Malko Malcuczynski	
CX1482	"More Songs You Love"	Mackerras	Schwarzkopf	
CX1483-5	Verdi: Il Trovatore	La Scala	Karajan Callas	
CX1486	Mozart: Symphonies 38, 39	Philh	Klemperer	
CX1487	Brahms: Double Concerto, Tragic Ov	Philh	Fournier Oistrakh	[SAX2264]
CX1488	Beethoven: Piano Sonatas Op 21, Op 13, Op 49/1, Op 49/2		Gieseking	
CX1489	Bellini: Norma (hlts)	La Scala	Serafin Callas	
CX1490	Beethoven: Piano Concerto 5	Philh	Ludwig Gilels	[SAX2252]
CX1491	Strauss,R: Horn Concertos	Philh	Sawallisch Brain	
CX1492-5	Strauss,R: Der Rosenkavalier	Philh	Karajan	[SAX2269-72]
	(The SAX and CX are different recordings of the same performance)			
CX1496	Wagner: Tristan and Isolde (Prelude & Liebestod),			
	Tannhauser Ov, Mastersingers Prelude	BPO	Karajan	
CX1497	Mendelssohn: Violin Concerto, Beethoven: Romances 1 & 2	Philh	Kletzki Martzy	
CX1498	Beethoven: Piano Sonatas Op 10/3, Op 22		Gieseking	
CX1499-1500	"Dinu Lipatti - His Last Recital" (Besancon Festival, 1950)		Lipatti	
CX1501	Tito Gobbi At La Scala (Leoncavallo, Verdi, Puccini)	Reissued from complete recordings		
CX1502	Verdi: La Forza Del Destino (excerpts)	La Scala	Serafin Callas	
CX1503	Rousseau: Le Devin du Village	Chamber Orch	Froment Gedda	
CX1504	Brahms: Symphony 1	Philh	Klemperer	[SAX2262]
CX1505	Delibes: Sylvia	ONDF	Cluytens	
CX1506	Brahms: Violin Concerto	PCO	Bruck Kogan	
CX1507-9	Rossini: The Barber of Seville	Philh	Galliera	[SAX2266-8]
CX1511	Mozart: Symphony 35, Divertimento K287	Philh	Karajan	
CX1512	Hindemith: Concert Music for Brass & Strings	Philh	Hindemith	
CX1513	Beethoven: Piano Sonatas Op 53 (Waldstein), Op 101		Arrau	
CX1514	Beethoven: Violin Concerto	Pro Arte	Schuchter Oistrakh	
CX1515	Bach: Cello suites 2, 5		Starker	
CX1516	Strauss,J: Die Fledermaus (hlts)	Philh	Karajan Streich Schwarzkopf	
CX1517	Brahms: Symphony 2, Tragic Overture	Philh	Klemperer	[SAX2362]
CX1518	Stravinsky: Firebird, Bizet: Jeux D'Enfants,			
	Ravel: Ma Mere L'Oye	Philh	Giulini	[SAX2279]
CX1519	Beethoven: Piano Sonatas 9, 10, 13, 14 (Moonlight)		Gieseking	[SAX2259]
CX1520-1	Gluck: Orfée	OdeP	De Froment Gedda	
CX1522	Verdi & Wagner (Ballo,Forza,Aida,Dutchman,Tannhauser,etc)	Philh	Ludwig Nilsson	

CX1523	Tchaikovsky: Symphony 2, Moussorgsky: Night on Bare Mt	Philh	Giulini	[SAX2416]
CX1524	Berlioz: Overtures Benvenuto Cellini, King Lear, Carnival Romain, Le Corsaire, Beatrice and Benedict	PCO	Cluytens	
CX1525	Tchaikovsky: Piano Concerto 1	Colonne Orch	Iturbi	
CX1526	Mozart: Piano Concerto K491, Chopin: Barcarolle	Philh	Karajan Gieseking	
CX1527	Haydn: String Quartets Op 64/5 & Op 76/2	Hungarian Quartet		
CX1528	Mozart: Arias from Idomeneo, Giovanni, Cosi, Zauberflote, etc	PCO	Cluytens Gedda	
CX1529-30	Playboy jazz	All Stars Concert		
CX1531	Grieg: Piano Concerto, Schumann: Piano Concerto	Philh	Galliera Arrau	
CX1532	Beethoven: Symphony 6	Philh	Klemperer	[SAX2260]
CX1533	Hindemith: Concerto for Clarinet and Orch, Nobilissima Visione	Philh	Hindemith	
CX1534-5	Orff: Der Mond	Philh	Sawallisch	
CX1536	Brahms: Symphony 3, Academic Festival Overture	Philh	Klemperer	[SAX2351]
CX1537	Beethoven: Piano Sonatas Op 2/2 & Op 2/3		Gieseking	
CX1538	Bruch: Scottish Fantasy, Wieniawski: Violin Concerto 1	Philh	Boult Rabin	
CX1539	Boccherini: Ov in Dmaj, Symphony in Cmin, Haydn: Symphony 94	Philh	Giulini	
CX1540	"Callas at La Scala" (Medea, La Vestale, I Puritani, Sonnambula)	La Scala	Serafin Callas	
CX1541	Mahler: Symphony 4	Philh	Kletzki Loose	[SAX2345]
CX1542	Wagner: Die Walkure, Dutchman (hlts)	Philh	Hotter Nilsson	[SAX2296]
CX1543	Menotti: The Unicorn, The Gorgon, and the Manticore	New York Ballet	Schippers	
CX1544	Berlioz: Romeo & Juliet Suite, Damnation of Faust Suite	Philh	Cluytens	
CX1545	"Italian Opera Intermezzi" (Mascagni, Wolf-Ferrari, etc)	Philh	Galliera	
CX1546	Tchaikovsky: Violin Concerto, Vivaldi: Violin Concerto P343, Locatelli: Sonata (arr Ysaye)	PCO	Vandernoot Kogan	
CX1547	Bartok: Mikrokosmos, Suite op 14, Rumanian Dances, etc		Solchany (piano)	
CX1548	Respighi: Pines of Rome, Berlioz: Carnaval Romain, Liszt	Philh	Karajan	
CX1549-50	Orff: Music for Children	Childrens Opera Group	Jellinek	
CX1551	Falla: Three Cornered Hat	FNRO	Toldra	
CX1552	Recital (Schubert, Brahms, Wolf, Strauss, Mahler)	Ludwig	Moore	
CX1553	Song Recital	Farrell	Trovillo	
CX1554	Beethoven: Symphonies 1, 8	Philh	Klemperer	[SAX2318]
CX1555-7	Puccini: Turandot	La Scala	Serafin Callas Schwarzkopf	
CX1558	Mozart: Marriage of Figaro (hlts)	VPO	Karajan Schwarzkopf Seefried	
CX1559	Prokofiev: Peter & the Wolf, Haydn: Toy Symphony	Philh	Karajan	[SAX2375]
CX1560	Rossini: Overtures (Barber, Scala di Seta, Tell, Cenerentola, etc)	FNRO	Markevich	
CX1561	Prokofiev: Symphony 5	Philh	Schippers	
CX1562	Paganini: Violin Concerto 1, Cantabile in Dmaj	PCO	Bruck Kogan	
CX1563	Chopin: Piano Concerto 2 etc	WarPh	Gorzynski Ashkenazy	
CX1564	Beethoven: Piano Sonatas Op 7, Op 10/1, Op 10/2		Gieseking	
CX1565	Tchaikovsky: Francesca Da Rimini, Overture 1812, Marche Slave	RPO	Kletzki	
CX1566	Schubert: Quartet in Gmaj Op 161	Hungarian Quartet		
CX1567	Palestrina: Church Music, Monteverdi: Madrigals	Netherlands Chamber Choir	Nobel	
CX1568	Wagner excerpts (Dutchman, Tannhauser, Parsifal, Lohengrin)	Philh	Ackermann Edelmann	
CX1569	Schubert: Wanderer Fantasy D 760, 3 Impromptus D946		Arrau	
CX1570	Schwarzkopf sings Operetta	Philh	Ackermann	[SAX2283]
CX1571	Tchaikovsky: 1812, Berlioz: Hungarian March, Sibelius etc	Philh	Karajan	[SAX2302]
CX1572	Mozart: Magic Flute (hlts)	VPO	Karajan Seefried	
CX1573	Brahms: Symphony 1	RPO	Kletzki	
CX1574-5	Beethoven: Symphony 9, Incidental Music to Egmont	Philh	Klemperer	[SAX2276-7]
CX1577	Faure: Dolly Suite (orch Rabaud), Masques et Bergamasques Suite, Pelleas et Melisande incidental music	Opera Comique	Tzipine	
CX1578	Mozart: Piano Concerto 22	Colonne Orch	Iturbi	
CX1579	St-Saens: Cello Concerto, Schumann: Cello Concerto	Philh	Giulini Starker	
CX1580	Brahms: Violin Sonata 3, Beethoven: Violin Sonata 3	Oistrakh	Yampolsky	
CX1581	Borodin: String Quartet 2, Tchaikovsky: String Quartet 1	Hungarian Quartet		
CX1582	Verdi: Rigoletto (hlts)	La Scala	Gobbi Callas	

CX1583-5	Puccini: Manon Lescaut	La Scala	Serafin Callas Di Stefano	
CX1586-7	Bruckner: Symphony 8	BPO	Karajan	
CX1588	Offenbach: Gaite Parisienne, Gounod: Faust, etc	Philh	Karajan	[SAX2274]
CX1589	Franck: Symphony, Psyché et Eros	Philh	Giulini	
CX1590	Bach,JS: The Musical Offering (Orchestral Version)	FNRO	Markevitch	
CX1591	Brahms: Symphony 4	Philh	Klemperer	[SAX2350]
CX1592	Haydn: String Quartets 72, 74	Amadeus Quartet		
CX1593	Bethhoven: Piano Sonatas 8, 21	Annie Fischer		
CX1594	Tchaikovsky: Violin Concerto, Saint-Saens: Intro & Rondo Capriccioso	Pro-Arte	Schuchter Igor Oistrakh	
CX1595	Dohnanyi: Konzertstuck Op 12, Kodaly: Sonata for Cello	Philh	Susskind Starker	
CX1596	Opera Excerpts (Gluck, Weber, Massenet, Debussy, Verdi, etc)	Philh	Schippers Farrell	
CX1597	Mendelssohn: Violin Concerto, St-Saens: Havanaise, Ravel: Tzigane	Philh	Boult Rabin	
CX1598	"Love Duets" (Verdi,Mascagni,Bizet,Gounod)	Di Stefano Carteri		
CX1599	Mozart: String Quartets 16, 18	Hungarian Quartet		
CX1600-2	Strauss: Capriccio	Philh	Sawallisch Schwarzkopf	
CX1603	Beethoven: Piano Sonatas Op 26, Op 28		Gieseking	
CX1604-5	Shostakovich: Symphony 11	ONDF	Cluytens	
CX1606	Recital by Fournier (Bach, Chopin, Granados, Kreisler, Haydn,etc)		Fournier	Moore
CX1607	Chopin: 17 Polish Songs	Eugenia Zareska Favaretto (piano)		
CX1608	Bizet: L'Arlesienne Suites 1 & 2, Carmen Suite 1	Philh	Karajan	[SAX2289]
CX1609	Tchaikovsky: Symphony 4	Philh	Schippers	
CX1610	Beethoven: Piano Sonatas Op 110, Op 111		Arrau	
CX1611-12	Schubert: Impromptus D899, D935 nos 1-4, Drei Klavierstucke	Gieseking		
CX1613	Handel: Messiah (hlts)	RLPO	Sargent	
CX1614	Kodaly: String Quartet 2, Villa-Lobos: String Quartet 10	Hungarian Quartet		
CX1615	Beethoven: Symphony 2, Overtures Coriolan, Prometheus	Philh	Klemperer	[SAX2331]
CX1616	Beethoven: Piano Concerto 3, Piano Sonata 26 (Les Adieux)	Philh	Galliera Arrau	
CX1617	"The Hoffnung Interplanetary Festival"	Royal Festival Hall 1958		
CX1618-20	Cherubini: Medea	La Scala	Serafin Callas	[SAX2290-2]
CX1621	Chopin: Sonata 3; Barcarolle Op 60; Valses 2,6; Mazurkas 35,36		Ashkenazy	
CX1622	Bach: Concertos in Dmin, Fmin etc	PCO	Vandernoot Casadesus	
CX1623	Tchaikovsky: Nutcracker Suite, Swan Lake Suite	Philh	Sawallisch	[SAX2285]
CX1624	Brahms: Piano Sonata 3, Intermezzi		Anda	
CX1625	Beethoven: Piano Concerto 1, Piano Sonata Op 78	Philh	Galliera Arrau	
CX1626	Lieder Recital Number 1 (Schubert, Schumann, Loewe, Wolf)	Hotter	Moore	
CX1627	Schubert: Trio in B flat Op 99	Oistrakh Oborin Knushevitsky		[SAX2281]
CX1628	"Callas portrays Verdi Heroines" (Macbeth, Nabucco, Ernani, etc)	Philh	Rescigno Callas	[SAX2293]
CX1629	Recital (Beethoven Mozart Weber)	Philh	Wallberg Nilsson	[SAX2284]
CX1630	Mozart: Piano Concertos K467, K482	Philh	Sawallisch Annie Fischer	
CX1631-3	Puccini: La Fanciulla Del West	La Scala	Matacic Nilsson	[SAX2286-8]
CX1634-5	Beethoven: Missa Solemnis	Philh	Karajan Schwarzkopf	
CX1636	Rimsky Korsakov: Scheherazade, Symphonic Suite Op 35	Philh	Von Matacic	
CX1637	Brahms: Piano Concerto 2	German St Op Orch Ludwig Ashkenazy		
CX1638	"Renata Scotto Operatic Arias"	Philh	Ferrari Scotto	
CX1639	Chopin: Piano Sonata 2 Op 35,Grande Valse Op 18, Nocturnes Op 48 & Op 15 2, Scherzo 3 Op 39		Malcuzynski	
CX1641	Victoria: Officium Defunctorum and other Sacred Works	Netherlands CO		
CX1642	Dvorak: Symphony 9, Smetana: Vltava	BPO	Karajan	[SAX2275]
CX1643	Beethoven: Archduke Trio D	Oistrakh Knushevitsky Oborin		[SAX2352]
CX1644	"Cello Encores" (Bach, Boccherini, Ravel, Debussy, Fauré)	Fournier	Moore	
CX1645	Mad Scenes from Anna Bolena, Hamlet, Il Pirata	Philh	Rescigno Callas	[SAX2320]
CX1647	Strauss,R: Le Bourgeois Gentilhomme, Intermezzo Suite	Philh	Sawallisch	
CX1648	Villa-Lobos: Bachianas Brasileiras 4 & 7	FNRO	Villa-Lobos	
CX1649-50	Donizetti: L'Elisir D'Amore	La Scala	Serafin Carteri	[SAX2298-9]

Cat. No.	Work	Orchestra	Conductor/Artist	[SAX]
CX1651	Soprano Arias (Tannhauser, Lohengrin, Walkure, Otello)	Philh	Susskind Nordmo Lövberg	[SAX2353]
CX1652	Weber: Overtures (Euryanthe, Freischutz, Abu Hassan, etc)	Philh	Sawallisch	[SAX2343]
CX1653	Beethoven: Piano Concerto 5	Philh	Galliera Arrau	[SAX2297]
CX1654	Borodin: Prince Igor, Mussorgsky: Bare Mountain	Philh	Von Matacic	[SAX2327]
CX1655	Wagner hlts (Tannhauser, Meistersinger, Gotterdammerung, etc)	Philh	Sawallisch	
CX1656	Bach: Cello suites 1 & 3		Starker	
CX1657	Wolf: Goethe Lieder		Schwarzkopf Moore	[SAX2333]
CX1658	Schwarzkopf portrays Romantic Heroines (Tannhauser, Freischutz, Lohengrin)	Philh	Susskind Schwarzkopf	[SAX2300]
CX1660	Mozart: Violin Concerto 3, Prokofiev: Violin Concerto 2	Philh	Galliera Oistrakh	[SAX2304]
CX1661	Lieder Recital Number 2 (Schubert, Strauss, Schumann, Wolf)		Hotter Moore	
CX1662	Schumann (re-orch Mahler) Symphony 3, Manfred-Overture	Philh	Giulini	
CX1663	Ravel: Daphnis St 2, Bizet: Carmen St 1, Respighi: Pines	Philh	Galliera	[SAX2303]
CX1664	Schumann: Fantasia and Carnaval		Annie Fischer	
CX1665	Haydn: Cello Concerto, Boccherini: Cello Concerto	Philh	Giulini Starker	
CX1666	Beethoven: Piano Sonatas 31, 32		Richter-Haaser	
CX1667	Beethoven: Piano Concertos 1, 2	PCO	Vandernoot Gilels	
CX1668-70	Handel: Messiah	RLPO	Sargent	[SAX2308-10]
CX1671	Mahler: Lieder Eines Fahrenden Gesellen, Kindertotenlieder	Philh	Vandernoot Ludwig	[SAX2321]
CX1672	Beethoven: Violin Concerto	FNRO	Cluytens Oistrakh	[SAX2315]
CX1673	Berlioz: Symphonie Fantastique	Philh	Cluytens	
CX1674	Tchaikovsky: Francesca Da Rimini, Romeo&Juliet, Marche Slave	Philh	Wallberg	
CX1675	Beethoven: Piano Sonatas Op 27("Moonlight"), Op 78, Op 109		Annie Fischer	
CX1676	Hindemith: Symphonia Serena, Concerto for Horn & Orch	Philh	Hindemith Brain	
CX1677	Dvorak: Symphony 9, Carnaval Overture	Philh	Sawallisch	[SAX2322]
CX1678	Bass Operatic Arias (Prince Igor, Eugene Onegin, Don Carlos, etc)	Philh	Fistoulari Ladysz	
CX1679	Walton: Belshazzar's Feast, Partita for Orchestra	Philh	Walton	[SAX2319]
CX1680	Brahms: Piano Concerto 2	BPO	Karajan Richter-Haaser	[SAX2328]
CX1681	"Callas sings Verdi at La Scala"	La Scala	Serafin/Votto Callas	
CX1682	Verdi: Il Trovatore (hlts)	La Scala	Karajan Callas	
CX1683	Lalo: Symphonie Espagnole, Tchaikovsky: Serenade Melancolique	Philh	Kondrashin Kogan	[SAX2329]
CX1684	Verdi: Overtures (Nabucco, Aida, Vespers, Traviata, Forza)	Philh	Serafin	[SAX2324]
CX1685	Chopin: Waltzes		Malcuzynski	[SAX2332]
CX1686	Mozart: Piano Concertos K466, K488	Philh	Boult Fischer	[SAX2335]
CX1687	Mozart: Divertimento K270, Ibert: 3 Pieces		Dennis Brain Ensemble	
CX1688-9	Strauss,J: Die Fledermaus	Philh	Ackermann	[SAX2336-7]
CX1690	Chopin: Polonaises		Malcuzynski	[SAX2338]
CX1691	Tchaikovsky: Nutcracker Suite, Romeo & Juliet Overture	Philh	Markevitch	[SAX2339]
CX1692	Brahms: Violin Concerto	Philh	Kondrashin Kogan	[SAX2307]
CX1693	Schumann: Frauenliebe und Leben, Brahms: Zigeunerlieder		Ludwig Moore	[SAX2340]
CX1694	Falla: Three Cornered Hat Suites 1 & 2, Ravel	Philh	Giulini	[SAX2341]
CX1695	Chopin: Piano Concerto 2, Fantaisie	LSO	Susskind Malcuzynski	[SAX2344]
CX1696	Beethoven: Piano Concerto 2, Piano Sonata 7	Philh	Galliera Arrau	[SAX2346]
CX1697	Wagner: Rienzi, Dutchman, Tannhauser, Lohengrin Prelude	Philh	Klemperer	[SAX2347]
CX1698	"Klemperer conducts Wagner" ((Mastersingers, Tristan, ,etc)	Philh	Klemperer	[SAX2348]
CX1699	Rimsky-Korsakov: Capricco Espagnol, Ravel: La Valse, Borodin: Steppes of Central Asia, Moussorgsky: Bare Mountain	Philh	Cluytens	[SAX2355]
CX1700	Transcriptions for Cello & Piano (Bach, Kreisler, Debussy, Popper, Chopin, Schubert, Paganini, St-Saens, Schumann, Moussorgsky)		Starker Moore	
CX1701	Chopin: Waltzes, Etudes, Polonaises, Mazurkas		Iturbi	
CX1702	Beethoven: Symphony 4, Ov Consecration of the House	Philh	Klemperer	[SAX2354]
CX1703	Mozart: Symphonies 29, 38	Philh	Karajan	[SAX2356]
CX1704	Tchaikovsky: Symphony 4	BPO	Karajan	[SAX2357]
CX1705	Mahler: Lieder Recital		Ludwig Moore	[SAX2358]
CX1706-8	Ponchielli: La Gioconda	La Scala	Votto Callas	[SAX2359-61]

CX1709	Schubert: Moments Musicaux, March Allegretto		Arrau	[SAX2363]
CX1710	Beethoven: Symphony 3	Philh	Klemperer	[SAX2364]
CX1711	Tchaikovsky: Violin Concerto, Meditation	PCO	Silvestri Kogan	[SAX2323]
CX1712	Lehar: Land of Smiles and Merry Widow	Philh Ackermann Schwarzkopf		
CX1713	Handel: Messiah Highlights	RLPO	Sargent	[SAX2365]
CX1714	Wolf: From the Italian Song Book	Schwarzkopf	Moore	[SAX2366]
CX1715	Strauss,R: Don Juan, Till Eulenspiegel, Salome's Dance	Philh	Klemperer	[SAX2367]
CX1716	Tchaikovsky: Symphony 6	Philh	Giulini	[SAX2368]
CX1717-20	Mozart: Don Giovanni	Philh	Giulini	[SAX2369-72]
CX1721	Beethoven: Symphony 5	Philh	Klemperer	[SAX2373]
CX1722	Schumann: String Quartet in A Op41, Stravinsky Three Pieces	Italian Quartet		
CX1723-4	Donizetti: Lucia di Lammermoor	Philh	Serafin Callas	[SAX2316-7]
CX1725	"Love Duets" (Tosca, Cav Rusticana, Boheme, etc)	La Scala	Callas Di Stefano	
CX1726	Rossini: Overtures, Verdi Overtures & Preludes	Philh	Giulini	[SAX2377]
CX1727	Mozart: String Quartet in G, Ravel: String Quartet in F	Italian Quartet		
CX1728	Coloratura Arias (Donizetti, Rossini, Bellini, Verdi)	Philh	Davis Moffo	[SAX2376]
CX1729	Rossini Overtures (Semiramide, Tell, Barber, Silken Ladder, etc)	Philh	Karajan	[SAX2378]
CX1730	Sibelius: Symphony 2	Philh	Karajan	[SAX2379]
CX1731	Tchaikovsky: Piano Concerto 1, Weber: Konzerstuck	Philh	Galliera Arrau	[SAX2380]
CX1732-5	Mozart: Marriage of Figaro	Philh Giulini Schwarzkopf		[SAX2381-4]
CX1736	Mendelssohn: Symphony 3, Hebrides Ov	Philh	Klemperer	[SAX2342]
CX1737	Beethoven: Piano Sonatas 17, 30		Richter-Haaser	[SAX2385]
CX1738	Beethoven: Violin Concerto	PCO	Silvestri Kogan	[SAX2386]
CX1739	Brahms: Piano Concerto 1	Philh	Giulini Arrau	[SAX2387]
CX1740	Brahms: Violin Sonatas 1, 2	Igor Oistrakh Ginzburg		[SAX2388]
CX1741	Mozart: Srnd 13, 3 German Dances, Ave Verum Corpus, Handel	BPO	Karajan	[SAX2389]
CX1742	Beethoven: Piano Sonatas 22, 23		Arrau	[SAX2390]
CX1743	Recital: (Albeniz: Asturias, Sevillanas, Tango, Cordoba; Granados: Allegro de Concierto, 3 Spanish Dances, etc		Iturbi	[SAX2391]
CX1744	Mozart: Violin Concerto K216, Mendelssohn: Violin Concerto	PCO	Silvestri Kogan	
CX1745	Bach: Cello suites 4, 6		Starker	
CX1746	Mendelssohn: Incidental Music to Midsummer Night's Dream	Philh	Klemperer	[SAX2393]
CX1747	Ravel: Piano Concerto in G, Concerto for Left Hand & Orchstra	PCO Cluytens Francoix		[SAX2394]
CX1748	Haydn: Symphonies 98, 101	Philh	Klemperer	[SAX2395]
CX1749	Schubert: String Quartet 14	Hungarian Quartet		
CX1750	Sibelius: Symphony 5, Finlandia	Philh	Karajan	[SAX2392]
CX1751	Mendelssohn: Symphony 4, Schumann: Symphony 4	Philh	Klemperer	[SAX2398]
CX1752-3	Leoncavallo: Pagliacci	La Scala	Matacic	[SAX2399-400]
CX1754	Schubert: Symphony 9	Philh	Klemperer	[SAX2397]
CX1755	Chopin: Piano Sonata No 3, Fantasia		Arrau	[SAX2401]
CX1756	Schubert: Sonata in Bflat maj D960, Impromptus		Annie Fischer	[SAX2402]
CX1757	Beethoven: Piano Concerto 4, Rondo 2	Philh Kertesz Richter-Haaser		[SAX2403]
CX1758	Concert: Waldteufel, Strauss, Chabrier, Weinberger, Offenbach	Philh	Karajan	[SAX2404]
CX1759	Dvorak: Symphony 9, Carnaval Ov	Philh	Giulini	[SAX2405]
CX1760	Mozart: The Four Horn Concerti	Philh	Klemperer Civil	[SAX2406]
CX1761	"Encores" Gieseking (Chopin, Mendelssohn, Debussy, etc)		Gieseking	
CX1762	Beethoven: Piano Sonatas Op 90, Op 106 ("Hammerklavier")		Richter-Haaser	[SAX2407]
CX1763-4	Bach,J.S: Brandenburg Concertos	Philh	Klemperer	[SAX2408-9]
CX1765	Brahms: Violin Concerto	ONRF Klemperer Oistrakh		[SAX2411]
CX1766-8	Bellini: Norma	Serafin	Corelli Callas	[SAX2412-4]
CX1769	Beethoven: Symphony 7	Philh	Klemperer	[SAX2415]
CX1770	Weber: Der Freischutz, Humperdinck: Hansel & Gretel, Gluck	Philh	Klemperer	[SAX2417]
CX1771	"Great Arias from French Operas" (Gluck,Meyerbeer,Delibes,etc)	Pretre	Callas	[SAX2410]
CX1772	Tchaikovsky: Capriccio Italien, Suite 3, etc	La Scala	Von Matacic	[SAX2418]
CX1773	Brahms: Symphony 1	Philh	Giulini	[SAX2420]
CX1774	Ballet Music from the Operas	Philh	Karajan	[SAX2421]

CX1775	Beethoven: Piano Concerto 5, etc	Philh	Kertesz Richter-Haaser	[SAX2422]
CX1776	Rossini-Respighi: Boutique Fantasque, Dukas: Sorcerer	Philh	Galliera	[SAX2419]
CX1777	Strauss,R: Rosenkavalier Highlights	Philh	Karajan	[SAX2423]
CX1778	Schubert: Symphony 8, Brahms: Haydn Variations	Philh	Giulini	[SAX2424]
CX1780	Mozart: Piano Concertos K453, K537	Philh	Kertesz Richter-Haaser	[SAX2426]
CX1781-2	Brahms: German Requiem	Philh	Klemperer Schwarzkopf	[SAX2430-1]
CX1783	Bartok: Music for Strings, Percussion & Celesta, Hindemith	BPO	Karajan	[SAX2432]
CX1784	Operatic recital (Rigoletto, Traviata, Tosca, La Boheme, etc)	La Scala	Di Stefano	
CX1785	The Hoffnung Astronautical Music Festival 1961			[SAX2433]
CX1786	Mozart: Symphonies 35, 36, Ov Entfuhrung aus dem Serail	Philh	Klemperer	[SAX2436]
CX1787	Puccini: Madame Butterfly Highlights	La Scala	Karajan Callas Gedda	
CX1788	Recital (Debussy: Children's Corner, etc; Ravel: Jeux D'Eau, etc)		Iturbi	[SAX2434]
CX1789	Strauss,R: Death & Transfiguration, Metamorphosen	Philh	Klemperer	[SAX2437]
CX1790	Rossini: Barber of Seville Highlights	Philh	Galliera	[SAX2438]
CX1791	Overtures (Freischutz, Dutchman, Lohengrin, Hebrides, etc)	BPO	Karajan	[SAX2439]
CX1792	Puccini: Turandot (hlts)	La Scala	Callas Schwarzkopf	
CX1793	Mahler: Symphony 4	Philh	Klemperer Schwarzkopf	[SAX2441]
CX1795-6	Bizet: Pearl Fishers	L'Opera Comique Dervaux		[SAX2442-3]
CX1797	Chopin: Piano Sonatas 2, 3		Malcuzynski	[SAX2444]
CX1798	Poulenc: Gloria, Organ Concerto	FNRO	Pretre Durufle	[SAX2445]
CX1799-1803	Bach,J.S: St. Matthew Passion	Philh	Klemperer	[SAX2446-50]
CX1804-6	Beethoven: Fidelio	Philh	Klemperer	[SAX2451-3]
CX1807	Beethoven: Sonatas 18, 32		Annie Fischer	[SAX2435]
CX1808-9	Bruckner: Symphony 7	Philh	Klemperer	[SAX2454-5]
CX1810	Orff: Die Kluge Highlights	Philh	Sawallisch	[SAX2456]
CX1811	Orff: Der Mond Highlights	Philh	Sawallisch	[SAX2457]
CX1812	Tchaikovsky: Symphony 6	Philh	Klemperer	[SAX2458]
CX1813	Liszt: Mephisto Waltz, Etudes d'Execution 5 - Feux Follets, Rachmaninov: Corelli Vns, Prokofiev: Piano Sonata 7		Ashkenazy	
CX1814	Weill: Suite from Threepenny Opera etc	Philh	Klemperer	[SAX2460]
CX1815	Dvorak: Symphony 8, Scherzo Capriccioso	Philh	Giulini	[SAX2461]
CX1816	Walton: Symphony 2, Partita for Orchestra	Cleveland	Szell	[SAX2459]
CX1817	Wagner: Wesendonk Lieder, Tristan, Brahms: Alto Rhapsody	Philh	Klemperer Ludwig	[SAX2462]
CX1818	Debussy: Nocturnes, La Mer	Philh	Giulini	[SAX2463]
CX1819	Humperdinck: Hansel & Gretel (hlts)	Philh	Karajan Schwarzkopf	
CX1820	'Klemperer Conducts More Wagner'	Philh	Klemperer	[SAX2464]
CX1821	Chopin: Mazurkas		Malcuzynski	[SAX2465]
CX1822	Brahms: Piano Concerto 2	Philh	Giulini Arrau	[SAX2466]
CX1823	Strauss,R: Also Sprach Zarathustra/Till Eulenspiegel	Philh	Maazel	[SAX2467]
CX1824	Mozart: Symphonies 38/39	Philh	Klemperer	[SAX2468]
CX1825	Debussy: L'Isle Joyeuse/etc		Samson Francois	[SAX2469]
CX1826-8	Mozart: "Haydn" String Quartets		Juilliard Quartet	[SAX2470-2]
CX1829-30	Mahler: Symphony 2	Philh	Klemperer	[SAX2473-4]
CX1831	Schumann: Symphonies 1/4	Clvlnd	Szell	[SAX2475]
CX1832-5	Ravel: Orch Works Vols 1-4	PCO	Cluytens	[SAX2476-9]
CX1836	Stravinsky: Serenade in A, Sonata, Schoenberg: Suite op 25, etc		Charles Rosen	[SAX2480]
CX1837	Gedda in Paris	PCO	Pretre Gedda	[SAX2481]
CX1838	Cherubini: Medea (hlts)	Paris Op	Pretre Gorr	[SAX2482]
CX1839	Brahms: Piano Music		Fleischer	
CX1840	Tchaikovsky: Romeo & Juliet, Francesca da Rimini	Philh	Giulini	[SAX2483]
CX1841	Moussorgsky-Ravel: Pictures at an Exhibition, Debussy: Faun	Philh	Maazel	[SAX2484]
CX1842	Schumann: Piano Concerto/Liszt Piano Conc 1	Philh	Klemperer Fischer	[SAX2485]
CX1843	Mozart: Symphonies 40/41	Philh	Klemperer	[SAX2486]
CX1844	'The Red Army Ensemble'		Red Army Ensemble	[SAX2487]
CX1845	Mahler: Symphony 10/Strauss: Death&Transfiguration	Clvlnd	Szell	[SAX2488]
CX1846	Arias from German Opera (Flute, Tannhauser, etc)	Berlin SO	Stein Prey	[SAX2489]

CX1847	"Szell conducts Russian music" (Borodin, Tchaikovsky, etc)	Clvlnd	Szell	[SAX2490]
CX1848	Ponchielli: La Gioconda (hlts)	La Scala	Votto Callas et al	[SAX2491]
CX1849	Debussy: 12 Etudes	Charles Rosen		[SAX2492]
CX1850	Beethoven: Symphony 8/Schubert: Symphony 8	Clvlnd	Szell	[SAX2493]
CX1851	Tchaikovsky: Symphony 4	Philh	Klemperer	[SAX2494]
CX1852	Strauss,R: Don Quixote/Don Juan	Clvlnd	Szell Fournier	[SAX2495]
CX1853	Schumann: Symphony 2	Clvlnd	Szell	[SAX2496]
CX1854	Tchaikovsky: Symphony 5	Philh	Klemperer	[SAX2497]
CX1855	Brahms: Symphony 2	Philh	Giulini	[SAX2498]
CX1856	Strauss,R: Till Eulenspiegel/Dvorak: Symphony 7	Clvlnd	Szell	[SAX2501]
CX1857	Schubert: Sonata in Amaj/Mozart: Rondo in Amin	Charles Rosen		[SAX2502]
CX1858	"Callas in Paris" (Berlioz, Bizet, Massenet, etc)	PCO	Pretre Callas	[SAX2503]
CX1859	Beethoven: Quartets 3/6	Drolc Quartet		[SAX2504]
CX1860	Beethoven: Songs	Prey Moore		[SAX2505]
CX1861	Schumann: Symphony 3, Manfred Ov	Clvlnd	Szell	[SAX2506]
CX1862	Brahms: Lieder	Prey	Malzer	
CX1863	Beethoven: Violin Concerto	Philh	Leinsdorf Milstein	[SAX2508]
CX1864	Chopin: Ballades 1-4		Malcuzynski	[SAX2509]
CX1865	Prokofiev: String Qt 1/Tchaikovsky: String Qt 1	Kroll Quartet		[SAX2507]
CX1866	Carl Loewe Ballads	Prey	Weissenborn	[SAX2511]
CX1867-8	Beethoven: Symphony 9/Wagner: Mastersingers Prelude	Clvlnd	Szell	[SAX2512-3]
CX1869	Beethoven: Symphony 7/Wagner: Tannhauser	Clvlnd	Szell	[SAX2510]
CX1870	Schubert: Symphonies 5/8	Philh	Klemperer	[SAX2514]
CX1871	Rachmaninov: Piano Concerto 3	WarPh Rowicki Malcuzynski		[SAX2515]
CX1872	Brahms: Symphony 3	Philh	Giulini	[SAX2516]
CX1874	Schubert: Symphony 9	Clvlnd	Szell	[SAX2517]
CX1875	Vivaldi: Violin Concerti (P234, P419, P88, P236)	Milstein Chamber Orchestra		[SAX2518]
CX1876	Schubert: String Quartet 14/Haydn: Strinq Quartet Op 64,5	Kroll Quartet		[SAX2519]
CX1877	Beethoven: String Qt 11/Hindemith: String Qt 3	Kroll Quartet		[SAX2520]
CX1878	Chopin: 24 Preludes Op 28	Samson Francois		[SAX2521]
CX1879	Schumann: Davidsbündlertänze	Charles Rosen		[SAX2522]
CX1880	Beethoven: Piano Sonatas 16/18	Richter-Haaser		[SAX2523]
CX1881	Mendelssohn: Symphony 4/Hebrides Ov/etc	Clvlnd	Szell	[SAX2524]
CX1882	Brahms: Piano Concerto 1	Clvlnd	Szell Fleisher	[SAX2526]
CX1883	Walton: Shakespeare Film Scores	Philh	Walton	[SAX2527]
CX1884	Franck: 4 Symphonic Poems/Le Chasseur Maudit/etc	ONB	Cluytens	[SAX2528]
CX1885	Haydn: Symphony 92/Mozart: Symphony 35	Clvlnd	Szell	[SAX2529]
CX1886	Beethoven: Quartets 4/5	Drolc Quartet		[SAX2530]
CX1887	Sonatas for 2 Violins	Kogan Elizabeth Gilels		[SAX2531]
CX1888	Ravel: Piano Works	Rosen		
CX1889	Prokofiev: Piano Concertos 3/5	Philh	Rowicki Francois	[SAX2533]
CX1890	Brahms: Piano Concerto 2	Clvlnd	Szell Fleisher	[SAX2534]
CX1891	Schubert: String Quartet 15	Juilliard Quartet		[SAX2535]
CX1892	Strauss,R: Horn Concerto 1	Clvlnd	Szell Bloom	
	Mozart: Clarinet Concerto	Clvlnd	Szell Marcellus	[SAX2536]
CX1893	Puccini: Tosca (hlts)	La Scala De Sabata Callas		
CX1894	Mozart: Mass in C K427	SW German CO Gonnenwein		[SAX2544]
CX1895	Handel: Dettingen Te Deum	German Madrigal Choir		[SAX2538]
CX1896	Debussy: La Mer/Ravel: Daphnis St 2/Pavane	Clvlnd	Szell	[SAX2532]
CX1897	Strauss,R: Arabella (hlts)	Philh Matacic Schwarzkopf		
CX1898	Berlioz: Symphonie Fantastique	Philh	Klemperer	[SAX2537]
CX1899	Bohemian Carnival	Clvlnd	Szell	[SAX2539]
CX1900	Callas sings Mozart, Weber, Beethoven	PCO	Rescigno Callas	[SAX2540]
CX1901	Brahms: Piano Quintet Op 34	Juilliard Quintet Fleisher		[SAX2541]
CX1902	Beethoven: Ovs Leonora 1-3/Fidelio	Philh	Klemperer	[SAX2542]
CX1903	Beethoven: Piano Concerto 3	Philh Giulini Richter-Haaser		[SAX2543]

Catalog	Work	Orchestra	Conductor/Performer	SAX
CX1904	Strauss,R: Sinfonia Domestica	Clvlnd	Szell	[SAX2545]
CX1905	Beethoven: Symphony 6	Clvlnd	Szell	[SAX2549]
CX1906	Mozart: Symphonies 31, 34	Philh	Klemperer	[SAX2546]
CX1907	Schumann: Symphony 3	Philh	Klemperer	[SAX2547]
CX1908	Debussy: Jeux/Images Pour Orchestre	PCO	Cluytens	[SAX2548]
CX1910	Verdi: Arias (Otello, Don Carlos, Araldo)	PCO	Rescigno Callas	[SAX2550]
CX1911	Beethoven: 33 Variations on a Waltz by Diabelli		Richter-Haaser	[SAX2557]
CX1912	Mozart: Symphony 41/Beethoven: Symphony 5	Clvlnd	Szell	[SAX2552]
CX1913	Mozart: Symphony 33/Div 2 K131	Clvlnd	Szell	[SAX2553]
CX1914	Dvorak: Symphony 9	Philh	Klemperer	[SAX2554]
CX1915	Britten: 4 Sea Intlds/Vns & Fugue on theme of Purcell	Philh	Giulini	[SAX2555]
CX1916	Stravinsky: Fairy's Kiss/Mussorgsky: Pictures	Clvlnd	Szell	[SAX2556]
CX1917	Mendelssohn: Quartets 2/3		Juilliard Quartet	[SAX2558]
CX1918	Mozart: Don Giovanni (hlts)	Philh	Giulini	[SAX2559]
CX1919	Rossini: Overtures	Philh	Giulini	[SAX2560]
CX1920	Beethoven: Piano Sonatas 3/22/26		Richter-Haaser	[SAX2561]
CX1921	Roussel: Bacchus & Ariadne etc	PCO	Cluytens	[SAX2562]
CX1922	"Music of Old Russia" (Tchaikovsky, Rimsky-Korsakov)	Orch cond Irving	Milstein	[SAX2563]
CX1923	Callas Sings Rossini and Donizetti Arias	PCO	Rescigno Callas	[SAX2564]
CX1924	Beethoven: Symphonies 1, 2	Clvlnd	Szell	[SAX2565]
CX1925	Bizet: L'Arlesienne Suites 1/2/Carmen: Suite 1	PCO	Cluytens	[SAX2566]
CX1926	Hagadah – The Telling (The Passover Story of the Life of Moses)	Written and Spoken by David Kossoff		
CX1927	Schumann : Dichterliebe, 9 Lieder from Kerner Lieder	Prey	Engel	[SAX2567]
CX1928	Bruckner: Symphony 4	Philh	Klemperer	[SAX2569]
CX1930	Beethoven: Overtures (Coriolan, Prometheus, Egmont, King Stephen, Consecration of the House)	Philh	Klemperer	[SAX2570]
CX1931	Haydn: Symphonies 88, 104	Philh	Klemperer	[SAX2571]
CX1932	Verdi: Aida (hlts)	La Scala	Serafin Callas	
CX1933	Brahms: Symphony 3/Haydn Variations	Clvlnd	Szell	[SAX2572]
CX1934	Mozart: Marriage of Figaro (hlts)	Philh	Giulini	[SAX2573]
CX1935	Walton Vns Theme of Hindemith/Hindemith: Sym Vns	Clvlnd	Szell	[SAX2576]
CX1936	Beethoven: Piano Sonatas Op 2/1 & Op 2/2		Richter-Haaser	[SAX2574]
CX1937	Barber: Piano Concerto, Schuman: Song of Orpheus	Clvlnd	Szell Rose	[SAX2575]
CX1938	Beethoven: Symphony 3	Clvlnd	Szell	[SAX2577]
CX1939	Verdi: Falstaff (hlts)	Philh	Karajan	[SAX2578]
CX1940	Bach: Concerto for 2 Violins, Sonata in Cmaj, Vivaldi		Milstein Morini	[SAX2579]
CX1941	Gounod: Romeo and Juliet (hlts)	ONDF	Gardelli	[SAX2580]
CX1943	Bruckner: Symphony 6	Philh	Klemperer	[SAX2582]
CX1944	Schumann: Kinderscenen, Kreisleriana		Annie Fischer	[SAX2583]
CX1945	Schütz: Christmas Oratorio	Small Orch	Hans Thamm	[SAX2584]
CX1946	Wolf: "Songs from the Romantic Poets"		Schwarzkopf Moore	
CX1948	Mozart: Overtures (Figaro/Giovanni/Magic Flute/etc)	Clvlnd	Szell	[SAX2587]
CX1949	Stravinsky: Symphony in 3 mvmts/Pulcinella St	Philh	Klemperer	[SAX2588]
CX5251	Roussel: Symphonies 3/4	PCO	Cluytens	[SAX5251]
CX5252	Handel: Concerto Grosso op 6/4, Mozart: Serenade 13, Symphony 25	Philh	Klemperer	[SBO2751] [SAX2278]
CX5253	Bach: Arias from St Matthew Passion	Philh	Klemperer	[SAX5253]
CX5254	Mozart: Violin Concertos 4/5	Philh	Milstein	[SAX5254]
CX5255	Schubert: Sonatas in Amin D784, Cmin D958		Richter-Haaser	[SAX5255]
CX5256	Mozart: Symphony 29/33	Philh	Klemperer	[SAX5256]
CX5257	Beethoven: Sonatas Hammerklavier/Op 110		Rosen	[SAX5257]
CX5258	Strauss,R: 4 Last Songs/etc	BRSO	Szell Schwarzkopf	[SAX5258]
CX5259	Mozart: Serenade for 13 Wind Insts K361	London Wind Qt	Klemperer	[SAX5259]
CX5260	Bartok: String Quartets 1, 2		Juilliard Quartet	[SAX5260]
CX5261	Bartok: String Quartets 3, 4		Juilliard Quartet	[SAX5261]
CX5262	Bartok: String Quartets 5, 6		Juilliard Quartet	[SAX5262]

CX5263	Bartok: Concerto for Orchestra/Janacek:Sinfonietta	Clvlnd	Szell	[SAX5263]
CX5264	Vivaldi: Violin Concertos (P163, P228, P208, P195)	Chamber Orch	Milstein	[SAX5264]
CX5265	Ravel: Rapsodie Espagnol, Pavane, Falla: Love the Magician	Philh Giulini	De Los Angeles	[SAX5265]
CX5266	Haydn: Symphony 100/102	Philh	Klemperer	[SAX5266]
CX5267	Virtuoso Piano Transcriptions (Chopin, Mendelssohn, Schubert, etc)		Rosen	[SAX5267]
CX5268	Lieder and Song Recital (Schubert, Schumann, Wolf, etc)	Schwarzkopf	Moore	[SAX5268]
CX5269	Schumann: Symphony 1, Manfred Ov	Philh	Klemperer	[SAX5269]
CX5271	Schubert: String Quartets D173, D804	Juilliard Quartet		[SAX5271]
CX5273	Chopin: Piano Concerto 2/Liszt: Piano Concerto 1	Philh	Pritchard Rosen	[SAX5273]
CX5274	Recital (Schubert, St-Saens, Brahms, Ravel)	Ludwig	Parsons	[SAX5274]
CX5275	Prokofiev: Violin Concertos 1/2	De Burgos/Giulini	Milstein	[SAX5275]
CX5276	Franck: Symphony in Dmin	Philh	Klemperer	[SAX5276]
CX5277	Wagner hlts (Faust Ov, Rienzi, Dutchman, Lohengrin, etc)	Clvlnd	Szell	[SAX5277]
CX5278	Lyric Songs	Gedda	Moore	[SAX5278]
CX5279	Brahms: Symphony 1	Clvlnd	Szell	[SAX5279]

Columbia 33C (10")

The 10" Columbia series was also released from October 1952 and the label is identical to the early dark blue 33CX label described under that series heading. There was no second label for this series. The final 33C release was 33C1066 in November 1964.

33C1001	Schumann: Piano Concerto	Philh	Karajan Lipatti
33C1002	Mozart: Symphony 41	RPO	Beecham
33C1003	Grieg: Piano Concerto	Philh	Karajan Gieseking
33C1004	Falla: El Amor Brujo	PCO	Argenta
33C1005	Chopin: Piano Sonata 3		Malcuzynski
33C1006	Mendelssohn: Symphony 4	RPO	Beecham
33C1007	Beethoven: Piano Concerto 4	Philh	Karajan Gieseking
33C1008	Sibelius: Violin Concerto	RPO	Beecham Stern
33C1009	Mahler: Kindertotenlieder	VPO	Walter Ferrier
33C1010	Stravinsky: Firebird Suite	NYPO	Stravinsky
33C1011	Recital: Eugen Onegin	Philh	Susskind Welitsch
	Salome (final scene)	Metropolitan Opera	Reiner Welitsch
33C1012	Mozart: Piano Concerto K488	Philh	Karajan Gieseking
33C1013	Wieniawski: Violin Concerto 2	NYPSO	Kurtz Stern
33C1014	Schumann: Scenes from Childhood,		
	Debussy: Children's Corner Suite		Gieseking
33C1015	Stravinsky: Petrouchka Suite	NYPSO	Stravinsky
33C1016	Walton: Orb & Sceptre, Portsmouth Point, Crown Imperial	Philh	Walton
33C1017	Delius: Over the Hills and Far Away, In a Summer Garden	RPO Beecham	
33C1018	Sibelius: Scenes Historiques Op 25 No 3 & Op 66	RPO Beecham	
33C1019	Smetana: Moldau (Vltava), From Bohemia's Woods and Fields	NYPO	Szell
33C1020	Schumann: Dichterliebe	Lotte Lehmann	Walter (piano)
33C1021	Bach,J.S: Partita 1 Mozart: Sonata K310		Lipatti
33C1022	Tchaikovsky: Violin Concerto	Phild	Hilsberg Stern
33C1023	Ravel: Rapsodie Espagnole, Piano Concerto for Left Hand	Phild	Ormandy Casadesus
33C1024	Mozart: Piano Concerto K467	NYPSO	Munch Casadesus
33C1025	Prokofiev: Symphony No 1, R-Korsakov: Russian Easter Festival	Phild	Ormandy
33C1026	Wagner: Wotan's Farewell, Magic Fire Music, Rienzi Ov	NYPSO	Stokowski
33C1027	Milhaud: Suite Francaise, Ibert: Escales	NYPSO	Milhaud Rodzinski
33C1028	Mozart: Piano Concerto K595	NYPSO	Barbirolli Casadesus
33C1029	Chausson: Poeme, St-Saens: Intro & Rondo Capriccioso	Phild	Ormandy Francescatti
33C1030	Berg: Violin Concerto	Philh	Kletzki Gertler
33C1031	Franck: Prelude,Chorale & Fugue, Liszt: Rapsodie Espagnole		Malcuzynski
33C1032	"Viennese Songs"		Erich Kunz

33C1033	Schumann: Piano Concerto	Philh	Karajan Gieseking	
33C1034	Ravel: Bolero, Le Tombeau de Couperin	ONRF	Cluytens	
33C1035	Wagner: Flying Dutchman (hlts)	Philh	Schuchter Björling Rysanek	
33C1036	Sibelius: Violin Concerto	Stockholm FO	Ehrling Oistrakh	
33C1040	Grieg: Piano Concerto	Philh	Galliera Lipatti	
33C1041	Khachaturian: Gayaneh - Ballet Suite	Philh	Khachaturian	
33C1042	Smetana: From Bohemia's Woods and Fields, Vltava (Ma Vlast)	Philh	Ackermann	
33C1043	Khachaturian: Masquerade Suite, In Memoriam	Philh	Khachaturian	
33C1044	Rawsthorne: Practical Cats	Philh	Rawsthorne Donat	
33C1045	Moussorgsky: Pictures at an Exhibition		Malinin	
33C1046	Bartok: Violin Sonata		Gertler	
33C1047	Beethoven: Kreutzer Sonata	Oistrakh	Oborin	
33C1049	Song Recital Vol 1	Soviet Army Ensemble		
33C1050	Song Recital Vol 2	Soviet Army Ensemble		
33C1051	Beethoven: Symphony 5	Philh	Klemperer	
33C1052	Operatic Arias (Pagliacci, Othello, Trovatore, Traviata, Chenier)	Philh	Galliera Panerai	
33C1053	Mozart: Eine Kleine Nachtmusik Handel: Concerto Grosso 4	Philh	Klemperer	[SBO2751]
33C1054	Walton: Facade - Ballet Suite., Johannesburg Festival Overture	Philh	Walton	
33C1055	Beethoven: Piano Concerto 4	Philh	Ludwig Gilels	[SBO2752]
33C1056	Schumann: Symphony No 4	BPO	Karajan	
33C1057	Chopin: Piano Concerto No 1	Philh	Galliera Anda	
33C1059	Lalo: Symphonie Espagnole Op 21	PCO	Bruck Kogan	
33C1060	Wagner: Siegfried Idyll, Strauss: Don Juan Op 20	Philh	Galliera	
33C1061	Mozart: Soprano Arias Vol 1 (Exsultate Jubilate, Magic Flute)	Philh	Galliera Moffo	
33C1062	Beethoven: Triple Concerto	Philh	Sargent Oistrakh Oborin Knushevitsky	[SBO2753]
33C1063	Mozart: Soprano Arias Vol 2 (Figaro, Cosi, Giovanni, Serail)	Philh	Galliera Moffo	[SBO2754]
33C1064	Mozart: Piano Concerto K467	Lucerne Festival Orch	Karajan Lipatti	
33C1065	Leoncavallo: Pagliacci (hlts)	La Scala	Matacic	[SBO2756]
33C1066	Red Army Ensemble vol 2			[SBO2757]

HMV ALP

HMV began issuing LP records in October 1952 with the series ALP (12") and BLP (10").

The labels are red with gold lettering, with the top half dominated by "Nipper" in colour and with the words "His Masters Voice" in a semi-circle around the picture. A later version of the ALP label replaced the gold lettering with black, the picture in the upper half is reduced in size, and the "His Masters Voice" is now in bold white letters.

ALP releases continued well into the stereo era, with the last of them (ALP2314) being published in 1967, by which time stereo (ASD) and mono (ALP) releases were issued with identical numbers.

Number	Work	Orchestra	Performer
ALP1001	Tchaikovsky: Symphony 5	La Scala	Cantelli
ALP1002	Tchaikovsky: Sleeping Beauty	Stokowski and his SO	
ALP1003	Ravel: Bolero/Mother Goose Suite	BSO	Koussevitsky
ALP1004-6	Verdi: Rigoletto	RCAVO	Cellini Berger Warren etc
ALP1007	Rossini: Overtures	NBCSO	Toscanini
ALP1008	Beethoven: Symphony 3	NBCSO	Toscanini
ALP1009	Mendelssohn: Trio in Dmin, Ravel: Trio in Amin	Heifetz Rubinstein Piatigorsky	
ALP1010	Nielsen: Symphony 4	DSRO	Grondahl
ALP1011	Brahms: Vrns on theme by Haydn/Haydn: Symphony 94	VPO	Furtwangler
ALP1012	Brahms: Symphony 1	NBCSO	Toscanini
ALP1013	Brahms: Symphony 2	NBCSO	Toscanini
ALP1014	Elgar: Violin Concerto	LSO	Sargent Heifetz
ALP1015	Chopin: Piano Concerto 1	RCAVO	Steinberg Brailowsky
ALP1016	Wagner: Gotterdammerung (Immolation,Funeral March,etc)	Philh	Furtwangler Flagstad
ALP1017	Rachmaninov: Piano Concerto 3	RCAVO	Reiner Horowitz
ALP1018	Dvorak: New World Symphony	CSO	Kubelik
ALP1019	Franck: Symphony in Dmin	San Francisco	Monteux
ALP1020-1	Puccini: Tosca	Rome Opera	Fabritiis Gigli etc
ALP1022-4	Rossini: Barber of Seville	Milan Orch	Serafin De Los Angeles
ALP1025	Tchaikovsky: Symphony 4	VPO	Furtwangler
ALP1026	Purcell: Dido and Aeneas	Mermaid Orch	Flagstad Schwarzkopf
ALP1027	Walton: Symphony 1	Philh	Walton
ALP1028	Chopin: Polonaises		Rubinstein
ALP1029	Brahms: Symphony 4	NBCSO	Toscanini
ALP1030-5	Wagner: Tristan & Isolde	Philh	Furtwangler Suthaus Flagstad
ALP1036-7	Schubert: Die Schone Mullerin	Fischer-Dieskau Gerald Moore	
ALP1038	Haydn: Symphonies 83 & 96	Halle	Barbirolli
ALP1039-0	Beethoven: Symphonies 1/9	NBCSO	Toscanini
ALP1041	Beethoven: Symphony 6	VPO	Furtwangler
ALP1042	Tchaikovsky: Symphony 6	Philh	Cantelli
ALP1043	"Through Childhood to the Throne" (Queen Eleizabeth II)		
ALP1044-7	Mussorgsky: Boris Godunov	ONRF	Dobrowen Christoff Gedda
ALP1049	Smetana: Bartered Bride,Mendelssohn: Midsmr Nts Dream	Philh	Kubelik
ALP1050	Beethoven: Violin Sonatas Op 12/1, Op 12/3	Menuhin	Kentner
ALP1051	Beethoven: Piano Concerto 5	Philh	Furtwangler Edwin Fischer
ALP1052	Elgar: Symphony 1	LPO	Boult
ALP1053-5	Shakespeare: Romeo & Juliet	Old Vic 1953 Production	
ALP1056-8	"The Coronation of Her Majesty Queen Elizabeth II"		
ALP1059	Beethoven: Symphony 4	VPO	Furtwangler
ALP1060	Beethoven: Symphony 3	VPO	Furtwangler
ALP1061	Haydn: Symphony 104, Schubert: Symphony 2	BSO	Munch

Catalog	Work	Orchestra	Performers
ALP1062	Beethoven: Piano Sonatas Op 13 ("Pathetique")/Op 109		Solomon
ALP1063	"Traditional Songs of Spain"		De Los Angeles Tarragao (Guitar)
ALP1064	Dvorak: Symphony 4(8)	Philh	Kubelik
ALP1065	Grieg: Piano Concerto/Falla: Nights in the Gardens of Spain	RCASO	Dorati Rubinstein
ALP1066	Beethoven: An Die Ferne Geliebte/Schubert: Heine Songs		Fischer-Dieskau Moore
ALP1067-8	Donizetti: L'Elisir D'Amore	RomeOp	Santini Gobbi
ALP1069	Chopin: Mazurkas/Schumann: Kinderscenen		Horowitz
ALP1070	Debussy: La Mer/Ravel: Daphnis & Chloe	NBCSO	Toscanini
ALP1071	"The Great Caruso" (from the film)		Mario Lanza
ALP1072-3	Verdi: La Traviata	NBCSO	Toscanini Albanese Merrill
ALP1074	Operatic Arias (Bellini, Borodin, Glinka, Mozart, Rossini)		Rossi-Lemeni
ALP1075	Dvorak: Symphony 2 (7)	Philh	Kubelik
ALP1076	Operatic and Song Recital (Cilea, Massenet, Weber, etc)	Philh	Susskind Joan Hammond
ALP1077-80	Handel: Messiah	RPO	Beecham Nash etc
ALP1081-2	Puccini: La Boheme	NBCSO	Toscanini Albanese Peerce
ALP1083	Tchaikovsky: Symphony 4	CSO	Kubelik
ALP1084	Bach,JS: Brandenburg Concertos 2, 5	Philh	Edwin Fischer
ALP1085	Mendelssohn: Violin Concerto in Dmin/Sonata in F	Philh	Boult Menuhin
ALP1086	Wagner: Siegfried Idyll, Tchaikovsky: Romeo and Juliet	Philh	Cantelli
ALP1087	Chopin: Sonata Op 35, Ballade Op 23, Nocturne Op 15/2, Liszt		Horowitz
ALP1088	Schubert: String Quartet "Death and the Maiden"		Amadeus Qt
ALP1089	Walton: Belshazzar's Feast		Liverpool Philh Walton
ALP1090-2	Verdi: Otello	NBCSO	Toscanini Vinay Nelli
ALP1093	Beethoven: Violin Sonata Op 47 ("Kreutzer")		Heifetz Moiseiwitsch
ALP1094	Beethoven: Sonatas Pathetique and Appassionata		Edwin Fischer
ALP1095-8	Wagner: Lohengrin	Hamburg	Schuchter Frick etc
ALP1099	Verdi: Operatic Arias (Nabucco, Forza, Ernani, Vespers)	Philh	Fistoulari Rossi-Lemeni
ALP1100	Beethoven: Violin Concerto	Philh	Furtwangler Menuhin
ALP1101	Respighi: Fountains of Rome/Pines of Rome	NBCSO	Toscanini
ALP1102	V-Williams: Symphony 7	Halle	Barbirolli
ALP1103	Bach: Concerto for 3 Pianos/Schubert: Moments Musiceaux	Philh	Edwin Fischer Matthews Smith
ALP1104	Brahms: Violin Concerto	Philh	Schwarz De Vito
ALP1105	Beethoven: Violin Sonatas Op 24 ("Spring"), Op 96	Menuhin	Kentner
ALP1106	Beethoven: Septet/Cherubini: Symphony	NBCSO	Toscanini
ALP1107	Prokofiev: Classical Symphony, Gershwin: American in Paris	NBCSO	Toscanini
ALP1108	Beethoven: Symphonies 5/8	NBCSO	Toscanini
ALP1109	Mozart: Overtures (Flute,Cosi,Figaro,Idomeneo,Giovanni,etc)	Philh	Kubelik
ALP1110	Liszt Recital		Brailowsky
ALP1111	Chopin: Ballades 3/4/Etude 3/Impromptu 1/etc		Horowitz
ALP1112-3	Verdi: Il Trovatore	RCAVO	Cellini Björling Milanov
ALP1114	Mozart: Symphony 38/Haydn: Symphony 60	Glynd	Gui
ALP1115-7	Bizet: Carmen	RCAVO	Reiner Merrill Stevens
ALP1118	Rachmaninov: Symphony 3	BBCSO	Sargent
ALP1119	Beethoven: Symphony 7	NBCSO	Toscanini
ALP1120	Schubert: Symphony 9	NBCSO	Toscanini
ALP1121	Bartok: Violin Concerto	Philh	Furtwangler Menuhin
ALP1122	Sibelius: Symphony 2	Halle	Barbirolli
ALP1123	Brahms: Piano Concerto 2	BSO	Munch Rubinstein
ALP1124	Mozart: Violin Concerto 5 K219/Bruch: Violin Concerto 1	LSO	Sargent Heifetz
ALP1125	Mozart: Quintet in C K515		Amadeus Qt Aronowitz.
ALP1126-8	Mascagni: Cavalleria Rusticana/Leoncavallo: Pagliacci	RCAVO	Cellini Björling De Los Angeles
ALP1129	Beethoven: Symphony 6	NBCSO	Toscanini
ALP1130-2	Beethoven: Fidelio	VPO	Furtwangler Mödl Windgassen
ALP1133	"The Heart of the Ballet"		Stokowski
ALP1134	Beethoven: Symphony 2	ABCSO	Goossens
ALP1135	Mendelssohn: Violin Concerto/Beethoven: Romances 1/2	Philh	Furtwangler Menuhin

ALP1136	Chopin: The 4 Scherzi		Rubinstein
ALP1137	Berlioz: Symphonie Fantastique	San Francisco SO	Monteux
ALP1138	Brahms: Alto Rhapsody, Mahler: Kindertotenlieder	RCASO	Monteux Anderson
ALP1139	Bach,JS: Goldberg Variations		Landowska (harpsichord)
ALP1140	A recital of songs by the Scandinavian Dorumsgaard	Flagstad	Moore
ALP1141	Beethoven: Piano Sonata 29 (Hammerklavier)		Solomon
ALP1142	Schumann: Carnaval/Etudes Symphoniques		Cortot
ALP1143	Wolf: Lieder Recital	Fischer-Dieskau	Moore
ALP1144	Boccherini: Quintet Op 29/1, Quintet Op 60/5	Quintetto Boccherini	
ALP1145	Beethoven: Symphonies 2/4	NBCSO	Toscanini
ALP1147-9	Rossini: La Cenerentola	Glynd	Gui Gabarain Oncina
ALP1150-1	Falla: La Vida Breve	Barcelona	Halffter De Los Angeles
ALP1152	Brahms: Symphony 1	Philh	Cantelli
ALP1153	Elgar: Enigma Vns, Wand of Youth Suite	LPO	Boult
ALP1154	Liszt: Piano Sonata in Bmin/Don Juan Fantasy		Cherkassky
ALP1155	Mozart: Symphony 39/Haydn: Symphony 95	Glynd	Gui
ALP1157	Chopin: Nocturnes		Rubinstein
ALP1158	Recital (Debussy, Liszt, Beethoven, Schumann, etc)		Iturbi
ALP1159	Christmas Carols	Royal Choral	Sargent
ALP1160	Beethoven: Piano Sonatas 21 Op 53 ("Waldstein")/32 Op 111		Solomon
ALP1162-5	Gounod: Faust	PCO	Cluytens De Los Angeles
ALP1166	Brahms: Symphony 3	NBCSO	Toscanini
ALP1168	Schumann: Fantasia, Carnaval		Brailowsky
ALP1169	Beethoven: Piano Sonatas 30, 31		Myra Hess
ALP1170	Chopin: Nocturnes Vol 2		Rubinstein
ALP1172	Brahms: Piano Concerto 1	Philh	Kubelik Solomon
ALP1173	Strauss,R:Don Juan/Wagner:Dawn & Siegfried's Rhine Journey	NBCSO	Toscanini
ALP1174	"Italian Classic Songs of the 17th & 18th Centuries"		Gigli
ALP1175	Rodgers: "Victory at Sea" (arr bennett)	NBCSO	Bennett
ALP1176-7	Shakespeare: Macbeth	Old Vic	Guinness
ALP1178	Schubert: Symphony 9	Halle	Barbirolli
ALP1179-0	Berlioz: Romeo & Juliet	BSO	Munch
ALP1181	Bizet: Symphony in C, L'Arlesienne Suites	SO	Stokowski
ALP1182-3	Beethoven: Missa Solemnis	NBCSO	Toscanini Marshall Merriman
ALP1184	Beethoven: "Archduke" Trio Op 97	Heifetz	Feuermann Rubinstein
ALP1185	Turina: Canto a Sevilla	LSO	Fistoulari De Los Angeles
ALP1186	Romberg: Student Prince	Mario Lanza etc	
ALP1187	Song recital by	Björling	Schauwecker (piano)
ALP1188-90	Bach,JS: St John Passion	RCASO	Shaw Addison Thebom
ALP1191	Song Recital (Schumann, Schubert, Brahms, Strauss, etc)	Flagstad	McArthur
ALP1192	Chopin: 24 Preludes		Rubinstein
ALP1193	Schubert: Rosamunde, Tchaikovsky: Nutcracker Suite	SO	Stokowski
ALP1194	Mozart: Piano Concerto K450/Sonata K331	Philh	Ackermann Solomon
ALP1195	Beethoven: Symphony 5	VPO	Furtwangler
ALP1196	Menotti: Amahl and the Night Visitors		Schippers
ALP1197	"Alfred Cortot Plays Popular Encores"		Cortot
ALP1199-01	Mozart: Don Giovanni	Glynd	Busch Souez Brownlee
ALP1202	Operatic Recital	Lanza	Malbin
ALP1203	Schumann: Symphony 1	BSO	Munch
ALP1204	Brahms: Haydn Variations/Elgar: Enigma Variations	NBCSO	Toscanini
ALP1205	Schönberg: Verklärte Nacht, V-Williams: Tallis Fantasia	SO	Stokowski
ALP1206	Recital	Heifetz	Bay
ALP1207	Ravel: Pavane, Falla: 3 Cornered Hat Suite, Debussy, Dukas	Philh	Cantelli
ALP1208	Strauss,R: Don Juan/Till Eulenspiegel	VPO	Furtwangler
ALP1209	Strauss,R: Ein Heldenleben	CSO	Reiner
ALP1210	Sibelius: Symphony 1	SO	Stokowski

ALP1211	Strauss,R: Don Quixote	BSO	Munch Piatigorsky Rubinstein
ALP1213	Brahms: Piano Recital		Rubinstein
ALP1214	Strauss,R: Also Sprach Zarathustra/Dance of the 7 Veils	CSO	Reiner
ALP1215-7	Puccini: Madama Butterfly	RomeOp	Gavazzeni De Los Angeles Gobbi
ALP1218	Mussorgsky: Pictures at an Exhibition, Franck: Psyché	NBCSO	Toscanini
ALP1219	Franck: Symphony	NBCSO	Cantelli
ALP1220	Wagner: Lohengrin Prelude act 1/Tannhauser Ov	VPO	Furtwangler
ALP1222	Dvorak: Symphony 5 (New World)	NBCSO	Toscanini
ALP1223	Busoni: Arlecchino	Glynd	Pritchard Evans Wallace
ALP1224	St-Saens: Carnival of the Animals,Strauss: Fantasy, etc	Halle	Barbirolli Rawicz Landauer
ALP1225-7	Berlioz: Damnation of Faust	BSO	Munch
ALP1228	Debussy: La Mer/Martyrdom of St Sebastian Suite	Philh	Cantelli
ALP1229-31	Verdi: Falstaff	NBCSO	Toscanini Valdengo Nelli
ALP1232	Grofé: Grand Canyon Suite	NBCSO	Toscanini
ALP1233	Brahms: Cello Sonatas Op 38, Op 99	Tortelier	Engel
ALP1234	Vivaldi: The Seasons	VdiR	Fasano
ALP1235	Beethoven:Egmont/Berlioz:Carnaval Romain/Sibelius:Finlandia	NBCSO	Toscanini
ALP1236	Tchaikovsky: Symphony 5	BBCSO	Sargent
ALP1239	Mozart: Symphonies 34/38	CSO	Kubelik
ALP1240	Stravinsky: Petruchka (original version)	SO	Stokowski
ALP1241	St-Saens:Violin Concerto Bmin/Vieuxtemps:Violin Concerto 5	Philh	Fistoulari Menuhin
ALP1242	Elgar: Symphony 2	HO	Barbirolli
ALP1243	Chopin: Piano Sonatas 2, 3		Schiöler
ALP1244	Ibert: Divertissement, Faure: Pelleas et Melisande	HO	Barbirolli
ALP1245	Ravel: Rapsodie Espagnole,St-Saens,Berlioz,Lalo	BSO	Munch
ALP1246	Recital of Harpsichord Music		Landowska
ALP1247	"Operatic Arias" (Force of Destiny, Aida, Gioconda, etc)	RCAVO	Cellini Zinka Milanov
ALP1249	Mozart: String Qt Dmin K421, Haydn: Qt in Cmaj Op 54/2	Amadeus Qt	
ALP1250	Chopin: Piano Concerto 1	LAPO	Wallenstein Rubinstein
ALP1251	Hindemith: Symphonic Metamorphosis, Schönberg: 5 Pieces	CSO	Kubelik
ALP1252-4	Verdi: Un Ballo in Maschera	NBCSO	Toscanini Peerce, Merrill, etc
ALP1255-6	Gilbert&Sullivan: The Mikado	D'Oyly Carte Opera	
ALP1257-61	Wagner: Die Walkure	VPO	Furtwangler Modl Suthaus
ALP1262-4	Shakespeare: Midsummer Nights Dream	BBCSO	Sargent
ALP1265	Shakespeare Songs and Lute Songs		Deller
ALP1266	Russian Folk Songs		Christoff
ALP1267	Mendelssohn: Symphonies 4 (Italian) & 5 (Reformation)	NBCSO	Toscanini
ALP1268	Beethoven: Symphony 6	NBCSO	Toscanini
ALP1269	Chausson: Poeme de l'Amour et de la Mer/French Song Recital	RCASO	Monteux Swarthout
ALP1270	Mahler: Lieder eines Fahrenden Gesellen/Brahms: 7 Songs	Philh	Furtwangler Fischer-Dieskau
ALP1271	Beethoven: Sonatas 7 in Fmaj Op 10/3, 32 in Cmin Op 111		Edwin Fischer
ALP1272	Beethoven: Piano Sonatas 23 Op 57 ("Appassionata")/28 Op 101		Solomon
ALP1273-5	Mozart: The Magic Flute	BPO	Beecham Lemnitz Berger
ALP1276	Wagner: Parsifal (Act 2), Lohengrin (Act 3)	RCASO	McArthur Flagstad Melchior
ALP1277	"Italian Operatic Choruses" (Verdi, Puccini, Mascagni)	RomeOp	Morelli
ALP1278-9	Rossini: Petite Messe Solenelle	AdSC	Fasano
ALP1280	Beethoven: Piano Concerto 5	RCAVO	Reiner Horowitz
ALP1281	Mozart: Violin Concertos 4 K218, 5 K219	Philh	Pritchard Menuhin
ALP1282	Brahms: Violin Sonatas 1 Op 78/3 Op 108	De Vito	Edwin Fischer
ALP1283	Mozart: String Quartets K465/K575	Amadeus Qt	
ALP1284	Opera Recital (Verdi, Puccini, Rossini, Mascagni, etc)	RomeOp	Morelli De Los Angeles
ALP1285	Chausson: Violin Concerto Op 21	Menuhin	Kentner
ALP1286-7	Beethoven: Symphony 9	Bayreuth	Furtwangler
ALP1288	Bruch: Scottish Fantasy	RCAVO	Steinberg Heifetz
	Korngold: Violin Concerto	LAPO	Wallenstein Heifetz
ALP1289-92	Verdi: Don Carlo	RomeOp	Santini Christoff Gobbi

ALP1293-4	Gilbert & Sullivan: HMS Pinafore	Sargent
ALP1295	Schubert: Lieder Recital	Fischer-Dieskau Moore
ALP1296	St-Saens: Symphony 3	NBCSO Toscanini
ALP1297	Brahms: Piano Concerto 1	CSO Reiner Rubinstein
ALP1298-9	Schubert: Winterreise	Fischer-Dieskau Moore
ALP1300	Beethoven: Piano Concerto 5	Philh Menges Solomon
ALP1301	"Homage to Pavlova"	Philh Kurtz
ALP1302	Seiber: String Quartet 2/Quartetto Lirico	Amadeus Qt
ALP1303	Beethoven: Piano Sonatas Op 31/2, Op 31/3	Solomon
ALP1304-5	Beethoven: Fidelio	NBCSO Toscanini Bampton Peerce
ALP1306	Dvorak: Cello Concerto	Philh Sargent Tortelier.
ALP1307	Mozart: String Quartet Dmaj K499, B flat maj K589	Amadeus Qt
ALP1308	St-Saens: Scenes from Samson&Delilah	NBCSO Stokowski Stevens Peerce
ALP1309	Song Recital (Schubert, Brahms, Strauss)	Flagstad McArthur
ALP1310	Chopin: Etudes Op 10, nos 1-12	Cherkassky
ALP1311	Chopin: Etudes Op 25/1-12, etc	Cherkassky
ALP1312-5	Mozart: Marriage of Figaro	Glynd Gui [ASD274-7]
ALP1316	Mozart: Piano Concertos K488/K491	Philh Menges Solomon
ALP1317-8	Beethoven: Songs Volumes 1 & 2	Fischer-Dieskau Klust
ALP1319	Beethoven: Kreutzer Sonata	De Vito Aprea
ALP1320	Granados: Goyescas	Amparo Iturbi (piano)
ALP1321	St-Saens: Piano Concerto 4/Chopin: Piano Concerto 2	BSO Munch Brailowsky
ALP1322	Shostakovich: Symphony 10	Philh Kurtz
ALP1323	Great Scenes from Boris Godunov	FNRO Dobrowen Christoff
ALP1324	Beethoven: Symphony 1/Overture Leonora 2	VPO Furtwangler
ALP1325	Schubert: Symphony 8/Mendelssohn: Symphony 4	Philh Cantelli
ALP1326-8	Puccini: Manon Lescaut	RomeOp Perlea Albanese Björling
ALP1329	"Gigli at Carnegie Hall" (17th, 20th, 24th April 1955)	Gigli
ALP1330	Mozart: Symphonies 40/41	CSO Reiner
ALP1331	Mozart: Violin Sonatas 10,15	Heifetz Smith
ALP1332	Boccherini: Quintet Op 13/3, Quintet Op 18/1	Quintetto Boccherini
ALP1333	Chopin: Waltzes 1-14	Rubinstein
ALP1334	Brahms: Violin Concerto	CSO Reiner Heifetz
ALP1335	Sibelius: Swan of Tuonela,Strauss,R: Danae,Villa-Lobos	HO Barbirolli
ALP1336	Tchaikovsky: Rococo Variations, St-Saens: Cello Concerto, Faure	Philh Menges Tortelier
ALP1337	Schubert: Quartet 10 Op 125/1,	Amadeus Qt
ALP1338	Beethoven: Violin Sonatas Op 12/2, Op 23	Menuhin Kentner
ALP1339	Rimsky-Korsakov: Scheherazade	Philh Stokowski Parikian
ALP1340	Clementi: Piano Sonatas	Horowitz
ALP1341-3	Shakespeare: Richard III	London Film Production
ALP1344	Concertos by Vivaldi/Valentini/Scarlatti	VdiR Fasano
ALP1345	Beethoven: Cello Sonata Op 5/1 etc	Piatigorsky Solomon
ALP1346	Beethoven: Cello Sonatas Op 5/2 and Op 69	Piatigorsky Solomon
ALP1347	Beethoven: Cello Sonatas Op 102/1 and Op 102/2	Piatigorsky Solomon
ALP1349	Prokofiev: Piano Concerto 2, Shostakovich: Concerto for Piano Trumpet and Strings	Philh Menges Cherkassky
ALP1350	Sibelius: Violin Concerto Paganini: Violin Concerto 1	LPO Boult Menuhin LSO Fistoulari Menuhin
ALP1351-2	Brahms: German Requiem	BPO Kempe Fischer-Dieskau Grummer
ALP1353	Operatic Recital (Bizet, Massenet, Donizetti, Mascagni)	Carosio Sanzogno
ALP1354	Beethoven: Violin Sonatas Op 30/1, Op 30/2	Menuhin Kentner
ALP1355	Puccini: Il Tabarro	Rome Opera Bellezza Gobbi
ALP1356	Tchaikovsky: Symphony 6	BSO Monteux
ALP1357	Gluck: Orfeo ed Euridice (Act 2)	NBCSO Toscanini Merriman Gibson
ALP1358	Brahms: Piano Sonata Op 5	Solomon
ALP1359	Elgar: Nursery Suite, In the South	LPO Boult

ALP1360	Bach,JS & Brahms Choruses		Robert Shaw Chorale
ALP1361	Boccherini: Quintet Op 28, Quintet Op 10/5, Quintet Op 41/2		Quintetto Boccherini
ALP1362	Bruch: Violin Concerto 2,Wieniawski: Violin Concerto 2	RCAVO	Solomon Heifetz
ALP1363	Verdi: Te Deum, Boito: Mefistofele (hlts)	NBCSO	Toscanini Moscona
ALP1365	Serenade (Film Sound Track)		Mario Lanza
ALP1366	Verdi: Soprano Arias	SO	Curiel Antonietta Stella
ALP1368	Debussy: La Damoiselle elue, Berlioz: Les Nuits d'Ete	BSO	Munch De Los Angeles
ALP1369-0	Boito: Mefistofele	RomeOp	Gui Christoff
ALP1371	Verdi: The Force of Destiny (hlts)	RCA	Cellini Milanov Peerce
ALP1372	Tchaikovsky: Suite 3/Dvorak: Symphonic Variations	Philh	Sargent
ALP1373	Schubert: Quintet op 163		Quintetto Boccherini
ALP1374	Ravel: Daphnis and Chloe (complete)	BSO	Munch
ALP1375	Shakespeare: Hamlet, Henry V (hlts)	Philh	Mathieson Olivier
ALP1376	Beethoven: Violin Sonatas 8 & 9	Menuhin	Kentner
ALP1377	Stravinsky: The Soldier's Tale	Pritchard	Helpmann
ALP1378	Friml: The Vagabond King		Henri Rene Orch etc
ALP1379	Elgar: Marches, Froissart, Dream Children	LPO	Boult
ALP1380-1	Verdi: Requiem	NBCSO	Toscanini
ALP1382-3	Bach,JS: Suites 1-4	RCA	Reiner
ALP1384	Berlioz: Symphonie Fantastique	BSO	Munch
ALP1385	Boccherini:Quintet Op 11/6,Largo Op 12/1,Quintet Op 40/4, etc		Quintetto Boccherini
ALP1386	Brahms: Symphony 2	BPO	Kempe
ALP1387	Restful Music	NBCSO	Toscanini
ALP1388-0	Verdi: Aida	RomeOp	Perlea Björling
ALP1391	Verdi: Il Trovatore (hlts)	RCAVO	Cellini Milanov Björling
ALP1392	Verdi: Rigoletto (hlts)	RCAVO	Cellini Peerce Warren Berger
ALP1393	"Five Centuries of Spanish Song"		De Los Angeles
ALP1394-7	Massenet: Manon		Opera Comique Monteux De Los Angeles
ALP1398-1400	Chopin: Mazurkas 1-51		Rubinstein
ALP1401	Chopin: Piano Sonatas 2 & 3		Brailowsky
ALP1402	Tchaikovsky: Piano Concerto 1	CSO	Reiner Gilels
ALP1403	Mozart: Symphonies 36, 39	CSO	Reiner
ALP1404	Strauss,R: Till Eulenspiegel, Death and Transfiguration	NBCSO	Toscanini
ALP1405	"The Magic Mario" (Romberg, Kern, etc)		Mario Lanza
ALP1406	Boccherini:Quintet Op 25/3,Largo Cantabile,Quintet Op 25/1,etc		Quintetto Boccherini
ALP1407	Verdi: Opera Recital (Aida, Traviata, Ballo, Forza, Falstaff, etc)	Philh	Curiel Hammond
ALP1408	Beethoven: Symphony 6	BPO	Cluytens
ALP1409-0	Puccini: La Boheme	RCAVO	Beecham De Los Angeles Björling
ALP1411	Prokofiev: Violin Sonata Op 80, Leclair: Violin Sonata 5, Locatelli/Ysaye: Violin Sonata in Fmin	Oistrakh	Yampolski
ALP1412	Cherubini: Requiem	NBCSO	Toscanini
ALP1413	Rachmaninov: Piano Concerto 2/Liszt: Piano Concerto 1	CSO	Reiner Rubinstein
ALP1414	Rachmaninov: Rhapsody on a theme of Paganini	CSO	Reiner Rubinstein
	Grieg: Piano Concerto	RCAVO	Wallenstein Rubinstein
ALP1415	Beethoven: Symphony 5/Schubert: Symphony 8 ("Unfinished")	BSO	Munch
ALP1416	Bizet: Carmen (hlts)	RCAVO	Reiner Stevens Merrill
ALP1417	Bizet: Carmen/Verdi: Force of Destiny/Weber: Oberon/etc.	NBCSO	Toscanini
ALP1418	Humperdinck: Hansel & Gretel/Berlioz: Romeo&Juliet/etc.	NBCSO	Toscanini
ALP1419-21	Verdi: la Traviata	RomeOp	Monteux Carteri Valletti
ALP1422-6	Beethoven: Violin Sonatas 1-10	Heifetz	Bay (No 9 with Moiseiwitsch)
ALP1427	Miaskovsky: Cello Concerto	Philh	Sargent Rostropovich
ALP1428	Puccini: Operatic Arias	LSO	Erede Antonietta Stella
ALP1429	Scriabin: Piano Sonata Op 23, Preludes from Op 11,13,15,16,27,48,51,59,67		Horowitz
ALP1430-1	Piano Recital (Schubert, Chopin, Scriabin, Liszt, Prokofiev)		Horowitz
ALP1432	Toscanini Anthology vol 3 (Dukas,St-Saens,Smetana)	NBCSO	Toscanini

ALP1435-6	Sir Winston Churchill (selection from Wartime speeches)		
ALP1437	Beethoven: Violin Concerto	BSO	Munch Heifetz
ALP1438	Berlioz: Harold in Italy	NBCSO	Toscanini
ALP1439	Vivaldi: Concertos	VdiR	Fasano
ALP1440	Sibelius: Symphony 2	NBCSO	Stokowski
ALP1441	Toscanini Anthology (Tchaikovsky, Rossini, Waldteufel)	NBCSO	Toscanini
ALP1443	Tchaikovsky: Swan Lake (hlts)	NBCSO	Stokowski
ALP1444	Mozart: Requiem	BPO	Kempe etc
ALP1446	Liszt: Hungarian Rhapsodies 2,6,12,15		Cziffra
ALP1449-51	Bach,JS: Sonatas and Partitas for Violin		Heifetz
ALP1452	Verdi : hlts from Nabucco,Lombardi,Forza,Luisa Miller	NBCSO	Toscanini Peerce Moscona
ALP1453	Verdi : Rigoletto act 4, etc	NBCSO	Toscanini Peerce Milanov Warren
ALP1454	Mozart: Piano Concertos 11, 24	Orch	G.Jones Kirkpatrick
ALP1455	Liszt: Piano Concerto 1, Hungarian Fantasia	PCO	Dervaux Cziffra
ALP1456	Elgar: Violin Concerto	LSO	Elgar Menuhin
ALP1460	Chausson: Poeme, St-Saens: Intro&Rondo Capriccioso, Berlioz	BSO	Munch Oistrakh
ALP1461	Mozart: Symphony 29/A Musical Joke K522	Philh	Cantelli
ALP1462	Sonatas and Duos by Purcell, Handel, Viotti, Spohr	De Vito	Menuhin
ALP1464	Elgar: Enigma, Serenade, Cockaigne	Various	Elgar
ALP1465	Chopin: Piano Concerto 2, Schumann: Piano Concerto	NBCSO	Steinberg Rubinstein
ALP1469	Berlioz: Romeo&Juliet, Tchaikovsky: Romeo&Juliet	NBCSO	Toscanini
ALP1470	Albeniz: Iberia, Scriabin: Poème de L'Extase	Philh	Goossens
ALP1471	Mozart: Symphony 34/Haydn: Symphony 104	Philh	Kempe
ALP1472	Beethoven Symphony 7	Philh	Cantelli [ASD254]
ALP1473-4	Rossini: Le Comte Ory	Glynd	Gui Barabas Oncina
ALP1475	Delibes: Sylvia & Coppelia	BSO	Monteux
ALP1476	Verdi: Ballo in Maschera (hlts)	Met	Mitropoulos Milanov Peerce
ALP1477	Chopin: Piano Sonata 2, Debussy: Preludes		Rubinstein
ALP1479	Sibelius: Violin Concerto/Suk: 4 Pieces	Philh	Susskind Neveu
ALP1480	Sibelius: Symphony 7, Oceanides, Pelleas	RPO	Beecham [ASD468]
ALP1481	Mascagni: Cavalleria Rusticana/Leoncavallo: Pagliacci (hlts)	RCAVO	Cellini De Los Angeles Björling
ALP1482-4	Shakespeare: Hamlet	Old Vic	Gielgud
ALP1485-6	Gilbert & Sullivan: The Mikado	Glynd	Sargent etc [ASD256-7]
ALP1487	Strauss,R: Songs		Fischer-Dieskau Moore
ALP1488	Mozart: String Quartet K458/Haydn: String Quartet Op 77/1	Amadeus Qt	
ALP1489	Chopin: Ballades, Mazurkas, Nocturnes, etc		Cherkassky
ALP1490	Balakirev: Islamey, Rimsky-Korsakov: Le Coq D'Or, etc	Philh	Goossens [ASD262]
ALP1491	Tchaikovsky: Symphony 5	Philh	Silvestri [ASD261]
ALP1492	Mozart: Symphony 39, Divertimento 15	NBCSO	Toscanini
ALP1493	Strauss,R: Don Quixote	NBCSO	Toscanini
ALP1494	Bartok: Concerto for Orchestra	CSO	Reiner
ALP1495	Tchaikovsky: Symphony 6	Philh	Silvestri [ASD273]
ALP1496	Mozart: Exsultate Jubilate K165, Benedictus Sit Deus K117, etc	BPO	Forster Erna Berger
ALP1497	Bizet: L'Arlesienne Suites 1/2	RPO	Beecham [ASD252]
ALP1498	Mozart: Symphony 40, Eine Kleine Nachtmusik, Cherubini	VPO	Furtwangler
ALP1499	V-Williams: Serenade, Greensleeves, Wasps Ov, Unknown Region	LSO	Sargent
ALP1501	Haydn: Cello Concerto, Vivaldi: Cello Concerto	DSRO	Woldike Bengtsson
ALP1503	Stravinsky: Petrushka	Philh	Kurtz
ALP1504-5	Gilbert&Sullivan: The Gondoliers	Pro Arte	Sargent [ASD265-6]
ALP1506-10	Wagner: The Mastersingers	BPO	Kempe Frick Neidlinger etc
ALP1511	Tchaikovsky: Symphony 4	Philh	Silvestri [ASD253]
ALP1512	Bach: Sonatas 1 & 2 for Violin		Menuhin
ALP1513	Wagner: Tannhauser/Dutchman/Gotterdammerung	BPO	Kempe
ALP1514	Dohnanyi: Nursery Song, Concerto 2	RPO	Boult Dohnanyi
ALP1515-7	Mozart: Idomeneo	Glynd	Pritchard Jurinac Simoneau
ALP1518	Recital (Byrd, Pachelbel, Bach, etc)		Kirkpatrick

ALP1520	Chausson: Poeme/Debussy: Sonata in Gmin/Ravel: Tzigane		Neveu	
ALP1521	Beethoven:Violin Sonata Op 30/2, Brahms:Violin Sonata Op 100	De Vito	Aprea	
ALP1522-4	Debussy: Pelleas & Melisande	ONDF	Cluytens De Los Angeles	
ALP1526	"Pops Concert" (Mendelssohn, Tchaikovsky, Weber, etc)	VPO	Furtwangler	
ALP1527	"Popular Piano Recital" (Beethoven, St-Saens, Poulenc, etc)		Cherkassky	
ALP1528	Bach: Cantatas 33 & 105	DSRO	Woldike etc	
ALP1530	Grieg: Peer Gynt	RPO	Beecham Hollweg	[ASD258]
ALP1531	Bach: Sonatas 3 & 4 for Violin		Menuhin	
ALP1532	Bach: Sonatas 5 & 6 for Violin		Menuhin	
ALP1533	Beecham Lollipops (Suppe,Sibelius,Berlioz,Debussy,Mozart,etc)	RPO	Beecham	[ASD259]
ALP1534	Liszt: Mephisto Waltz/Valse Oubliee no 1/Rhaps Espagnol		Cziffra	
ALP1535	"The Art of Guido Cantelli" (mvmts from popular symphonies)	Philh	Cantelli	
ALP1536	Mozart: Symphony 41/Div K131	RPO	Beecham	
ALP1537	Dvorak: Symphony 8, Ov Carnaval	LPO	Silvestri	[ASD470]
ALP1538	Rachmaninov: Piano Concerto 4/Ravel: Concerto in Gmaj	Philh	Gracis Michelangeli	[ASD255]
ALP1539	Mozart: Quintets Dmaj K593, Eflat K614	Amadeus Qt		
ALP1540	Recital (Mozart, Schumann, Brahms, Wolf, Pfitzner, Strauss)	Loose	Werba	
ALP1541	Boccherini: Cello Concerto,Haydn: Cello Concerto	Pro Arte	Previtali Baldovino	
ALP1542	Sibelius: Symphony 1	BBCSO	Sargent	[ASD260]
ALP1543	Mendelssohn/Tchaikovsky: Violin concertos	Philh	Silvestri Ferras	[ASD278]
ALP1544	Schubert: Octet op 166	BPO Chamber Ensemble		
ALP1545	Brahms: Symphony 4	BPO	Kempe	
ALP1546	Beethoven: Piano Concerto 3/etc	Philh	Menges Solomon	[BSD751]
ALP1547	Mozart: Violin Sonatas 32, 34	Menuhin	Kentner	
ALP1548-9	Bach,J.S: Goldberg Variations		Tureck	
ALP1550	Dvorak: Symphony 9	FNRO	Silvestri	
ALP1551	Schumann: Songs including Liederkries	Fischer-Dieskau Moore		
ALP1552	Dohnanyi: 6 Pieces, Intermezzo, Pastorale, Burletta, Vns op 29,etc		Dohnanyi	
ALP1553	Dohnanyi: Winterreigen, Suite in Olden Style, Valses Nobles, etc		Dohnanyi	
ALP1554	Prokofiev: Symphony 1,Shostakovich: Symphony 1	Philh	Kurtz	[ASD263]
ALP1555-63	Winston Churchill: A Selection from his Speeches			
ALP1564	Rimsky Korsakov: Scheherazade	RPO	Beecham	[ASD251]
ALP1565	Beethoven: Andante Favori, Chopin: Impromptus, Liszt		Kentner	
ALP1566	Tchaikovsky: Symphony 6	Philh	Kempe	
ALP1567	Bruckner: Mass in Emin/Te Deum	BPO	Forster	
ALP1568	Brahms: Violin Concerto	BPO	Kempe Menuhin	[ASD264]
ALP1569	Mendelssohn: Symphony 3, Ov Calm Sea	RPO	Previtali	
ALP1570	Grieg: Holberg Suite/2 Elegaic Melodies	Philh	Fistoulari	
ALP1571	Lalo: Symphonie Espagnole, St-Saens Intro & Rondo Capriccioso	Philh	Goossens Menuhin	[ASD290]
ALP1572	Bach,J.S: St Matthew Passion (hlts)	St Hedwig's Berlin Karl Forster		
ALP1573	Beethoven: Piano Sonatas 1,7		Solomon	
ALP1574	Bach: Chaconne, Schubert: Impromptu in Aflat, Hindemith: Sonata 3		Cherkassky	
ALP1575	Handel: Arias	LSO	Sargent Lewis	[ASD291]
ALP1576	Beethoven: Symphony 7/Egmont Ov	BPO	Cluytens	
ALP1577	Puccini: Suor Angelica	RomeOp	Serafin De Los Angeles	
ALP1578	Sibelius: Karelia, En Saga, Swan, Romance	RPO	Collins	
ALP1579	Haydn: String Quartets 57, 65	Amadeus Quartet		
ALP1580	Chopin: Piano Concertos 1,2	RPO	Goossens Simon	
ALP1581	Schumann: Symphony 1,Ov Manfred	BPO	Kempe	
ALP1582	Tchaikovsky: The Tempest, Glazunov: Stenka Razin, Borodin	Philh	Fistoulari	
ALP1583	Beethoven: Piano Concerto 1/Sonata Op 90	Philh	Menges Solomon	[ASD294]
ALP1584	Brahms: Songs	Fischer-Dieskau Engel		
ALP1585	Opera Recital (Verdi and Bellini)	Rome	Gui Christoff	
ALP1586	Delius: Brigg Fair,Song Before Sunrise, etc	RPO	Beecham	[ASD357]
ALP1587	Schumann: Frauenliebe und Leben Op 42, Mendelssohn: Songs	Berger	Scherzer (piano)	

ALP1588	Bartok: Piano Concerto 3/Dance Suite	Philh	Markevitch Annie Fischer
ALP1589	Concert (Albinoni, Vivaldi, Pergolesi)	VdiR	Fasano
ALP1590	Brahms: Serenade 1 Op 11	PCO	Vandernoot
ALP1591	Strauss,R: Don Juan, Feuersnot Love Scene, Smetana:The Moldau	VPO	Cluytens
ALP1592	Haydn: String Quartets 72,74	Amadeus Quartet	
ALP1593	St-Saens: Piano Concertos 1/3	ONDF	Fourestier Darre
ALP1594	Rossini: String Sonatas 1 & 5/Bellini/etc	VdiR	
ALP1595	Dvorak: Cello Concerto	RPO Boult	Rostropovich [ASD358]
ALP1596	Beethoven: Symphony 2, Ruins of Athens Ov	RPO	Beecham [ASD287]
ALP1597	Bartok: Divertimento, Hindemith: Mathis der Maler	Philh	Silvestri
ALP1598	Beethoven: Symphony 4, Ov Leonora 1	BBCSO	Toscanini
ALP1599	Microgroove Frequency Test Record		
ALP1600	Holst: The Planets	BBCSO	Sargent [ASD269]
ALP1601-2	Gilbert & Sullivan: Yeoman of the Gurad	Glynd	Sargent [ASD364-5]
ALP1603	Villa-Lobos: Bachianas Brasilieras 2, 5, 6, 9	ONDF	Villa-Lobos De Los Angeles
ALP1604	Piano Recital (Paraphrases, Transcriptions, Improvisations)		Cziffra
ALP1605	Strauss,R: Tod und Verklarung etc	Philh	Rodzinski [ASD270]
ALP1606-8	Haydn: The Seasons	RPO	Beecham [ASD282-4]
ALP1609	Tchaikovsky: Nutcracker Ballet	Philh	Kurtz [ASD289]
ALP1610-2	Leoncavallo: Pagliacci, Mascagni: Cavalleria Rusticana	La Scala	Ghione/Mascagni Gigli
ALP1613-5	Glinka: A Life for the Tsar	Lamoureux	Markevitch Christoff S-Randall
ALP1616	Rachmaninov: Rhapsody, Stravinsky: Petrushka	LSO	Menges Cherkassky
ALP1617-9	Wolf: Morike Lieder	Fischer-Dieskau Moore	
ALP1620	Recital of Operatic Arias		Björling
ALP1621	Beethoven: Waldstein & Appassionata Sonatas		Kentner
ALP1622	Dvorak: String Quartet Op 96, Janacek: String Quartet 2	Vlach Quartet	
ALP1623	Dvorak: New World Symphony	BPO	Kempe [ASD380]
ALP1624-6	Haydn: Symphonies 93-98	RPO	Beecham
ALP1627	Moussorgsky: Pictures, Ravel: Bolero	RPO	Goossens
ALP1628	Walton: Belshazzar; Handel: Zadok etc.	RLPO	Sargent
ALP1629	Vivaldi: L'Estro Armonico, Op3;Concertos,P.280.320.321	VdiR	Fasano
ALP1630	Rachmaninov: Piano Concerto 2	Phild	Stokowski Rachmaninov
ALP1631	Mozart: Concertos for 2 Pianos K242/K365	LMP	Blech Vronsky Babin
ALP1632	Rimsky-Korsakov: Capriccio Espagnol, Prokofiev: Ov on Hebrew Themes, Liadov:Kikimora, etc	RPO	Kurtz
ALP1633	Berlioz: Symphonie Fantastique	FNRO	Beecham [ASD399]
ALP1634-6	Verdi: Simon Boccanegra	RomeOp	Santini Gobbi De Los Angeles
ALP1637	Nights in Vienna	VPO	Kempe [ASD279]
ALP1638	Wagner: Tristan & Isolde/Lohengrin/Parsifal	VPO	Kempe
ALP1639	Sibelius: Symphony No2	BBCSO	Sargent
ALP1640	Prokofiev: Sinfonia Concert, Rachmaninov	Rostropovich	
ALP1641	Ochestral Concert (Respighi, Albinoni, Bassani, etc)	VdiR	Fasano
ALP1642	Opera Recital by Lois Marshall	LSO	Pedrazzoli Marshall
ALP1643	Grieg/Schumann: Piano Concertos	Philh	Menges Solomon [ASD272]
ALP1644	Tchaikovsky: Swan Lake (hlts)	Philh	Kurtz Menuhin [ASD271]
ALP1645	Bach,J.S: Partitas 1/2		Tureck
ALP1648	Liszt: Symphonic Poems: Les Preludes/Tasso	Philh	Silvestri
ALP1649	Orchestral Concert (Sibelius, St-Saens, Chabrier, etc)	RPO	Collins
ALP1650-1	Sullivan: H.M.S. Pinafore	Gyndebourne	Sargent [ASD415-6]
ALP1652-5	Moussorgsky: Songs (complete)	Christoff	Labinsky (piano)
ALP1656	"French Ballet Music" (Delibes, Gounod, Massenet, Bizet, etc)	RPO	Beecham
ALP1657	Beethoven: Symphony 5, Leonora 3 Ov	BPO	Cluytens [ASD267]
ALP1658	A night at the proms	BBC	Sargent Cherkassky [ASD536]
ALP1659-60	Puccini: Madama Butterfly	Rome Op	de Fabritiis Gigli Del Monte
ALP1661-2	Galuppi: Il Filosofo di Campagna, Cimarosa: Maestro di Capella	Collegium Musicum Italicum Fasano	
ALP1663	Beethoven: Ovs Leonora 3,Fidelio,Coriolan, Prometheus, Egmont	BPO	Kempe [ASD336]

Cat. No.	Work	Performer(s)	Stereo
ALP1664	Beethoven: Symbhony 6	BBCSO Toscanini	
ALP1665	Music of India (Ragas and Talas)	Shankar Rakha	
ALP1666	Franck: Sonata in Amaj/Faure: Sonata in Amaj	Ferras Barbizet	
ALP1667	Tchaikovsky: Symphony 4	RPO Beecham	
ALP1668	Tchaikovsky: Manfred Symphony	FNRO Silvestri	
ALP1669	Mendelssohn: Violin Concerto, Bruch: Violin Concerto 1	Philh Kurtz Menuhin	[ASD334]
ALP1670	Bach Cantatas 56 & 82	Geraint Jones Orch Souzay	
ALP1671	British Folk Songs	Lois Marshall	
ALP1672	Opera Excerpts (Verdi, Puccini)	Rome Santini	
ALP1673	Schubert: String Quartet D112/Brahms: String Quartet Op 67	Amadeus Quartet	
ALP1674	Beethoven: Mass in Cmay,OP.86	RPO Beecham	[ASD280]
ALP1675	Janacek:Taras Bulba, Martinu: Frescoes	RPO Kubelik	
ALP1676	Mozart: Flute Concertos	Phil Kurtz Schaffer	
ALP1677	Schubert: Lieder Recital Vol 2	Fischer-Dieskau Moore	
ALP1678	Grieg/Liszt No2:Concertos	Philh Vandernoot Cziffra	[ASD301]
ALP1679	Rimsky Korsakov, Glinka, Tchaikovsky	Philh Kletzki	[ASD343]
ALP1680	Operatic Recital (Puccini, Mascagni, Smetana, Dvorak)	Philh Susskind Hammond	[ASD302]
ALP1681	"The Best of Gigli"	Gigli	
ALP1684	Ravel: Bolero/Dukas: Danse Macabre/Debussy: Faun Prelude	PCO Silvestri	
ALP1685	Beethoven: Symphony No3	PCO Schuricht	
ALP1686	Franck: Symphony in Dminor	FNRO Beecham	[ASD458]
ALP1687	Kodaly: Missa Brevis	Hungarian State Kodaly	
ALP1688	Falla: Tricorne Suites stc, Granados, Albeniz	RPO Rodzinski	[ASD281]
ALP1689	Debussy: La Mer/Nocturnes	PCO Silvestri	
ALP1690	Brahms: Cello Sonata Op 99, Debussy, Scriabin, etc	Rostropovich Dedyukhin	
ALP1691	"Cziffra plays Miniatures" (Mozart, Beethoven, Hummel, etc)	Cziffra	
ALP1692	Bach,J.S: Partitas 3/6	Tureck	
ALP1693-5	Haydn: Symphonies 99-104 ("Salomon")	RPO Beecham	[ASD339-41]
ALP1696	Brahms: St Anthony Vns, Wagner: Siegfried Idyll	Philh Kletzki	
ALP1697	Delius: Florida Suite, Over the Hills etc	RPO Beecham	[ASD329]
ALP1698-9	Beethoven: Symphonies Nos8 & 9	BPO Cluytens	
ALP1700	Verdi: Don Carlos (hlts)	Rome Santini Stella Gobbi	
ALP1701	Chopin: Nocturnes vol 1 (Nos 1-10)	Rubinstein	
ALP1702	Chopin: Nocturnes vol 2 (Nos 11-19)	Rubinstein	
ALP1703	Bach: Cantata Arias	BPO Foster Fischer-Dieskau	[ASD342]
ALP1704	Brahms: Piano Concerto No2	Philh Boult Kentner	[ASD268]
ALP1705	Bartok: Sonata for Solo Violin, Sonata 1 for Violin & Piano	Menuhin H Menuhin	
ALP1706	Debussy: Iberia, Ravel: Rapsodie Espagnole,Alborada, Dukas	RPO Goossens	
ALP1707	Beethoven: Symphony No7	PCO Schuricht	
ALP1708	Liszt: Piano Sonata in Bmin, Schubert: "Wanderer" Fantasy	Gheorghiu	
ALP1709	"Songs of Many Lands"	Gerard Souzay Baldwin (piano)	
ALP1710	Handel: Water Music, Fireworks, Samson etc	RPO Sargent	[ASD286]
ALP1711	Tchaikovsky, Glinka, Moussorgsky, Rimsky:	RPO Rodzinski	[ASD288]
ALP1712	Grieg: Complete Violin Sonatas	Menuhin Levin	
ALP1713	Schumann: Fantasiestucke Op 12/Chopin: Fantasie in Fmin	Cziffra	
ALP1714	Bach,J.S: Partitas 4 & 5	Tureck	
ALP1717	Beethoven: Piano Variations	Cziffra	
ALP1718	Tchaikovsky: Piano Concerto 1	Philh Vandernoot Cziffra	[ASD315]
ALP1719	Liszt: Paganini Studies, Franck:Prelude,Chorale&Fugue,Schumann	Abbey Simon	
ALP1720	Operatic Highlights (Donizetti,Massenet,Puccini,Verdi,Giordano)	Rome Santini	
ALP1721-4	Gounod: Faust	OTNO Cluytens De Los Angeles	[ASD307-10]
ALP1725	Schubert: Symphony No8, Rosamunde	RPO Kletzki	[ASD296]
ALP1726	Puccini: Gianni Schicchi	RomeOp Santini Gobbi	[ASD295]
ALP1727	Falla, Ravel, Chabrier	Philh Vandernoot	[ASD297]
ALP1728	St-Saens: Carnival of the Animals, Prokofiev: Peter & the Wolf	Philh Kurtz Flanders	[ASD299]

ALP1729	Handel-Beecham: Love in Bath	RPO Beecham	[ASD298]
ALP1731	Glyndebourne: The First Twenty Five Years		
ALP1732	Sibelius: Symphony 5, Pohjola's Daughter	BBCSO Sargent	[ASD303]
ALP1733	Schubert: Piano Quintet (Trout)	Amadeus Quartet	[ASD322]
ALP1734-5	Schubert: Die Winterreisse	Souzay Baldwin	
ALP1736	Popular movements from the classics	VPO Cluytens	[ASD304]
ALP1737-8	Liszt: A Faust Symphony, Symphonic Poem Orpheus	RPO Beecham	[ASD317-8]
ALP1739	Beethoven: Violin Sonatas 5 ("Spring"), 9 ("Kretuzer")	Yehudi & Hephzibah Menuhin	[ASD389]
ALP1743	Schubert: Symphonies Nos 3&5	RPO Beecham	[ASD345]
ALP1744	Bartok: Concerto for Orchestra	RPO Kubelik	[ASD312]
ALP1745	Stravinsky: Le Sacre du Printemps	Philh Markevitch	[ASD313]
ALP1746	Bruch: Violin Concerto 1, Lalo: Sym Espagnole	Philh Susskind Ferras	[ASD314]
ALP1747	Recital: "An Introduction to Bach"	Tureck	
ALP1748	Beethoven: Symphony 7	RPO Beecham	[ASD311]
ALP1749	Overtures (Humperdinck, Glinka, Mendelssohn, etc)	Philh Silvestri	[ASD338]
ALP1750	Wolf: Spanisches Liederbuch	Fischer-Dieskau Moore	[ASD378]
ALP1751	Schubert: Symphony 9	RPO Kubelik	[ASD325]
ALP1752-4	Weber: Der Freischutz	BPO Keilberth	[ASD319-21]
ALP1755-6	Bach: Brandenburg Concertos 1-6	BFCO Menuhin	[ASD327-8]
ALP1757-8	Sullivan: Iolanthe	Pro Arte Sargent	[ASD323-4]
ALP1759	Strauss: Don Quixote, Till Eulenspiegel	BPO Kempe Tortelier	[ASD326]
ALP1760	Bach: Concertos in A and E/Double Concerto	Menuhin Ferras	[ASD346]
ALP1761	Bizet: Symphony in C/Lalo: Symphony	ONRF Beecham	[ASD388]
ALP1762-4	Bizet: Carmen	FNRO Beecham	[ASD331-3]
ALP1765	Overtures Bartered Bride, Hebrides, Oberon, etc	VPO Kempe	[ASD330]
ALP1766	Purcell: Songs and Anthems	Various	[ASD335]
ALP1767	Schubert: Lieder Recital Vol 3	Fischer-Dieskau Engel	[ASD337]
ALP1768	Mozart: Clarinet Concerto/Bassoon Concerto	RPO Beecham Brymer	[ASD344]
ALP1769	Brahms: Hungarian Dances, Dvorak: Scherzo Capriccioso	RPO Kubelik	[ASD347]
ALP1770	Brahms: Symphony 2	RPO Beecham	[ASD348]
ALP1771	Beethoven: Symphony 6	RPO Kubelik	[ASD349]
ALP1772	Brahms: Symphony 1	BPO Kempe	[ASD350]
ALP1773-4	Mahler: Das Lied Van der Erde, Symphony 5 (adagietto)	Philh Kletzki Fischer-Dieskau	[ASD351-2]
ALP1775-6	Verdi: Requiem Mass	Rome Serafin	[ASD353-4]
ALP1777	Folksongs of the British Isles	Mackerras Lewis	
ALP1778	Wolf: Eichendorff Songs	Fischer-Dieskau Moore	[ASD356]
ALP1779	Schumann: Symphony 3/Manfred Ov	BPO Cluytens	
ALP1780-2	Verdi: La Traviata	Rome Serafin	[ASD359-61]
ALP1783	Wolf: Songs	Fischer-Dieskau Moore	[ASD362]
ALP1784	Wagner: Excerpts (Gotterdammerung, Tannhauser)	Berlin SO Konwitschny	[ASD363]
ALP1785	Respighi: Fountains of Rome/Bartered Bride	Philh Goossens	[ASD366]
ALP1786-8	Vivaldi: Il Cimento dell'Armonia e dell Invenzione	VdiR Fasano	[ASD367-9]
ALP1789	Brahms: Liebeslieder Walzer	Morison Thomas Lewis Bell etc	
ALP1790	Tchaikovsky: Sleeping Beauty Suite	Philh Kurtz Menuhin	[ASD371]
ALP1791	Bach,J.S: Overture in the French Style/Italian Concerto	Tureck	[ASD372]
ALP1792	Christmas Carols	Royal Choral Society Sargent	[ASD383]
ALP1793	Tchaikovsky: Songs	Christoff Labinsky	[ASD390]
ALP1794	Chopin: Piano Concerto 1	Philh Kletzki Pollini	[ASD370]
ALP1795-7	Puccini: Madama Butterfly	Rome Santini	[ASD373-5]
ALP1798	Famous Marches	Philh Kurtz	[ASD376]
ALP1799	Beethoven: Violin Concerto	VPO Silvestri Menuhin	[ASD377]
ALP1800	Tchaikovsky: Symphony 5	BPO Kempe	[ASD379]
ALP1801-2	Sullivan: The Pirates of Penzance	Pro Arte Sargent	[ASD381-2]
ALP1803	Recital (Spring Song, Fur Elise, Traumerei, etc)	Cziffra	
ALP1804	Bach: Cantata No203, Handel: Arias	Fischer- Dieskau	[ASD397]
ALP1805	Operatic duets	RPO Tausky	[ASD384]

ALP1806-8 Wagner: The Flying Dutchman	Berlin Opera	Konwitschny	[ASD385-7]
ALP1809-11 Vivldi: L'Estro Armonico, OP3	VdiR	Fasano	[ASD391-3]
ALP1812-13 Strauss: Der Zigeunerbaron	VPO	Hollreiser	[ASD394-5]
ALP1814 Dvorak: Symphony No7	VPO	Silvestri	[ASD396]
ALP1815 Tchaikovsky: Symphony No4	VPO	Kubelik	[ASD398]
ALP1816-7 Liszt: Transcendental Studies 1-12		Cziffra	
ALP1818 Prokofiev, Khachaturian, Rimsky-Korsakov	VPO	Silverstri	[ASD400]
ALP1819 Stravinsky: Symphony in 3 Movs, Le Rossignol	Philh	Silvestri	[ASD401]
ALP1820-1 Dvorak: Slavonic Dances Op46, Op72, Serenade in E major	BBCSO	Schwarz	[ASD402-3]
ALP1822-3 Bach: Suites Nos 1-4 BWV 1066-9	BFCO	Menuhin	[ASD404-5]
ALP1824 Brahms: Symphony 3/Tragic Ov	BPO	Kempe	[ASD406]
ALP1825 Verdi: Opera arias (Falstaff, Rigoletto, Don Carlos)	BPO Erede	Fischer-Dieskau	[ASD407]
ALP1827 Schubert: Lieder	Fischer-Dieskau Moore		
ALP1828 Bach: Cantatas 11 & 140	LGO	Thomas	
ALP1829 Haydn: Songs	Fischer-Dieskau Moore		
ALP1830 Rachmaninoy: Songs	Christoff	Labinsky	
ALP1831 Franck: Symphony in D min	Philh	Silvestri	[ASD408]
ALP1832-3 Verdi: Il Trovatore	RCA	Cellini Milanov Bjoerling	
ALP1834-6 Haydn: The Creation	Berlin	Forster	[ASD409-11]
ALP1837 Gounod: Faust-exc	French Op	Cluytens	[ASD412]
ALP1838 'The Fabulous Victoria de Los Angeles' (recital)	De Los Angeles Moore		[ASD413]
ALP1839 Bach: Musical Offering	BFCO	Menuhin	[ASD414]
ALP1840 Schumann: Carnaval op 9/Carnival of Vienna		Cziffra	
ALP1841 Operatic Recital (Mascagni, Puccini, Verdi, Giordano)		Björling	
ALP1842 Enesco: Rhapsody, Liszt, Ravel	VPO	Silvestri	[ASD417]
ALP1843 "French Romantic Music" (Faure, Chabrier, Bizet)	FNRO	Beecham	
ALP1844 Schubert: Symphonies 3/4	VPO	Kubelik	[ASD418]
ALP1845 Schubert: Lieder Recital No. 6 (Goethe, Schiller, Mayrhofer, etc)	Fischer-Dieskau Engel		
ALP1846 Overtures (Rossini, Mendelssohn, Berlioz)	RPO	Beecham	[ASD420]
ALP1847 Strauss: Ein Heldenleben	RPO	Beecham	[ASD421]
ALP1848 Borodin: Symphony 2, Prince Igor	VPO	Kubelik	[ASD422]
ALP1849 Mozart: Piano Trio K542/Ravel: Piano Trio	Menuhin	Kentner Cassado	[ASD423]
ALP1850 Schubert: Mayrhofer Lieder	Fisher-Dieskau Engel		
ALP1851 Sullivan: Trial by Jury	Pro Arte	Sargent	[ASD419]
ALP1852-3 Wolf: Goethe Lieder	Fisher-Dieskau Moore		[ASD424-5]
ALP1854 Beethoven: Symphony 3	BPO	Kempe	[ASD426]
ALP1855 Tagore: Shyama Parts1-12	Various Soloists		
ALP1856 Bach: Violin Concerto BWV1042, Mozart: Violin Concerto No3	RPO	Kubelik De Vito	[ASD429]
ALP1857 Songs and Ballads	Bjoerling cond. Grevillius		
ALP1858 Mozart: Violin Concertos K218, K219	PCO	Vandernoot Ferras	[ASD427]
ALP1859 Tchaikovsky: Symphony No5	VPO	Kubelik	[ASD428]
ALP1860 Berlioz: Damnation de Faust	Paris Op	Cluytens	[ASD430]
ALP1861 Viennese Bonbons: Strauss Family	VPO	Kempe	[ASD431]
ALP1862 Berlioz: Debussy: Mozart: Saint-Saens ect	RPO	Beecham	[ASD432]
ALP1863 Beethoven: Symphony No6	BPO	Cluytens	[ASD433]
ALP1864 Busoni-Liszt: Piano Works		Ogdon	[ASD434]
ALP1865 Rossini: Overtures (Tell, Semiramide, etc)	VPO	Sargent	[ASD435]
ALP1866-8 Verdi: Rigoletto	MMF	Gavazzeni Kraus	[ASD436-8]
ALP1869 Delibes: Coppelia, Sylvia	Philh	Irving Menuhin	[ASD439]
ALP1870-1 "A Beecham Anthology" (Memorial edition)			
ALP1872 Paganini: Violin Concertos 1 & 2	RPO	Erede Menuhin	[ASD440]
ALP1873 Britten: Simple Symphony, Holst: Fool, Walton: Facade	RPO	Sargent	[ASD443]
ALP1874 Rehearsal Sequences		Beecham	
ALP1875 Strauss,J: Fledermaus, Zigeunerbaron	VPO	Hollreiser	[ASD444]
ALP1876-9 Wagner: Tannhauser	GSOpB	Konwitschny	[ASD445-8]
ALP1880 Smetana: Dvorak, Weinberger	RPO	Kempe	[ASD449]

ALP1881	Beethoven: Tempest Sonata/Schumann: Fantasia		Richter	[ASD450]
ALP1882	Mozart: Symphonies 36/38	VPO	Kubelik	[ASD451]
ALP1883	Spanish Songs of the Renaissance		De Los Angeles	[ASD452]
ALP1884	Bach,JS: Chromatic Fantasia & Fugue in Dmin, Rameau, Couperin		Tureck	[ASD453]
ALP1885	Stainer: Crucifixion	Leeds Philh	Bardgett	[ASD454]
ALP1886	Shostakovich: Symphony 5	VPO	Silvestri	[ASD455]
ALP1887	Opera Recital (Wagner, Massenet, Verdi, Mascagni)	Paris	Cluytens Gorr	[ASD456]
ALP1888	Bach: Cantatas 211 & 212	BPO	Forster	[ASD457]
ALP1889	Delius Centenary 1862-1962 Vol 1	RPO	Beecham	
ALP1890	Delius Centenary 1862-1962 Vol 2	RPO	Beecham	
ALP1891	Duets		De Los Angeles Fischer-Dieskau	[ASD459]
ALP1892	Mendelssohn: Midsummer Nights Dream, Humperdinck	RPO	Kempe	[ASD460]
ALP1893	Music of India		Shankar	[ASD463]
ALP1894	Brahms: Symphony 4	RPO	Kempe	[ASD461]
ALP1895	Tchaikovsky: Symphony 6	VPO	Kubelik	[ASD462]
ALP1896	Piano Recital		Cziffra	[ASD464]
ALP1897	Gluck: Iphigenie en Tauride	Paris	Pretre	[ASD465]
ALP1898	Italian Overtures (Verdi, Bellini, Rossini, Donizetti)	Philh	Serafin	[ASD466]
APL1899	Coleridge-Taylor: Hiawatha	Royal Choral	Sargent	[ASD467]
ALP1900	Beethoven: Piano Sonatas 13 Op 27/1 & 31 Op 110		Solomon	
ALP1901	Schubert: Piano Sonatas in Amaj D664/Amin D784		Solomon	
ALP1902	Song Recital	di Stefano	Cond Guarino	[ASD469]
ALP1903	Pearls of Viennese Operetta	VPO	Loibner	[ASD471]
ALP1904	Gilbert & Sullivan (hlts)	Pro Arte	Sargent	[ASD472]
ALP1905	Mozart: Violin Concertos 3, 5	BFCO	Menuhin	[ASD473]
ALP1906-7	Brahms: Sonatas 1-3, Schubert: Fantaisie D934	Menuhin	Kentner	[ASD474-5]
ALP1908	Neapolitan Songs		di Stefano	[ASD476]
ALP1909	Bach,J.S: Recital		Tureck	[ASD477]
ALP1910	Schubert: Rosamunde, Gluck: Ballet Suite	VPO	Kempe	[ASD478]
ALP1911	Twentieth Century Spanish Songs		De Los Angeles Soriano	[ASD479]
ALP1912	Handel: The Gods Go A'Begging, Arrival of the Queen of Sheba, Rossini: Semiramide, etc	RPO	Beecham	[ASD480]
ALP1913	Schubert: Die Schone Mullerin		Fiescher-Dieskau Moore	[ASD481]
ALP1915-6	Liszt: Transcendental Studies 1-12, Hungarian Rhaps 9, 10, 13		Cziffra	
ALP1917	Mahler: Symphony 1	VPO	Kletzki	[ASD483]
ALP1918-9	Sullivan: Patience	Pro Arte	Sargent	[ASD484-5]
ALP1921	Puccini La Boheme (hlts)	RCAVO	Beecham	
ALP1922	Gilbert & Sullivan: (hlts)	Pro Arte	Sargent	[ASD487]
ALP1923	Neapolitan Songs		Corelli	[ASD488]
ALP1924-5	Bach: Six Violin Sonatas	Menuhin	Malcolm	[ASD489-90]
ALP1926	Dohnanyi: Suite, Rossini-Respighi: Boutique	RPO	Sargent	[ASD497]
ALP1927	Handel: Concerti Grossi,OP6,Nos7,8,9,11	BFCO	Menuhin	[ASD491]
ALP1928	Rachmaninov: Piano Concerto 2, Preludes	Philh	Pritchard Ogdon	[ASD492]
ALP1929	Bruckner: Symphony 9	VPO	Schuricht	[ASD493]
ALP1930	Kodaly: Hari-Janos, Gotovac, Tchaikovsky: Suite 3	VPO	Kempe	[ASD494]
ALP1932	Gilbert & Sullivan: (hlts)	Pro Arte	Sargent	[ASD495]
ALP1933-6	The Living Bible		Laurence Olivier D Fairbanks (narr)	
ALP1937-40	The Living Bible		Laurence Olivier D Fairbanks (narr)	
ALP1941-4	The Living Bible		Laurence Olivier D Fairbanks (narr)	

These were also available in large 12 disc presentation box with lavish illustrations

ALP1945	Poulenc: Les Biches, Milhaud, Dutilleux	PCO	Pretre	[ASD496]
ALP1946	Music of India-Ragas		Vilayat Khan	[ASD498]
ALP1947	Sibelius: Symphony 2 (Live performance 1954)	BBCSO	Beecham	
ALP1948	Bliss: Piano Concerto	Philh	Sargent Barnard	[ASD499]
ALP1949	Bach: Handel:Vivaldi:	BFCO	Goossens Menuhin	[ASD500]
ALPS1950-3	Bach: Christmas Oratorio	LGO	Thomas	[ASD501-4]

ALP1954	Cantos de Espana	PCO De Burgos	De Los Angeles	[ASD505]
ALP1955	Mozart: Serenata Notturna, Eine Kleine Nachtmusik, Haydn	BFCO	Menuhin	[ASD506]
ALP1956	Stravinsky: Pulcinella, Baiser de la Fée	Philh	Vandernoot	[ASD507]
ALP1957	V-Williams: Symphony 5	Philh	Barbirolli	[ASD508]
ALP1958	Borodin, Mussorgsky, Rimsky-Korsakov	RPO	Pretre	[ASD509]
ALP1959	Beethoven: Violin Sonatas 7&10		Yehudi & Hephzibah Menuhin	[ASD510]
ALP1960	Stravinsky: Oedipus Rex	RPO	Davis	[ASD511]
ALP1961	Tippett: Conc for Double String Orch, Prokofiev: Visions Fugitive	Moscow CO	Barshai	[ASD512]
ALP1962	Glinka: Life for the Tsar, Gounod: Faust	Philh	Kurtz	[ASD513]
ALP1963	Schubert: Symphony 8, Mozart: Eine Kleine Nachtmusik	VPO	Kubelik	[ASD514]
ALP1964	Bruckner: Mass 3	Berlin SO	Forster	[ASD515]
ALP1965	Neapolitan Songs		Corelli	[ASD516]
ALP1966	Hungarian, Slavonic and Polovtsian Dances	PCO	Silvestri	[ASD519]
ALP1967	Poulenc: Concerto for 2 Pianos, Concert Champêtre	PCO	Pretre Poulenc	[ASD517]
ALP1968	Sibelius, Delius, Dvorak, Grieg	RPO	Beecham	[ASD518]
ALP1969	"Richter in Italy" (Schumann: Papillons, Sonata in Gmin, etc)		Richter	[ASD520]
ALP1970	V Williams: Tallis,Greensleeves,Elgar: Intro & Allegro, Serenade	SOL	Barbirolli	[ASD521]
ALP1971-3	Smetana: Bartered Bride	BamSO	Kempe Lorengar	[ASD522-4]
ALP1974	Vienna Philharmonic on Holiday	VPO	Kempe	[ASD525]
ALP1975-7	Bach: St John Passion	Berlin SO	Forster	[ASD526-8]
ALP1978	Opera Recital (Giordano, Donizetti, Puccini, Bellini)		Corelli	[ASD529]
ALP1979	A French Recital (Ravel, Duparc, Debussy)	PCO Pretre	De Los Angeles	[ASD530]
ALP1980	Enescu: Violin Sonata 3, Debussy: Violin Sonata, Ravel: Tzigane	Ferras	Barbizet	[ASD531]
ALP1981	Kabalevsky: The Comedians, Rimsky-Korsakov: Le Coq d'Or	Philh	Kurtz	[ASD532]
ALP1982	Mozart: Violin Concertos 4 & 6	BFCO	Menuhin	[ASD533]
ALP1983	Delius: Songs of Sunset, etc	RPO	Beecham	
ALP1984	Wagner: Rheingold (hlts)	German SO	Kempe	[ASD535]
ALP1985	Bach: Cantata 208, Telemann: Kanarienvogel	Berlin SO	Forster	[ASD534]
ALP1986	Berlioz: Harold in Italy	Philh	Davis Menuhin	[ASD537]
ALP1987	Liszt: Piano Works		Kentner	[ASD538]
ALP1988	Music of India		Khan	[ASD539]
ALP1989	Elgar: Symphony 1	Philh	Barbirolli	[ASD540]
ALP1990	Sibelius: En Saga, Karelia, Finlandia, Swan of Tuonela	VPO	Sargent	[ASD541]
ALP1991	Tchaikovsky: Piano Concerto 1, Franck: Symphonic Variations	Philh	Barbirolli Ogdon	[ASD542]
ALP1992	Verdi: Traviata (hlts)	Rome	Serafin	[ASD543]
ALP1993	Schubert: Schwanengesang		Fischer-Dieskau Moore	[ASD544]
ALP1994	Falla: Nights in the Gardens of Spain, Concerto for harpsichord	PCO	de Burgos Soriano	[ASD545]
ALP1995	Piano Recital		Ogdon	[ASD546]
ALP1996	Glinka: Songs	Chrisfoff	Labinsky	[ASD547]
ALP1997	Gluck: Orfeo ed Euridice (hlts)	Berlin SO	Stein Prey	[ASD550]
ALP1998	Elgar: Enigma, Cockaigne	Philh	Barbirolli	[ASD548]
ALP1999	Brahms: Double Concerto, Beethoven: Violin Sonata Op 12/1	Philh Kletzki	Ferras Tortelier	[ASD549]
ALP2000	Wagner: Opera & Song Recital	FNRO	Pretre Crespin	[ASD553]
ALPS2001-2	Schubert: Winterreise		Fischer-Dieskau Moore	[ASD551-2]
ALP2003	Dvorak: Symphony No8; Wagner: Meistersinger Prelude	RPO	Beecham	
ALP2004	Corelli: Concerti Grossi, Op 6 Nos 2, 6, 7, 8	VdiR	Fasano	[ASD554]
ALP2005	Wagner: Tannhauser hlts		Konwitschny Fischer-Dieskau	[ASD555]
ALP2006	Wagner: Hollander hlts		Konwitschny Fischer-Dieskau	[ASD556]
ALP2007	Mozart: Stamitz Torelli		Cologne Soloists Muller-Bròhl	[ASD557]
ALP2008	Great Sopranos of our time			[ASD558]
ALP2009	Shostakovich: Symphony No12 etc	Philh	Pretre	[ASD559]
ALP2010	Operatic recital (Handel, Weber, Wagner, Donizetti)		Klobucar (cond) Traxel	[ASD560]
ALP2011	Schubert: Wanderer Fantasie/Sonata Op 120		Richter	[ASD561]
ALP2012	Weber: Freischutz hlts	BPO	Keilberth	[ASD562]
ALP2013-4	Sullivan: Ruddigore	PRO Arte	Sargent	[ASD563-4]
ALP2015	Lieder Recital (Schubert, Schumann, Wolf)	Koth	Engel	[ASD565]

ALP2016	Tchaikovsky: Onegin Spades exc.	Wunderlich, Prey ect [ASD566]
ALP2017	Haydn: Concerto in C Mozart: K364	Menuhin, Bath, Barshai [ASD567]
ALP2018	Christmas Carols-Royal Choral Socy	Royal Choral Society Sargent [ASD568]
ALP2019	Mozart: Missa Brevis K220, Palestrina	Berlin SO Forster [ASD569]
ALP2020	Falla: El Amor Brujo, Turina, Albeniz, etc	PCO de Burgos [ASD570]
ALP2021	Massenet: Herodiade hlts	Paris Op Pretre Crespin [ASD571]
ALP2022	Berg: Violin Concerto	PCO Pretre Ferras [ASD572]
ALP2023	Brahms: Haydn Vns, Tragic Ov, Academic Ov	Philh Krips [ASD573]
ALP2025	Christoff sings 'Tsars and Kings'	PCO Cluytens Christoff [ASD574]
ALP2026	Mozart: Flute & Harp Concertos	Menuhin Shaffer Costello [ASD575]
ALP2027	Gluck: Alceste (hlts)	Paris Op Pretre [ASD576]
ALP2028	Handel: Water Music	BFCO Menuhin [ASD577]
ALP2029	Prokofiev: Symphony 5	Philh Kletzki [ASD578]
ALP2030	Vivaldi: Marcello	VdiR Fasano [ASD579]
ALP2031-2	Nicolai: Die Lustigen Weiber Von Windsor	Bavarian Heger [ASD580-1]
ALP2033	Rimsky Korsakov: Tsar Saltan, Snow Maiden, Khachaturian	Philh Kurtz [ASD582]
ALP2034	Poulenc: Stabat Mater, Motets	PCO Pretre Crespin [ASD583]
ALP2035	Bloch: Violin Concerto	Philh Kletzki Menuhin [ASD584]
ALP2036	Saint - Saens: Symphony No 3	Paris Pretre Durufle [ASD585]
ALP2038	Brahms: Sextet No1	Menuhin Masters Aronowitz etc [ASD587]
ALP2039	Rossini: Stabat Mater	Berlin SO Forster Lorengar [ASD588]
ALP2040	Gounod: Sainte Cecile Mass	PCO Hartemann Lorengar [ASD589]
ALP2041	Bizet: Carmen exc	FNRO Beecham [ASD590]
ALP2042	Mozart: Violin Concertos Nos1 & 2	BFCO Menuhin [ASD591]
ALP2043	Mozart: Violin Concerto No 7 Two Violins	BFCO Menuhin [ASD592]
ALP2044	Schumann: Strauss: Lieder	Della Casa Peschko [ASD593]
ALP2045	Strauss: Ariadne exc	BPO Erede Della Casa [ASD594]
ALP2046	Haydn: Symphony No 49, Mozart: Symphony No 29	BFCO Menuhin [ASD595]
ALP2047-8	Mahler: Symphony 9	BPO Barbirolli [ASD596-7]
ALP2049	Handel: Concerti Grossi Op6 Nos 3,6,10,12	BFCO Menuhin [ASD598]
ALP2050	Religious Music	Franco Corelli (cond) [ASD599]
ALP2051	Liszt: Sonata; Hungarian Fantasia etc	Philh Pritchard Ogdon [ASD600]
ALP2052	Carter: Piano Sonata, Double Concerto	Rosen, cond, Meier [ASD601]
ALP2053-4	Bruckner: Symphony 8	VPO Schuricht [ASD602-3]
ALP2055	Handel: Concerti Grossi Op6,Nos 1,2,4,5	BFCO Menuhin [ASD604]
ALP2056	Mozart: Clarinet Trio, Clarinet Quintet	de Peyer Melso [ASD605]
ALP2057-8	Opera and Song Recital	Gobbi Moore [ASD606-7]
ALP2059	Falla: Three Cornered Hat	Philh de Burgos De los Angeles [ASD608]
ALP2060	Puccini: Madam Butterfly exc	De Los Angeles Björling [ASD609]
ALP2061-2	Elgar: Symphony 2, Falstaff	HO Barbirolli [ASD610-11]
ALP2063	Gerhard Symphony 1, Don Quixote Dances	BBCSO Dorati [ASD613]
ALP2064	Schoenberg: Lutyens: Britten	RPO Del Mar Tyler [ASD612]
ALP2065	Bizet: Lutoslawski: Rachmaninov	Vronsky & Babin [ASD614]
ALP2066	18th Century Music	Fischer-Dieskau [ASD615]
ALP2067	Verdi: Simone Boccanegra (hlts)	Rome Op Santini De Los Angeles Gobbi
ALP2068	On Wings Of Songs	Joan Hammond Ivor Newton [ASD616]
ALP2069	Mozart: Symphonies 35, 41	VPO Kubelik [ASD617]
ALP2070	Beethoven Romances 1, 2, Wieniawski, Chausson, Berlioz	Philh Menuhin [ASD618]
ALP2071	Thomas: Mignon exc	Opera Comique Hartemann [ASD619]
ALP2072	Brahms & Reger: Clarinet Quintets	Melos de Peyer [ASD620]
ALP2073	Tippett: Piano Concerto; Sonata No2	Philh Davis Ogdon [ASD621]
ALP2074	Operatic Arias (Bellini, Verdi, Mozart, Charpentier)	Rome Op Ferraris Freni [ASD622]
ALP2075	Frescobaldi&Bach: Organ Works	Fernando Germani [ASD623]
ALP2076	Bach: Easter Oratorio;	SW German Gonnenwein [ASD624]
ALP2077	Mendelssohn: Elijah exc	Philh Sargent [ASD625]
ALP2079	Mozart: Serenade No7 K250	BFCO Menuhin [ASD627]

ALP2080	Couperin: Concerts Royaux and Nouveaux	Toulouse CO Auriacombe	[ASD628]
ALP2081	Sir Winston Churchill - The State Funeral		
ALP2082	Liszt: Concerto No1 Totentanz	Philh Vandernoot Cziffra	[ASD629]
ALP2083	Brahms: Lieder	Fischer-Dieskau Moore	[ASD630]
ALP2084	Telemann: Suite in C Concertos	Moscow CO Barshai	[ASD631]
ALP2085	Schubert: Symphony No 9	HO Barbirolli	
ALP2086	Bach: Flute Sonatas - Vol 1	Shaffer Malcolm	[ASD633]
ALP2088	Purcell - An Anthology - Vol 1	Menuhin etc	[ASD635]
ALP2089	Tchaikovsky: Symphony No5	Philh Pretre	[ASD636]
ALP2090	Britten: Bridge, Corelli: Tippett	BFCO Menuhin Tippett	[ASD637]
ALP2092	Boulez: Koechlin: Messiaen:	BBCSO Dorati	[ASD639]
ALP2093	Goehr & R.R. Bennett & P.M. Davis & McAuley	Melos Ensemble	[ASD640]
ALP2094	Choral Recital (Byrd, Palestrina, Lassus, etc)	Kings College Choir Willcocks	[ASD641]
ALP2095	20th Century Spanish Piano Music	Soriano	[ASD642]
ALP2096	Brahms: Sextet No 2; Schubert: Trio D471	Menuhin etc	[ASD643]
ALP2097	Delius: Cello Concerto, Songs of Farewell etc	RPO Sargent Du Pre	[ASD644]
ALP2098	Piano Works by 20th Century British Composers	Ogdon	[ASD645]
ALP2099	Arensky: Vars Tchaikovsky: Serenade	LSO Barbirolli	[ASD646]
ALP2101/2	Elgar: The Dream Of Gerontius	HO Barbirolli Baker Lewis	[ASD648-9]
ALP2103	Schumann: Lieder	Fischer-Dieskau Moore	[ASD650]
ALP2104	Song Recital	SOL De Burgos De los Angeles	[ASD651]
ALP2105	Massenet: Manon (hlts)	Paris Monteux De Los Angeles	
ALP2106	Elgar: Cello Concerto/Sea Pictures	LSO Barbirolli Du Pre	[ASD655]
ALP2111	From Christmas to Candlemas	King's College Choir Willcocks	[ASD653]
ALP2112	Stravinsky: Firebird Suite, Strauss: Rosenkavalier	Philh Krips	[ASD654]
ALP2113	Mahatma Gandhi Centenary Commemoration Record	St Pauls Cathedral 1969	
ALP2114	Hugo Wolf Recital	Schwarzkopf Furtwangler (piano)	
ALP2115	French Song Recital	Claire Croiza (Mezzo)	
ALP3799	Operatic Arias by Puccini	Callas	
ALP3803	Villa-Lobos: Bachianas Brasilieras	FNRO Villa-Lobos De Los Angeles	
ALP3824	"Maria Callas sings Operatic Arias" (Verdi, Rossini, etc)	Callas	
ALP3843	Schubert:Song Recital (An die Musik,Gretchen am Spinnrade +)	Schwarzkopf Edwin Fischer	

HMV BLP (10")

This 10" series was also released in October 1952 (at the same time as the ALP series) and the label is identical to the first label described in the ALP section above. The series, which ended at BLP1107 was completed by late 1959.

BLP1001	V Williams: Symphony 6	LSO	Boult
BLP1002	Moussorgsky: Pictures at an Exhibition	CSO	Kubelik
BLP1003	Recital (Prince Igor, Boris Godunov)	Philh	Dobrowen Christoff
BLP1004	Tchaikovsky: Swan Lake, Bizet: L'Arlesienne	Halle	Barbirolli
BLP1005	Vieuxtemps: Violin Concerto 4	Philh	Susskind Menuhin
BLP1006	Debussy: The First Book of Preludes		Alfred Cortot
BLP1007	Schubert: 4 Impromptus D 899		Schnabel
BLP1008	Mendelssohn: Violin Concerto	LSO	Sargent De Vito
BLP1009	Smetana: Vltava (Moldau)/Schumann: Manfred Ov	VPO	Furtwangler
BLP1010	Hindemith: Mathis Der Maler	NBCSO	Cantelli
BLP1011	Respighi: Feste Romane	NBCSO	Toscanini
BLP1012	Tchaikovsky: Violin Concerto	Philh	Susskind Heifetz
BLP1013	Liszt: Piano Concerto 1, Chopin: Fantasie in Fmin, Mazurka, etc	Philh	Fistoulari Cherkassky
BLP1014	Beethoven Moonlight Mozart: Sonata K332		Horowitz
BLP1015	Brahms: Symphony 3	Halle	Barbirolli
BLP1016	Bantock: Fifine at the Fair	RPO	Beecham

Cat. No.	Work	Performers
BLP1017	Brahms: Sonata No3 in Fminor	Fischer
BLP1018	Paganini: Violin Concerto 2	Philh Fistoulari Menuhin
BLP1019	Vaughan Williams: Tallis Elgar: Wand of Youth 2	BBCSO Sargent
BLP1020	Memories of Coronation Day 2 June 1953	narrated by Richard Dimbleby
BLP1021	Rubbra: Symphony 5	Halle Barbirolli
BLP1022	Beethoven: Romances, Saint Saens: Havanaise	RCA Steinberg Heifetz
BLP1023	Melba-film Sound track	Patrice Munsel
BLP1024	Beethoven: Piano Concerto 2	Philh Cluytens Solomon
BLP1025	Nielsen: Violin Concerto	DSRO Woldike Menuhin
BLP1026	Bach: Violin Sonatas 1, 2	Menuhin Kentner
BLP1027	Chopin: Polonaises Fantaise & Brillante OP22	Rubinstein
BLP1028	Brahms: Double Concerto	Philh Schwarz De Vito Baldovino
BLP1029	Lalo: Symphonie Espagnole	RCASO Steinberg Heifetz
BLP1030	Schubert: Impromptus Op 142	Schnabel
BLP1031	Schumann: Piano Quintet Op44	Paganini Quartet Rubinstein
BLP1032	Bartok: Music for strings Percussion ect	CSO Kubelik
BLP1033	Wagner: Parsifal, Prelude & Good Friday Music	NBCSO Toscanini
BLP1034	"Neapolitan Songs"	Gigli
BLP1035	Wagner: Siegfried Act 3 - Finale	Philh Sebastian Flagstad Svanholm
BLP1036	Beethoven: Piano Concerto 4	Philh Cluytens Solomon
BLP1037	Falla: 7 Popular Spanish Songs, Granados, etc	De Los Angeles Moore
BLP1038	Schubert: Symphony 8	NBCSO Toscanini
BLP1039	Schumann: Piano Concerto	Philh Schwarz Myra Hess
BLP1040	Faure Piano Quartet OP15	Paganini Quartet Rubinstein
BLP1041	Clementi: Symphony, Corelli: Concerto Grosso op6	VdiR Fasano
BLP1042	Vivaldi Concertos in F and C	VdiR Fasano
BLP1043	Elgar: Cello Concerto	BBCSO Sargent Tortelier
BLP1044	Schumann: Symphony 4	Philh Cantelli
BLP1045	Mendelssohn Symphony 3	ABC Sydney Goossens
BLP1046	Bach: Double Concerto, Handel: Trio Sonata 2	Philh Menuhin De Vito
BLP1047	Walton: Violin Concerto	Philh Walton Heifetz
BLP1048	A Liszt Recital	Horowitz
BLP1049	V Williams: Dives & Lazarus, Elgar: Introduction	Halle Barbirolli
BLP1050	Debussy: Children's Corner, Schumann: Scenes from Childhood	Alfred Cortot
BLP1051	Beethoven: Piano Sonatas 14 (Moonlight), 26 (Les Adieux)	Solomon
BLP1052	"Neapolitan Songs"	Di Stefano
BLP1053	Operatic Duets (Verdi, Puccini, Bizet)	RCA Cellini Merrill Bjoerling
BLP1055	"Great Tenor Arias" (from Pagliacci,Faust,Boheme,etc)	Bjoerling
BLP1056	Brahms: Trio in Bmaj Op 8	Heifetz Feuermann Rubinstein
BLP1058	Rimsky-Korsakov: Capriccio Espagnol, Debussy, Chabrier	Halle Barbirolli
BLP1059	Handel (Arr Harty): Water & Fireworks Music	BBCSO Sargent
BLP1060	Negro Spirituals	Marian Anderson
BLP1061	Schumann: Etudes Symphoniques Op 13	Myra Hess
BLP1063	Beethoven: Piano Concerto 3	Philh Edwin Fischer
BLP1064	Schumann: Dichterliebe	Schiotz Moore
BLP1065	Elgar: Cockaigne Ov, Elizabethan Suite	Halle Barbirolli
BLP1066	Mozart: Piano Concerto K466	Philh Edwin Fischer
BLP1067	Beethoven: Piano Concerto 4	Philh Edwin Fischer
BLP1068	Schumann: Liederkreis Op 39	Fischer-Dieskau Moore
BLP1069	Schubert: String Quartet D804	Amadeus Quartet
BLP1070	Bach: Violin Concertos 1/2	LAPO Wallenstein Heifetz
BLP1071	Songs of Romance	Lanza
BLP1072	Chausson: Poeme, Conus: Violin Concerto	RCASO Solomon Heifetz
BLP1073	Beethoven Berlioz Saint - Saens	Philh Susskind Hammond
BLP1074	Bach Toccata & Fugue etc- Transcribed	SO Stokowski
BLP1075	Tchaikovsky: Eugen Onegin, Villa Lobos: Bachianas Bras. 5	SO Stokowski Albanese

BLP1076	Mozart: Piano Sonata K576, Haydn: Piano Sonata in Cmaj		Solomon
BLP1077	Schubert Trio OP99		Schioler Holst Bengtsson
BLP1078	VWilliams: Tuba & Oboe Concertos	LSO	Barbirolli
BLP1079	Chopin: Andante & Grand Pol Op 22, Nocturne Op 55/1, etc		Horowitz
BLP1080	Barber: Souvenirs, Shostakovich: Golden Age	Philh	Kurtz
BLP1081	Mahler: Kindertotenlieder	BPO	Kempe Fischer-Dieskau
BLP1082	Franck: Violin Sonata	Menuhin	Kentner
BLP1083	Brahms: Symphony 3	Philh	Cantelli
BLP1084	"Favourite Songs by John McCormack"		McCormack
BLP1085	Mussorgsky/Ravel: Pictures at an Exhibition	NBCSO	Cantelli
BLP1086	Puccini: Operatic Arias	Philh	Curiel Hammond
BLP1087	Franck: Violin Sonata in Amaj	De Vito	Aprea
BLP1088	Mozart: Eine Kleine Nachtmusik, Ovs: Figaro, Cosi, Magic Flute	Philh	Kempe
BLP1089	Debussy: 2 Nocturnes, Ravel: Daphnis & Chloe St 2	Philh	Cantelli
BLP1090	Elgar: Falstaff (recorded 1931-2)	LSO	Elgar
BLP1091	Popular Broadway Songs		Mario Lanza
BLP1092	Simpson: Symphony 1	LPO	Boult
BLP1093	Schumann Symphony No 3	NBCSO	Toscanini
BLP1094	Recital		Mario Lanza
BLP1095	"Italian Songs"		Gigli
BLP1096	Brahms: Schumann Variations	Gorini	Lorenzi
BLP1097	Mozart: Opera Arias	BPO	Schuchter Koth
BLP1098	Nicolai: Merry Wives of Windsor (hlts)	Berlin State Opera Schuchter	
BLP1099	Song Recital		Gigli
BLP1100	Neapolitan Songs		Gigli
BLP1101	Holst: Beni Mora, Britten: Purcell Variations	BBCSO	Sargent [BSD754]
BLP1102	Beethoven: Septet op20	BPO Chamber Ensemble	
BLP1103	Recital (Beethoven, Bach, Scarlatti, etc)		Myra Hess
BLP1104	Rossini - Respighi: Boutique Fantasque	RPO	Goossens [BSD752]
BLP1105	Mozart: Quintet in Gmin K516	Amadeus Quartet	
BLP1106	Faure: La Bonne Chanson op61	Fisher - Dieskau Moore	
BLP1107	John McCormack: Sings to the Children		McCormack

HMV CLP

When HMV first issued LPs in 1952 the CLP and DLP series were at a lower price than the premium priced ALP/BLP series. The CLP/DLP recordings were generally performed by artists who, in the opinion of HMV, did not command the same status as those on the more expensive labels. We may wish to disagree with HMV's opinion in many cases (Lympany, Moiseiwitsch, Brain, Bachauer, for example)

The CLP/DLP label is the same as that used for ALP/BLP except that the background colour is plum instead of red.

This is only a sample of the most important of the CLP series.

CLP1001	Tchaikovsky: Piano Concerto 1	Philh	Dobrowen Solomon
CLP1002	Franck: Vns Symphonique, Schumann: Etudes Symphoniques op 13	Philh	Susskind Lympany
CLP1003	Stravinsky: Rite of Spring	Philh	Markevitch
CLP1004	Offenbach: (arr Rosenthal): Gaite Parisienne	Boston Proms Fiedler	
CLP1006	Schubert: String Quintet in Cmaj Op 163	Amadeus Quartet	
CLP1007	Rachmaninov: Piano Concerto 2, Mendelssohn: Capriccio	Philh	Malko Lympany
CLP1008	Grieg & Schumann: Piano Concertos	Philh	Ackermann Moiseiwitsch

CLP1009	Mozart: Symphony 40, Haydn: Symphony 86	LMP	Blech
CLP1010	Schubert: Symphonies 4, 5	LMP	Blech
CLP1011	Arnold: Homage to the Queen	Philh	Irving
CLP1012	Mozart: Piano Concerto K449, Liszt: Gnomenreigen, Etude 3, etc	Philh	Cameron Horsley
CLP1013	Schumann: Carnaval, Chopin: Les Sylphides	Philh	Irving
CLP1014	Mozart: Sinfonia Concertante K364, Symphony 35	LMP	Blech
CLP1015	Popular Symphonic Mvmts (Beethoven 5,Schubert 8,Dvorak 9,etc)	Boston Proms	Fiedler
CLP1016	Concert by Band of HM Royal Marines		
CLP1017	Brahms: Handel Variations, Schumann: Fantasia in Cmaj		Moiseiwitsch
CLP1018	Tchaikovsky: Swan Lake	Philh	Irving
CLP1019-20	Dvorak: Slavonic Dances 1-16, Grieg: Lyric Suite op 54	Philh	Malko
CLP1021	Recital of works by Tartini (Kreisler, Paganini, Falla, etc)	Haendel	Moore
CLP1022	Schubert: Symphony 8 Liszt: Les Preludes, Weber: Euryanthe ov	Philh	Schwarz
CLP1025	Bach,JS: Organ Works vol 1		Germani
CLP1026	Bach,JS: Organ Works vol 2		Germani
CLP1028	Haydn: Symphonies 92, 100	Copenhagen	Malko
CLP1029	Mozart: Quintet K452, etc	Dennis Brain Wind Ensemble	
CLP1030	Gilbert & Sullivan: Overtures	Boston Proms	Fiedler
CLP1031	Mozart: Mass K317, Haydn: Salve Regina 3 in Gmin	LMP	Blech Cantelo Thomas
CLP1032	Brahms: Violin Concerto	LSO	Celibidache Haendel
CLP1033	Liszt: Hungarian Rhapsodies 1,2,3,6	Philh	Schwarz
CLP1034	Bizet/Hammerstein: Carmen Jones	From the Film soundtrack	
CLP1037	Grieg: Piano Concerto in Amin, Rachmaninov: Piano Concerto 1	Philh	Menges Lympany
CLP1038	Mozart: Piano Concertos K414, K467	Philh	Menges Lympany
CLP1040	"Mr Strauss comes to Boston"	Boston Pops	Fiedler
CLP1043	Dohnanyi: Suite for Orch in F#min, Tchaikovsky: Hamlet Ov	Philh	Irving
CLP1044	Prokofiev: Symphonies 1 ("Classical"), 7	Philh	Malko
CLP1045	Tchaikovsky: Symphony 4	Philh	Malko
CLP1046	Delibes: Coppelia	ROHCG	Irving
CLP1048	Franck: Prelude,Aria&Finale,Rachmaninov: Preludes 2,3,5,6,10,11		Horsley
CLP1049	Tchaikovsky: Piano Concerto 1	London Orch	Sherman Bachauer
CLP1051	Chopin: 24 Preludes Op 28		Lympany
CLP1052-3	Austin: Beggar's Opera (arranged Gay-Pepusch)	Pro-Arte	Sargent
CLP1055	Mozart: Symphony 31, Haydn: Symphony 104	LMP	Blech
CLP1056	Rawsthorne: Sym Studies, Tippett: Conc for Double String Orch	Philh	Lambert Goehr
CLP1057	Liszt: Piano Sonata in Bmin, Chopin: Barcarolle, Shostakovich		Bachauer
CLP1058	Delibes: Sylvia	Philh	Irving
CLP1059	Verdi-Mackerras: The Lady and the Fool ballet	Philh	Mackerras
CLP1060	Tchaikovsky: Nutcracker St, Prokofiev: Love of 3 Oranges	Philh	Malko
CLP1061	Haydn: Notturno 5 in C (arr Geiringer), Symphony 80, Mozart	Philh	Pritchard
CLP1063	Mozart: Symphonies 34, 36	LMP	Blech
CLP1065	Waldteufel: Waltzes, Polkas, etc	Boston Pops	Fiedler
CLP1066	Mozart: Symphony 33, Haydn: Symphony 103	LMP	Blech
CLP1067	Debussy: Pour le Piano, 3 Preludes, Ravel: Gaspard de la Nuit, Mompou: Jeunes Filles au Jardin		Bachauer
CLP1068	"Music for the Nostalgic Traveller" (Offenbach, Brahms, Albeniz)	Melachrino Orch	
CLP1069	Schumann: Humoreske Op 20, Faure: Impromptu op 102, Nocturne Op 63, etc		Johannesen
CLP1070	"Sadlers Wells Ballet Silver Jubilee"	ROHCG	Irving
CLP1071	Schumann: Davidsbundlertanze op 6, Mendelssohn: Studies op 104		Edith Fischer
CLP1072	Rachmaninov: Paganini Vns, Chopin: Barcarolle, etc	Philh	Rignold Moiseiwitsch
CLP1073-4	Tchaikovsky: Sleeping Beauty	ROHCG	Irving
CLP1075	Borodin: Symphonies 2, 3	Philh	Malko
CLP1076	Concert	Band of the Irish Guards	
CLP1089	St-Saens: Piano Concerto 2, Faure: Ballade, Couperin	London Orch	Sherman Bachauer
CLP1090	Schubert: Symphonies 3, 6	LMP	Blech

CLP1094	Rachmaninov: Piano Concerto 2	Philh	Rignold Moiseiwitsch	
CLP1096	Mozart: Piano Concerto K271, Piano Sonata K283	London Orch	Sherman Bachauer	
CLP1097	Piano Recital (Debussy, Liszt, Handel, Chopin, Rachmaninov)		Semprini	
CLP1101	Offenbach: Operetta hlts	Boston Pops	Fiedler	
CLP1102	Mozart: Symphonies 28, 32, Arriaga: Sinfonia a Gran Orquesta	LMP	Blech	
CLP1106	Waltzes by Johann Strauss 2nd, Josef Strauss, Eduard Strauss	Boston Pops	Fiedler	
CLP1110	Overtures: Ruy Blas, Hebrides, Prince Igor, Russlan&Ludmilla,etc	Philh	Malko	
CLP1111	Bach,JS: Piano Concerto in Fmin, Concerto for 2 Pianos in C, Bach (arr Busoni): Toccata in C	London Orch	Sherman Bachauer	
CLP1112	Schubert: Fantaisie D934, Rondeau Brillante D895, Sonatina D384	Rostal	Horsley	
CLP1113	Schubert: Violin Sonata D574, Violin Sonatatinas D385, D408	Rostal	Horsley	
CLP1114	Chopin: Les Sylphides, Strauss,J: Graduation Ball	Boston Pops	Fiedler	
CLP1115	Four Quartets		T.S.Eliot	
CLP1118	Rawsthorne: Piano Concerto 1, Britten: Piano Concerto Op 13	Philh	Menges Lympany	
CLP1120	Bach: Concerto in C for 3 Hpsds, Concerto in Amin for 4 Hpsds	Malcolm	Joyce Dart Vaughan	
CLP1124	Schumann: Violin Sonata op 105, Debussy, Stravinsky	Rostal	Horsley	
CLP1125	Dvorak: "New World" Symphony	Philh	Malko	
CLP1126	Prokofiev: Piano Concertos op 10, op 26	Philh	Susskind Lympany	[CSD1253]
CLP1127	Oratorio Arias (Handel, Haydn, Mendelssohn)	LSO	Bernard Marshall	
CLP1128	Bach,JS: Magnificat in D, Purcell: Queeen Mary Funeral Music	Geraint Jones Chorus and Orch		
CLP1133	Turina: Danzas Fantasticas, Procession del Rocio, Debussy	RPO	Irving	[CSD1261]
CLP1135	Gershwin: Porgy and Bess (hlts)	Harlem SO	Fuller	
CLP1138	Rachmaninov: Piano Concerto 3	London Orch	Sherman Bachauer	
CLP1139	Strauss,R: Der Rosenkavalier (hlts)	BPO	Schuchter Rysanek Grummer	
CLP1140	Glazunov (arr Irving): Birthday Offering ballet	RPO	Irving	[CSD1252]
CLP1144	Prokofiev: Cinderella ballet suite op 87	RPO	Irving	[CSD1256]
CLP1145	Bach: Organ Rectial		Germani	
CLP1146	Schubert: Impromptus op 90, op 142		Goldsand	
CLP1148	Schubert: Piano Sonata Op 120, Moments Musicaux Op 94		Goldsand	
CLP1149	St-Saens: Piano Concerto op 44, Milhaud: Le Carnival D'Aix	Philh	Tzipine Johannesen	
CLP1153	Chopin: Piano Concerto 1	Netherlands Philh	Goehr Mewton-Wood	
CLP1164	Rawsthorne: Piano Concerto 2, Rubbra: Piano Concerto Op 85	BBCSO	Sargent Matthews	
CLP1167	Bliss: Piano Concerto	Utrecht SO	Goehr Mewton-Wood	
CLP1168	"The Waltzes of Strauss in HiFi"	Sym Orch	Valentino	
CLP1172	Britten: Matinee Musicales op 24, Soirees Musicales op 9, Arnold: 4 Scottish Dances, 8 English Dances	Philh	Irving	
CLP1173	Brahms: 16 Waltzes Op 39, Scriabin: 24 Preludes Op 11		Bachauer	
CLP1178	Bach: Cantata 147	Geraint Jones Chorus and Orch etc		[CSD1512]
CLP1181	Mozart: Symphony 41, 12 Minuets K568	LMP	Blech	
CLP1182	Ireland: Piano Concerto, Stravinsky: Capriccio	RPO	Cameron Horsley	
CLP1195	Delibes: La Source, Messager: Les Deux Pigeons	ROHCG	Mackerras	
CLP1208	Schumann: Fantasiestucke op 12, Chopin: Piano Sonata in Bmin		Johannesen	
CLP1209	Mozart: Serenade K320, 4 Minuets K601,3 German Dances K605	LMP	Blech	
CLP1210-1	Adam: Giselle	ROHCG	Fayer	
CLP1212	English Organ Music (Boyce,Byrd,Gibbons, etc)		Thurston Dart	
CLP1224	Stravinsky: Firebird (revised edn), Feux D'Artifice op 4, Bartok	RPO	Previtali	
CLP1225	Philharmonic Pops (Brahms,Kreisler,Tchaikovsky, etc)	London Sinfonia	Irving Simon	[CSD1262]
CLP1226	Lehar: Merry Widow (hlts)	Sadlers Wells	Reid	[CSD1259]
CLP1239	"Immortal pas de Deux"	RPO	Irving	[CSD1286]
CLP1240	Concert	Irish Guards Band		
CLP1243	Chopin: Berceuse op 57, Stravinsky: Tango, Chabrier, etc		Johannesen	
CLP1255	D'Indy: Symphony on a French Mt Air, Faure: Fantaisie op 111, St-Saens: Wedding Cake op 76, etc	LSO	Goossens Johannesen	
CLP1268	Rachmaninov: Preludes op 23/6, op 32/1,3,4,5,10,12,13, etc		Horsley	
CLP1282	Chopin Recital		Moiseiwitsch	
CLP1305-7	Bach: Organ Music (Preludes and Fugues, Choral Preludes, etc)		Germani	

CLP1324	Beethoven: Piano Sonata op 2/2, Bach: Toccata & Fugue in Dmin, etc	Bachauer	
CLP1349	Chopin: Waltzes 1-14	Lympany	[CSD1301]
CLP1442	North German Organ Music	Flor Peters	
CLP1461	Piano Concerto Mvmts	RPO Goossens Moiseiwitsch [CSD1373]	
CLP1749	Janacek: Concertino for Piano & Chamber Ensemble, Dumka for Violin & Piano, Violin Sonata, Suite for Strings	Barylli Ensemble Holetschek Barylli Swoboda	[XWN19069,18750]
CLP1780	"Two Pianos" (Brahms, Debussy, Ravel)	Smith Sellick	[CSD1557]
CLP1812	Prokofiev: Piano Sonatas 1,2,3,4	Yuri Boukoff	
CLP1835	Prokofiev: Piano Sonatas 8,9	Yuri Boukoff	
CLP1843	Glazunov: Raymonda, Tchaikovsky: Storm	Philh Matacic	[CSD1590]
CLP1904	St-Saens: Carnival of the Animals, Faure, Poulenc	Smith Sellick	[CSD1624]

HMV DLP (10")

This is only a sample of the most important of the DLP series.

DLP1001	Prokofiev: Peter and the Wolf op 67	Philh Markevitch Pickles
DLP1002	Franck: Charale 3 in Amin, Bach: Prelude & Fugue in Emin	Germani
DLP1003	Mozart: String Quartet K387	Amadeus Quartet
DLP1004	Adam (arr Jacob): Giselle	ROHCG Irving
DLP1005	Strauss,J: Waltzes	Boston Pops Fiedler
DLP1006	Mozart: Piano Concerto K537 ("Coronation")	New London Orch Sherman Bachauer
DLP1009	Liszt: Rapsodie Espagnole, Funerailles, Hungarian Rhapsody 12	Bachauer
DLP1019-20	Concert	Glasgow Orpheus Choir
DLP1032	Rossini-Respighi: Boutique Fantasque	Philh Irving
DLP1033	Grieg: Peer Gynt suites 1,2	Boston Pops Fiedler
DLP1035	Marches (Sousa, Meacham, Carter)	Boston Pops Fiedler
DLP1037	Handel Organ Concertos op 4/2, op 4/4	Philh Schuchter Jones
DLP1038	Rossini: William Tell Ov, Dukas: Sorcerer's Apprentice, Verdi	Rome SO Previtali
DLP1043	Mozart: Fantasia in Fmin K608, Franck: Chorale in E	Germani
DLP1051	Offenbach: Gaite Parisienne	ROHCG Susskind
DLP1052	Handel: Organ Concertos op 6/11, op 7/4	Philh Schuchter Jones
DLP1053	Organ Recital (Couperin, Distler, Buxtehude, etc)	Piet Kee
DLP1061	Beethoven: Overtures Leonora 3, Coriolan, Prometheus	Philh Malko
DLP1064	Bizet: Carmen Suite 1, Kodaly: Dances of Marosszek	LSO Previtali
DLP1069	Overtures 1812, Oberon, Zampa	Philh Malko
DLP1079	Orch Concert (Offenbach, Suppe, Paganini, etc)	Boston Pops Fiedler
DLP1080	Fricker: Symphony 2	Liverpool Philh Pritchard
DLP1092	Liadov: 8 Russian Folk Songs, Glazunov, Borodin	Philh Malko
DLP1100	Sibelius: Karelia (hlts), King Christian Suite, Kodaly	LPO Cameron
DLP1115	Opera hlts (Meyerbeer, Bizet, Verdi, Gounod, etc)	various
DLP1117	Butterworth: Songs from "A Shropshire Lad"	Cameron Moore
DLP1120	Strauss,J: Die Fledermaus (hlts)	NWDR Orch Schuchter Rothenberger
DLP1121	Song Recital (Haydn, Schubert)	Ritchie De Peyer Malcolm
DLP1124	Mozart: Piano Concerto K491	London Orch Sherman Bachauer
DLP1128	Concert	Glasgow Orpheus Choir
DLP1133	"Carols at Christs Hospital"	Sung by the Choir under Cecil Cochrane
DLP1141	Ravel: Sonatine in F#, Debussy: Preludes	Edith Fischer
DLP1142	"The Music of Leroy Anderson"	Boston Pops Fiedler
DLP1148	Gershwin: Rhapsody in Blue, American in Paris	Morton Gould Orch
DLP1152	Operatic Music arranged for Orchestra	BPO Fiedler
DLP1154	Moussorgsky: Pictures at an Exhibition	Bachauer

DLP1155	"The Incomparable Voice of Paul Robeson"		Robeson	
DLP1158	Mozart: Piano Concerto K453	London Orch	Sherman	Bachauer
DLP1165	"Emperor of Song"		Robeson	
DLP1168	Berlioz: Damnation of Faust suite op 24, Trojan March, etc	Philh	Mackerras	
DLP1170	Concert (Glinka, Moussorgsky, Gliere, Rimsky-Korsakov, etc)	Philh	Mackerras	
DLP1185	Verdi: Overtures (Force of Destiny, Luisa Miller, Nabucco)	Philh	Mackerras	
DLP1186	Mozart: Arias	RPO	Susskind	Brannigan
DLP1187	Chopin: Andante Spianato & Grande Polonaise Brillante op 22, etc		Gimpel	
DLP1190	Tchaikovsky: Violin Concerto	RPO	Goossens	Haendel
DLP1193	Wolf-Ferrari: Il Segreto di Susanna (orch hlts)	Philh	Mackerras	
DLP1199	Bach: Organ Recital		Vollenweider	
DLP1200	Handel: Arias	Philomusica	Farncombe	Brannigan
DLP1208	Handel: Organ Concertos op 4/4, Bach		Vollenweider	
DLP1209	Berkeley: 4 Poems of St Theresa of Avila, etc	Hemsley	Lush	
DLP1210	Lehar: Graf von Luxembourg (hlts)	Chorus & Orch	Fox	[DSD1754]
DLP1213	Rothenberger Operatic recital (J Strauss, Lehar, R-Korsakov, etc)	FFB Orch	Schmidt-Boelcke	[DSD1756]
DLP1214	Rothenberger Recital (Mozart, Beethoven, Weber, Verdi)	Berlin Opera Orch	Zanotelli	[DSD1757]
DLP1215	Theodorakis: Suite 1 for Piano & Orch	Strasbourg SO	Bruck	

HMV COLH
"Great Recordings of the Century"

In 1957 HMV and Columbia launched a series of 12" LPs under the title "Great recordings of the Century". These were reissues of recordings originally issued on 78 rpm discs by some of their leading artists. The prefix COLH related to HMV material and COLC to Columbia.

There is some variation in the label and jacket designs, particularly when comparing English and French issues.

COLH 1	Beethoven: Piano Concerto 1	LSO	Sargent	Schnabel
COLH 2	Beethoven: Piano Concerto 2	Philh	Dobrowen	Schnabel
COLH 3	Beethoven: Piano Concerto 3	Philh	Dobrowen	Schnabel
COLH 4	Beethoven: Piano Concerto 4	Philh	Dobrowen	Schnabel
COLH 5	Beethoven: Piano Concerto 5	Philh	Dobrowen	Schnabel
COLH 6	Beethoven: Violin Sonatas op 12/1, op 12/2	Kreisler	Rupp	
COLH 7	Beethoven: Violin Sonatas op 12/3, op 23	Kreisler	Rupp	
COLH 8	Beethoven: Violin Sonatas Op 24 (Spring), Op 30/1	Kreisler	Rupp	
COLH 9	Beethoven: Violin Sonatas op 30/2, op 96	Kreisler	Rupp	
COLH 10	Beethoven: Violin Sonatas op 30/3, op 47	Kreisler	Rupp	
COLH 11	Beethoven: Violin Concerto	LPO	Barbirolli	Kreisler
COLH 12	Schubert: Trio in Gmaj, Haydn: Trio in Bflat maj	Cortot	Thibaud	Casals
COLC 13	Bach: Brandenburg Concertos 1,2,6	Adolph Busch Chamber Orch	Busch	
COLC 14	Bach: Brandenburg Concertos 3,4,5	Adolph Busch Chamber Orch	Busch	
COLH 15	Bach: Clavier Concerti 1 in Dmin, 4 in A, 5 in Fmin	Edwin Fischer and his Chamber Orch		
COLH 16	Bach,JS: Cello Suites 1,2	Casals		
COLH 17	Bach,JS: Cello Suites 3,4	Casals		
COLH 18	Bach,JS: Cello Suites 5,6	Casals		
COLH 20	Monteverdi: Madrigali Guerrieri et Amorosi	Vocal Ensemble	Nadia Boulanger	
COLH 21	Brahms: Symphony 1	VPO	Furtwangler	
COLC 27-28	Beethoven: Symphony 9	VPO	Weingartner	
COLH 29	Beethoven: Archduke Trio	Cortot	Thibaud	Casals
COLH 30	Dvorak: Cello Concerto	Czech Philh	Szell	Casals
COLH 31	Franck: Symphonic Variations, Schumann: Piano Concerto op 54	LPO	Ronald	Cortot
COLH 32	Chopin: Les Quatorze Valses	Cortot		
COLH 33	Schubert: Piano Sonata D960, Allegretto D915	Schnabel		
COLH 34	Prokofiev: Piano Concerto op 26, Piano Sonata op 29, etc	LSO	Coppola	Prokofiev
COLH 35	Brahms: Violin Concerto	LPO	Barbirolli	Kreisler
COLH 36	Mozart: Piano Concerto 20, Eine Kleine Nachtmusik	VPO	Walter (conductor & pianist)	
COLH 37	Mozart: Symphonies 38, 41	VPO	Walter	
COLH 38	Chopin: 24 Preludes Op 28, 4 Impromptus Valses	Cortot		
COLH 39	Chopin: 24 Etudes op 10 & 25	Cortot		
COLH 40	Schubert: Quintet Op 114 (Trout)	Pro Arte	Schnabel	
COLH 41	Brahms: Horn Trio, Violin Sonata 2	Adolf Busch	Serkin	Aubrey Brain
COLH 42	Mozart: String Quintet K478, String Quintet K516	Pro Arte	Schnabel	
COLH 43	Schubert: Piano Trio D929	A.Busch	H.Busch	Serkin
COLH 44	Mozart: Piano Concerto K453	LSO	Collingwood	Edwin Fischer
COLH 45	Bach: Chromatic Fantasia and Fugue in Dmin, toccata in D, etc	Edwin Fischer		
COLH 46-50	Bach: Well Tempered Klavier (48 Preludes and Fugues)	Edwin Fischer		
COLH 51	Beethoven: Piano Sonatas Op 2/1, Op 2/2	Schnabel		
COLH 52	Beethoven: Piano Sonatas Op 2/3, Op 7	Schnabel		
COLH 53	Beethoven: Piano Sonatas Op 10/1, Op 10/2, Op 10/3	Schnabel		
COLH 54	Beethoven: Piano Sonatas Op 13 (Pathetique), Op 14/1, Op 14/2	Schnabel		

COLH 55	Beethoven: Piano Sonatas Op 22, Op 26		Schnabel
COLH 56	Beethoven: Piano Sonatas Op 27/2, Op 28		Schnabel
COLH 57	Beethoven: Piano Sonatas Op 31/1, Op 31/2		Schnabel
COLH 58	Beethoven: Piano Sonatas Op 31/3, Op 49/1, Op 49/2		Schnabel
COLH 59	Beethoven: Piano Sonatas Op 53 (Waldstein), Op 54, Op 57 (Appassionata)		Schnabel
COLH 60	Beethoven: Piano Sonatas Op 78, Op 79, Op 81a (Les Adieux), Op 90		Schnabel
COLH 61	Beethoven: Piano Sonata Op 106		Schnabel
COLH 62	Beethoven: Piano Sonatas Op 101, Op 109		Schnabel
COLH 63	Beethoven: Piano Sonatas Op 110, Op 111		Schnabel
COLH 64	Beethoven: Diabelli Variations Op 120		Schnabel
COLH 65	Beethoven: Eroica Variations, Rondos, etc		Schnabel
COLH 66	Beethoven: Bagatelles, Fur Elise, Fantasia in Gmin		Schnabel
COLH 67	Mozart: Piano Concertos K467, K595	LSO	Barbirolli Schnabel
COLH 68	Schubert: 4 Impromptus D899		Edwin Fischer
COLH 69	Franck: Prelude, Chorale and Fugue, Schumann: Sym Studies op 13		Cortot
COLH 71	Bach,JS: Italian Concerto, Chromatic Fantasia&Fugue, Partita 1, Toccata in D		Landowska
COLH 72	Liszt: Bmin Piano Sonata, Funerailles, Schumann: Arabesque, etc		Horowitz
COLH 73	Scarlatti: Sonatas		Landowska
COLH 74	Franck: Sonata in Amaj, Faure: Sonata in Amaj	Cortot	Thibaud
COLH 75	Brahms: Double Concerto, Mendelssohn: Piano Trio op 49/1	Barcelona Orch	Cortot Thibaud Casals
COLH 76	Faure: Piano Quartet op 45	Long	Thibaud Vieux Fournier
	Impromptu 5, Nocturnes 4&6, Barcarolle 6	Long	
COLH 77	Bach: Violin Concertos in Amin, E, Dmin for 2 violins	Paris SO	Monteux Menuhin Enesco
COLH 80	Brahms: Violin Concerto	Philh	Dobrowen Neveu
COLH 81	Liszt: Piano Concertos 1, 2	PCO	Weingartner Sauer
COLH 82	Brahms: Piano Concerto 2	BBCSO	Boult Schnabel
COLH 83	Schubert: Piano Sonata D850		Schnabel
COLH 84	Schubert: Piano Sonata D959		Schnabel
COLH 85	Schumann: Piano Quintet op 44, Kinderscenen		Pro Arte Quartet Schnabel
COLH 86	Schumann: Kreisleriana, Davidsbundlertanze		Cortot
COLC 89	Bach: Organ Preludes and Fugues, Toccatas and Fugues		Schweitzer
COLH 90	Mozart: Concerto for 2 Pianos K365, Piano Concerto K459	LSO	Boult A&K.U.Schnabel
COLH 91	Chopin: Fantaisie Op 49, Ballades 1-4		Cortot
COLH 92	Beethoven: Violin Sonata op 47	Thibaud	Cortot
	7 vns on Mozart's "Bei Mannern"	Casals	Cortot
COLH 93	Debussy: Preludes book 1, Children's Corner Suite		Cortot
COLH 94	Mozart: Piano Concerto K482, Rondo K485	Sym Orch	Barbirolli Edwin Fischer
COLH 95	Mozart: Piano Concerto K537, Piano Sonata K576		Goehr Landowska
COLH 96	Violin Recital	Thibaud	Janopopoulo
COLH 97	Brahms: Symphony 1	VPO	Furtwangler
COLH 98	Ravel:Concerto for Left Hand and Orch,St-Saens:Piano Conc 4	PCO	Munch Cortot
COLH 99	Lalo: Cello Concerto, Debussy: Cello Sonata in Dmin		Marechal
COLH100	Scenes from Russian Opera		Chaliapin
COLC101	Operatic Arias		Claudia Muzio
COLH102	Lieder by Wolf and R Strauss		Elizabeth Schumann
COLH103	Faure: Song Recital		Panzera
COLH104	Duparc: Song Recital		Panzera
COLH105	Wagner: Die Walkure, Gotterdammerung (hlts)	Melchior	Schorr Leider
COLH108-9	Verdi: Requiem Mass	Rome Op	Serafin Gigli Pinza etc
COLH110-11	Strauss,R: Der Rosenkavalier	VPO	Heger Lehmann Schumann
COLH112	Opera Recital		Lotte Lehmann
COLH113	Spanish Songs		Conchita Supervia
COLC114	Italian Operatic Arias		Eva Turner
COLH115	Operatic Arias	Thill	Feraldy
COLH116	Operatic Arias		Mattia Battistini
COLH117	Opera and Song Recital		Tito Schipa

COLH118	Operatic Arias		Gigli
COLH119	"The Young Caruso" (Operatic Arias)		Caruso
COLH120	"The Years of Triumph" (Operatic Arias)		Caruso
COLH123	Songs and Ballads		John McCormack
COLH124	Songs and Ballads		John McCormack
COLH125	Songs and Operatic Arias		Nellie Melba
COLH127	"11 Famous Singers - an Operatic Anthology"		Pinza, Rethberg, Schipa, etc
COLH129	Singers of Imperial Russia		Chaliapin, etc
COLH130	"Schubert Songs Vol 1"		Elisabeth Schumann
COLH131	"Schubert Songs Vol 2"		Elisabeth Schumann
COLH132	Operatic scenes (1928-1931 recordings)		Frida Leider Lauritz Melchior
COLH133	Wagner: Die Walkure act 1	VPO	Walter Lehmann Melchior
COLH134	Songs by Debussy		Maggie Teyte
COLH135	Operatic Arias		Frieda Hempel
COLH136	Recital of Operatic Arias and Songs		Tetrazzini
COLH137	Wagner: Scenes from Mastersingers		Friedrich Schorr
COLH138	French Songs vol 1		Maggie Teyte Moore
COLH141	Arias and Songs		Chaliapin
COLH142	Wolf: Songs		Elena Gerhardt
COLH143	Operatic Arias		Gigli
COLH144	Operatic Arias and Duets		Gigli
COLH146	Operatic Arias		Gigli
COLH147	Recital		Florence Austral
COLH152	Canteloube: Chants D'Auvergne, Ravel: Chants Hebraiques, etc		Madeleine Grey
COLH154	Mozart: Operatic Arias, Strauss,R: Lieder		Elizabeth Schumann
COLH155	Operatic Arias		Ruffo
COLH300	Piano Recital		Horowitz
COLH301	Schumann: Piano Trio op 63	Cortot	Thibaud Casals
COLH302	Rameau: Harpsichord Suites 1, 2, 3, 4, Couperin: Passacaille		Landowska
COLH303	Debussy: String Quartet, Ravel: String Quartet	Calvet Quartet	
COLH304	Scarlatti: Sonatas Vol 2		Landowska
COLH305	Mozart: Piano Sonatas K310, K332, K570, K570, Rondo K511		Schnabel
COLH306	Schumann: Carnaval op 9, Kinderscenen op 15, Papillons op 2		Cortot
COLH308	Schubert: Moments Musicaux D780		Schnabel
COLH309	Mozart: Piano Sonatas K330, K331, Fantaisie K475		Edwin Fischer
COLH310	Handel: Harpsichord Suites 2,5,7,10,14		Landowska
COLH311	Strauss,R: Alpine Symphony	BavSO	R.Strauss
COLH312	Mozart: Violin Sonatas K378, K526	Thibaud	Long
COLH313	Chausson: Concerto for Piano, Violin, & SQ, Faure: Berceuse	Cortot	Thibaud etc
COLH315	Schumann: Piano Concerto, Franck: Symphonic Variations		Yves Nat
COLH316	Bach,JS: Preludes and Fugues in Cmin, Cmaj, Amin, Emin		Schweitzer

HMV RLS

EMI introduced their Library series to house multi-record sets using both boxes and gatefold sleeves. Mono sets were given an RLS number and stereo sets an SLS number (see ARCH)

RLS 600	Coronation Service of Queen Elizabeth II	Westminster Abbey June 2nd, 1953	
RLS 684	Wagner: Tristan and Isolde	Philh	Furtwangler Flagstad Suthaus
RLS 689	Wagner: Die Walkure	VPO	Furtwangler Modl Suthaus
RLS 691	Weber: Der Freischutz	BPO	Keilberth Grummer Frick
RLS 696	Wagner: The Mastersingers	BPO	Kempe Frick Grummer
RLS 697	Beethoven: Fidelio	VPO	Furtwangler Mödl Windgassen
RLS 701	"A Tribute to Solomon" (Commemorates his 70th birthday)		Solomon
RLS 702	Wagner: The Ring	RAI Rome SO Furtwangler	(1953)
RLS 703	Wagner: Das Rheingold	RAI Rome SO Furtwangler	(1953)
RLS 707	Stars of the Old Vic & Sadlers Wells		
RLS 708	"Images of Elgar" 1927 3 Choirs & studio. Includes Northrop Moore book		
RLS 709	Elgar: Dream of Gerontius	RLPO	Sargent (1944)
RLS 710	Recital by Chaliapin (Godunov hlts & other unpublished from 1910-1930)		Chaliapin
RLS 711	Operatic Arias & Songs		Adelina Patti (1905-6)
RLS 712	Bach,J.S: 6 Cello Suites		Casals (1936-9)
RLS 713	"Elgar on Record"		(1926-34)
RLS 714	An anthology of the greatest recordings of Isobel Baillie		Isobel Baillie (1926-51)
RLS 715	"The Art of Jussi Björling" (Opera, Operettas, etc)		Björling (1929-50)
RLS 716	Operetta & Song Recital		Maggie Teyte (1908-48)
RLS 717	The Art of Felix Weingartner (Beethoven, Brahms, Wagner)		(1931-40)
RLS 718	"Yehudi Menuhin - his Famous Early Recordings" (Bach, Mozart, Paganini, Mendelssohn, etc)		
RLS 719	Dame Nellie Melba - The London recordings		(1904-26)
RLS 721	"Shostakovich plays Shostakovich" (Piano Concerto 2, Cello Sonata, Piano Quintet, etc)		
RLS 722	Beethoven: Piano Sonatas		Solomon (1948-56)
RLS 723	"The Art of Pablo Casals" (Concertos by Brahms, Boccherini, etc)		Casals
RLS 724	"The Record of Singing" vol 1 (Includes book by Michael Scott "The Record of Singing")		
RLS 725	Gluck: Orfeo ed Euridice	Netherlands Op Bruck Ferrier	(1951)
RLS 726	Mozart: Piano Concertos K450, K488, K491/Piano Sonatas K331, K576		Solomon (1955-7)
RLS 727	Beethoven: Symphonies 1, 9	VPO/Bayreuth Furtwangler	(1952/51)
RLS 728	Strauss,J: Die Fledermaus	Philh	Karajan (1955)
RLS 729	"The Art of Gigli vol 1 (1918-1946)"		Gigli
RLS 730	Mendelssohn: Elijah	RLPO	Sargent Baillie Johnston
RLS 731	Beethoven: The Cello Sonatas (complete)	Solomon	Piatigorsky
RLS 732	"The Art of Gigli Vol 2 (1947-1955)"		Gigli
RLS 733	Romantic Symphonies (Brahms, Franck, Schubert, Tchaikovsky)	LPO	Beecham (1936-40)
RLS 734	Beethoven: Symphony 2, Haydn: Symphonies 93, 99, 104	LPO	Beecham (1935-9)
RLS 735	"Boris Christoff: The 1949-1952 recordings"		Christoff
RLS 736	Verdi: Un Ballo in Maschera	La Scala	Votto Callas (1957)
RLS 737	Puccini: Manon Lescaut	La Scala	Serafin Callas (1959)
RLS 738	Art of Tito Gobbi (Early recordings, unpublished 1955 recordings)		Gobbi
RLS 739	"The Complete Recorded Legacy of Ginette Neveu"		Neveu (1938-48)
RLS 740	Wagner: The Mastersingers	BPO	Kempe Frantz (1957)
RLS 741	Puccini: Turandot	La Scala	Serafin Callas (1958)
RLS 742	"Historic Recordings of Actual Performances at Royal Opera House Covent Garden"		(1926-36)
RLS 743	"The Record of Singing" vol 2 (includes Michael Scott's book)		
RLS 744	Rossini: Le Comte Ory	Glynd	Gui Barabas (1957)
RLS 745	"The Art of Segovia"		Segovia (1927-39)
RLS 746	Bach,JS: Mass in Bmin	Vienna Soc of Friends of Music Karajan	(1952-3)
RLS 747	Rossini: Italian in Algiers	La Scala	Giulini Simionato (1955)

RLS 748	Song Recital (Britten, Grainger, Schubert, Purcell)	Pears Britten		(1942-50)
RLS 749	Recital (Mozart, Chopin, Bach, Scarlatti, Liszt, Ravel, Enesco)		Lipatti	(1943-50)
RLS 751	Strauss,R: 4 Last Songs, Capriccio (hlts), Arabella (hlts)	Philh	Ackermann Schwarzkopf	
RLS 752	Debussy: Preludes Books 1 & 2, Estampes, Images		Gieseking	(1953-5)
RLS 753	The Beethoven Piano Sonatas Vol 1 (Nos 1-7)		Schnabel	
RLS 754	The Beethoven Piano Sonatas Vol 2 (Nos 8-15)		Schnabel	
RLS 755	The Beethoven Piano Sonatas Vol 3 (Nos 16-22 & 24)		Schnabel	
RLS 756	"The Young Di Stefano"		Di Stefano	(1943-57)
RLS 757	Verdi: La Traviata	Lisbon Opera	Callas Sereni	(1958)
RLS 758	The Beethoven Piano Sonatas Vol 4 (Nos 23 & 25-32)		Schnabel	
RLS 759	"The Hugo Wolf Society Volumes 1-7, The 1931-1938 Recordings"			(1931-38)
RLS 760	Strauss,R: Ariadne Auf Naxos	Philh	Karajan	(1955)
RLS 761	"Dinu Lipatti - His Last Recital" (Besancon Festival)		Lipatti	(1950)
RLS 763	"Elizabeth Schwarzkopf: The Early Years"		Schwarzkopf	(1946-1955)
RLS 764	"Stars of the Vienna Opera 1946-53" (Hotter,Welitsch,Kunz,Lipp,Ludwig,Schwarzkopf,Seefried,etc)			
RLS 765	Schubert: String Quintet, Brahms: Piano Quintet, Smetana, Dvorak	Hollywood Quartet Aller		
RLS 766	"Schubert Lieder on Record - An Anthology of 64 Great Singers"			(1898-1952)
RLS 767	String Quartets by Schubert & Mozart	Amadeus Qt Pleeth		
RLS 769	Beethoven Piano Music Vol 5 (Diabelli Vns/Eroica Vns/Bagatelles/etc)		Schnabel	
RLS 920	Brahms: Deutsche Volkslieder		Schwarzkopf Fischer-Dieskau Moore	
RLS5094	Piano Concertos: Brahms 1&2, Grieg, Schumann, Tchaikovsky 1, etc		Solomon	
RLS7700	"The Art of Richard Tauber"			
RLS7701	"The Art of Dennis Brain" (Mozart, Beethoven, Strauss, Hindemith,etc)		Dennis Brain	(1943-57)
RLS7703	"Never Sing Louder Than Lovely"		Isobel Baillie	
RLS7704	Strauss,R: Der Rosenkavalier	VPO	Heger Lehmann	(1933)
RLS7705	"The Record of Singing" vol 1			
RLS7706	"The Record of Singing" vol 2			
RLS7707	Beethoven: late Quartets	Hollywood Quartet		
RLS7708	Wagner: The Mastersingers	Bayreuth	Karajan	(1951)
RLS7709	Mozart: Cosi fan Tutte	Philh	Karajan	(1955)
RLS7710	"The Art of Beniamino Gigli Vol 3" (The Operatic Recordings)		Gigli	(1918-43)
RLS7711	"Wagner on Record (1926-1942)" (Ring, Dutchman, Lohengrin, Tannhauser, Tristan, Mastersingers)			
RLS7713	Schubert: Piano Sonata 17,Impromptus 1-4, Moments Musicaux		Schnabel	
RLS7714	"Karajan at 75"	VPO	Karajan	(1946-9)
RLS7715	"Karajan & the Philharmonia 1947-60: 75th Birthday Edition"	Philh	Karajan	
RLS7716	Elgar: Orchestral Works (Symphony 1, Falstaff, Enigma, etc)	LPO	Boult	(1949-55)

HMV XLP

The HMV 'Concert Classics' series (XLP) was first published in 1959. The series is a mixture of original recordings and reissues of material from the Nixa, Westminster, HMV, Columbia and Parlophone catalogues. These are cross referenced within the listing.

This handbook lists those records that were issued only in mono, the corresponding stereo listing for SXLP can be found in ARCH.

Label: This is blue with silver lettering with a small rectangular 'Nipper' logo also in blue and silver.

XLP20001-2	Beethoven: Symphonies 5 & 9	PCO	Schuricht Lipp Hoffgen Dickie Frick
XLP20005	Ballet Music (Delibes: Coppelia&Sylvia,Gounod: Faust)	Colonne Concert	Dervaux
XLP20006	Mozart: Symphonies 40, 41	PCO	Vandernoot
XLP20009	Tchaikovsky: Symphony 5	Nordwestdeutsche Philh	Schuchter
XLP20010	Brahms: Piano Concerto 1	BPO	Kempe Gimpel

XLP20011 Wagner: Tannhauser,Die Walkure,Lohengrin,Tristan (hlts)	PCO	Dervaux	
XLP20012 Beethoven: Symphony 6	PCO	Schuricht	
XLP20013 Tchaikovsky: Piano Concerto 1, Liszt: Mephisto Waltz	FNRO	Silvestri Ciccolini	
XLP20014 Dvorak: Symphony 9 ("New World")	Nordwestdeutsche Philh Schuchter		
XLP20016 Beethoven: Symphonies 1, 4	PCO	Schuricht	
XLP20017 Chopin: Piano Concerto 2, Schumann: Piano Concerto	FNRO	Kletzki Francois	
XLP20018 Grieg: Peer Gynt Suites 1&2, Smetana: Ma Vlast	Nordwestdeutsche Philh Schuchter		
XLP20020 Mozart: Symphonies 38, 39	PCO	Vandernoot	
XLP20021 Chopin: Piano Works		Gheorghiu (piano)	
XLP20022 Beethoven: Symphonies 2, 8	PCO	Schuricht	
XLP20039 Ovs (Weber, Brahms, Wagner, Nicolai, J Strauss, Rossini)	PCO	Dervaux	
XLP20054 Dvorak: Piano Quintet in Amaj, String Quartet 7	Barylli Quartet Farnadi		[WLP5337]
XLP20055 Beethoven: Piano Sonatas 8, 14, 23	Badura-Skoda		[WLP5184]
XLP20056 Schumann: Quintetes op 44, op 47	Barylli Qt Demus		[XWN18575]
XLP20057 Bach,JS: Suite 1, Concerto for Flute&Hpsd	LBE	Haas Pougnet/Malcolm/Morris	
XLP20062 Beethoven: Trio 6 (Archduke)	Badura-Skoda Fournier Janigro		[WLP20018]
XLP20063 Dvorak: Slavonic Dances op 46, op 72	Philh SO Rodzinski		[WLP20013]
XLP20066 Schubert: Trio Op 99, Haydn: Trio in Gmaj	Badura-Skoda Fournier Janigro		[WLP5188/5202]
XLP20067 Haydn: Piano Trio 17, Schubert: Piano Trio 2	Badura-Skoda Fournier Janigro		[WLP5293/5121]
XLP20068 Chopin: Piano Concertos 1, 2	VSOO Rodzinski Badura-Skoda		[WLP5308]
XLP20070 Guitar Recital (Bach, Frescobaldi, Dowland, Falla, etc)		Oscar Ghiglia (guitar)	
XLP20072 Brahms: Piano Quartet op 25	Members of Barylli Qt Demus		
XLP20073 Brahms: Piano Quartet op 26	Members of Barylli Qt Demus		
XLP20074 Brahms: Piano Quartet op 60	Members of Barylli Qt Demus		
XLP20076 Mozart: Piano Trios 1, 3, 6	Badura-Skoda Fournier Janigro		[WP108]
XLP20077 Mozart: Piano Trios 2, 4, 5	Badura-Skoda Fournier Janigro		
XLP20079 Beethoven: Piano Trio op 1/3, Trio op 11	Badura-Skoda Fournier Janigro		
XLP20081 Schubert: String Quartets 10, 11, 12	Vienna Konzerthaus Quartet		
XLP20082 Chopin: Preludes op 28/1-24		Bakst (piano)	
XLP20083 Beethoven: Diabelli Variations op 120		Barenboim (piano)	
XLP20084 Liszt: Hungarian Rhapsodies 16-19, Rhapsodie Espagnole, etc		Farnadi (piano)	
XLP20085 Franck: Violin Sonata in Amaj, Grieg: Violin Sonata 3	Gertler Farnadi (piano)		
XLP20086-7 Bach,JS: Partitas		Demus (piano)	
XLP20095 Haydn: String Quartets 67, 77, 78	Vienna Konzerthaus Quartet		
XLP30001 Prokofiev: Symphony 1,Falla: 3 Cornered Hat,Ravel Dukas	Philh	Markevitch	[CX1049]
XLP30003 Rimsky-Korsakov: Le Coq d'Or Suite, Tsar Saltan Suite	Philh	Issay-Dobrowen	[SX1010]
XLP30004 Mozart: Quintet in Eflat K452 Piano Concerto K449	Wind Ensemble Brain Horsley		[CLP1029/1012]
XLP30005 Beethoven: Sonatas Op 109, 110		Myra Hess	[ALP1169]
XLP30006 Verdi-Mackerras: The Lady and the Fool	Philh	Mackerras	[CLP1059]
XLP30007 An Evening of Ballet (Weber,Tchaikovsky,Stravinsky,etc)	Philh	Markevitch	
XLP30008 Elgar: Sea Pictures, Overture In the South	LSO	Weldon Ripley	[SX1028]
XLP30009 "Memories of Kreisler" (Schon Rosmarin, Liebesfreud, etc)	Kreisler Rupp		
XLP30010 Borodin: Symphonies 2, 3	Philh	Malko	[CLP1075]
XLP30011 Dvorak: Serenade in Dmin, Gounod: Petite Symphonie	LBE	Haas	[PMB1001]
XLP30013 Mozart: Piano Concertos 9, 17	LSO	Sherman Bachauer	[CLP1096/DLP1158]
XLP30014 Berlioz: Ovs Corsaire, Benvenuto, Beatrice, Francs Juges	Philh	Kletzki	[CX1003]
XLP30015 Tchaikovsky: Manfred Symphony	Philh	Kletzki	[CX1189]
XLP30016 Haydn: Notturno in C, Div in C, Mozart: Serenade 12	LBE	Haas	[PMA1013]
XLP30020 Beethoven: Piano Concerto 4, Piano Sonata 27	Philh	Cluytens Solomon	[ALP1583/BLP1036]
XLP30021 Strauss,R: Symphony for Wind Instruments	LBE	Haas	[PMA1006]
XLP30023 Brahms: Symphony 1	Philh	Cantelli	[ALP1152]
XLP30025 Mendelssohn: Midsummer Nts Dream (Ov & Inc Music)	Philh	Kletzki	[CX1174]
XLP30026 Handel: Israel in Egypt (hlts)	RLPO	Sargent	[CX1347-8]
XLP30028 Schubert: Symphony 6, Grieg: Concert Ov In Autumn, etc	RPO	Beecham	[CX1363]
XLP30030 Brahms: Symphony 3, Schumann: Symphony 4	Philh	Cantelli	[BLP1083/1044]
XLP30031 Tchaikovsky: Mozartiana, Suite 4, Rimsky-Korsakov	Philh	Fistoulari	[PMC1028/1031]

XLP30034 Mozart: Symphony 29, A Musical Joke K522	Philh	Cantelli	[ALP1461]
XLP30036 Tchaikovsky: Fantasy Ov Hamlet	Philh	Irving	[CLP1043]
Francesca da Rimini	RPO	Kletzki	[CX1565]
XLP30039 Haydn: Cello Concerto op 101, Vivaldi: Cello Concerto	DSRO	Woldike Bengtsson	[ALP1501]
XLP30040 Wagner: Tannhauser, Dutchman, Gotterdammerung (hlts)	BPO	Kempe	[ALP1513]
XLP30041 Schubert: Rosamunde, inc music	Philh	Kletzki	[CX1157]
XLP30042 Rossini: Ovs (Cenerentola,Semiramide,Tell,Tancredi,etc)	various	Gui/Gracis/Previtali	[Various HMV]
XLP30043 Brahms: Symphony 2	BPO	Kempe	[ALP1386]
XLP30044 Mahler: Lieder Eines Fahrenden Gesellen	Philh	Furtwangler F-Dieskau	[ALP1270]
Kindertotenlieder	BPO	Kempe F-Dieskau	[BLP1081]
XLP30045 Mendelssohn: Symphony 3, etc	IPO	Kletzki	[CX1219]
XLP30048 Wagner: Parsifal, Tristan und Isolde,Lohengrin (hlts)	VPO	Kempe	[ALP1638]
XLP30049 Holst: The Perfect Fool,St Paul's St, Somerset Rhapsody	Philh/LSO	Weldon	[SX1019/etc]
XLP30050-2 Handel: Messiah	RLPO	Sargent	[CX1146-8]
XLP30053 Mozart: Sonata K331, Schubert: Sonata D664, Haydn		Solomon	[Various HMV]
XLP30058 Vivaldi: The Four Seasons	Philh	Giulini Parikian (vln)	[CX1365]
XLP30059 "Favourite Italian Opera Choruses" (Boito, Puccini, etc)	Rome Op various		
XLP30064 Britten: Young Person's Guide, Prokofiev: Peter & Wolf	Philh	Markevitch	[CX1175/DLP1001]
XLP30069 "The Unashamed Accompanist"		Gerald Moore	[SX1043]
XLP30071 Coates: London St, Three bears, etc	LSO	Mackerras Coates	
XLP30072 Grieg and Schumann Piano Concertos	Philh	Karajan Lipatti	[33C1040/1001]
XLP30073-4 Brahms: German Requiem	BPO	Kempe Grummer	[ALP1351-2]
Bruckner: Te Deum	BPO	Forster	[ALP1567]
XLP30079 Concert (Mozart, Beethoven, Rossini, Brahms, etc)	BBCSO	Toscanini	
XLP30082 Wagner: Lohengrin,Tannhauser,Gotterdammerung (hlts)	VPO	Furtwangler	[ALP1220/1016]
XLP30090 Ovs Beethoven Leonora 3, Weber: Freischutz, Euryanthe	VPO	Furtwangler	[Various HMV]
XLP30092 Ravel: Daphnis & Chloe St, Debussy, Dukas	Philh	Cantelli	[ALP1207/BLP1089]
XLP30093 Brahms: Piano Concerto 2	Philh	Dobrowen Solomon	[78s]
XLP30095 Schubert: An Die Musik etc (Wanderer,Sylvia,etc)	Moore	Fischer-Dieskau	[ALP1677]
XLP30096 Handel: Messiah (hlts)	RLPO	Sargent	[CX1146-8]
XLP30097 Overtures: Rosamunde, Merry Wives, Fingal's Cave, etc	VPO	Furtwangler	[Various HMV]
XLP30102-3 Schubert: Lieder (Winterreise, Schwanengesang)	Hotter	Moore	[CX1222-3/1269]
XLP30104 Mozart: Symphony 40, Eine Kleine Nachtmusik, Schubert	VPO	Furtwangler	[Various HMV]
XLP30106 Smetana: Vltava, Liszt: Les Preludes, Schubert, etc	VPO	Furtwangler	[Various HMV]
XLP30109 Lalo: Symphonie Espagnol	Philh	Martinon Oistrakh,	
Bruch: Violin Concerto 1	LSO	Matacic Oistrakh	[Various Columbia]
XLP30116 Beethoven: Sonatas Op 101, Op 106 ("Hammerklavier")		Solomon	[ALP1141/1272]
XLP30118 Concert (Respighi, Debussy, Wolf-Ferrari)	AdSC	De Sabata	[78s]

The following were issued in the early 1980s.

XLP60001 Balakirev: Symphony 1	Philh	Karajan	[78s]
XLP60002 Britten: Frank Bridge Vns op 10, V-Williams: Tallis Fantasia	Philh	Karajan	[CX1159]
XLP60003 Roussel: Symphony 4, Stravinsky: Jeu de Cartes	Philh	Karajan	[78s]
XLP60004 Mozart: Sinfonia Concertante K297b, Clarinet Conc K622	Philh	Karajan Walton Brain	[CX1178/CX1361]

HMV CSLP
"The Golden Treasury of Immortal Performances"

This short lived series of reissues from '78' originals was launched in Sept 1956. The end of the agreement between HMV and the American Victor label caused the deletion of recordings in the HMV catalogue which had originated in America with the Victor company, and this series was deleted in its entirety from Sept 1958.

The jackets are white with gold lettering and with a framed colour picture of 'Nipper' displayed on an artist's easel. The label is also white with gold lettering but with a monochrome picture of 'Nipper' in the upper half.

CSLP500	50 Years of Great Operatic Singing, Vol 1 1900-1910			
CSLP501	50 Years of Great Operatic Singing, Vol 2 1910-1920			
CSLP502	50 Years of Great Operatic Singing, Vol 3 1920-1930			
CSLP503	50 Years of Great Operatic Singing, Vol 4 1930-1940			
CSLP504	50 Years of Great Operatic Singing, Vol 5 1940-1950			
CSLP505	Tchaikovsky: Piano Concerto 1	NBCSO	Toscanini	Horowitz
CSLP506	Violin Recital			Kreisler (violin)
CSLP507	Beethoven: Violin Concerto (rec 1940)	NBCSO	Toscanini	Heifetz
CSLP508	Sacred Music		Caruso	McCormack
CSLP509	Rachmaninov: Piano Concerto 1, Paganini Variations	Phild	Ormandy/Stokowski	Rachmaninov
CSLP510	The Art of Caruso Vol 1			Caruso
CSLP511	The Art of Caruso vol 2			Caruso
CSLP512	The Art of Caruso vol 3			Caruso
CSLP515	Rachmaninov: Piano Concerto 4 (rec 1941)	Phild	Ormandy	Rachmaninov
CSLP516	50 Years of Great Operatic Singing, Vol 6 supplement			
CSLP517	Rachmaninov: Piano Concerto 2 (rec 1929)	Phild	Stokowski	Rachmaninov
CSLP518	Operatic Duets			
CSLP520	Rachmaninov: Piano Concerto 3 (rec 1939-40)	Phild	Ormandy	Rachmaninov

Parlophone
Parlophone PMA (12")

Parlophone commenced the issue of LPs during 1952 in four series. PMA/PMB were full priced and devoted exclusively to classical music, while PMC/PMD were lower priced and include much non classical music.

Label: This is black with gold lettering with the Parlophone £ trademark in the upper half above the word 'Parlophone' in black with gold shading.

Cat No	Work	Orchestra	Artists
PMA1001	Haydn: Symphonies 1, 13, 28	VSO	Sternberg
PMA1002	Haydn: Symphony 47, Symphony 84	Vienna CO / Collegium Musicum Vienna	Litschauer / Heiller
PMA1003	Mozart: Violin Concertos K216, K218	Philh	Susskind Goldberg
PMA1004	Haydn: Symphony 22, Dittersdorf: Concerto in Gmaj	LBE	Haas
PMA1005	Handel: Te Deum	Danish Radio	Wöldike
PMA1006	Strauss,R: Symphony for Wind Instruments	LBE	Haas
PMA1007	Bach: Violin Concerto in Emaj, Haydn: Violin Conc in Cmaj	Philh	Susskind Goldberg
PMA1008	Chopin: Ballades 1-4		Siki
PMA1009	Bach,CPE: Concerto in Eflat for harpsichord & piano, Bach,JS: Concerto in Cmin for 2 harpsichords	LBE	Haas Salter Spinks
PMA1010	Haydn: Mass 8 (Heiligenmesse)	Denmark Royal Op	Wöldike
PMA1011	Chopin the 4 Scherzi		Siki
PMA1012	Mozart: Piano Concerto K449, Haydn: Concerto for violin and harpsichord	Grete / LBE	Scherzer / Haas Pougnet Salter
PMA1013	Mozart: Serenade K388, Haydn: Notturno in C, Div in C	LBE	Haas
PMA1014	Haydn: Symphonies 7, 8	Vienna CO	Litschauer
PMA1015	Haydn: Mass in Time of War (Paukenmesse)	Vienna SO	Gillesberger
PMA1016	Haydn: Symphonies 26, 36	Vienna CO	Heiller
PMA1021	Handel: Double Concertos in F, Bflat	Collegium Musicum Copenhagen	Friisholm
PMA1022	Schumann: Carnaval op 9, Chopin		Siki
PMA1023	Bach,JS: Cantata, M Haydn: Mass in Bflat	LBE	Haas
PMA1024	Conchita Supervia Sings Carmen		Supervia
PMA1025	Rossini: Operatic excerpts		Supervia
PMA1026-8	Shaporin: 'The Decembrists'	Bolshoi	Melik-Pashaev Ivanov Petrov
PMA1029-32	Tchaikovsky: The Enchantress	MPO	Samosud
PMA1033-6	Glinka: Russlan & Ludmilla	Bolshoi	Kondrashin Firsova Petrov
PMA1037	Rachmaninov: Piano Concerto 1, Bach,JS: Piano Conc in Dmin	USSR	Sanderling Richter
PMA1038	Rachmaninov: Symphony 2	USSR	Gauk
PMA1039	Kabalevsky: Piano Concerto 3, Rakov: Violin Concerto	USSR / USSR	Kabalevsky Gilels / Rakov I Oistrakh
PMA1040	Shostakovich: String Quartet op 73, Piano Quintet op 57	Tchaikovsky Quartet / Beethoven Quartet	Shostakovich (piano)
PMA1042	Franck: Piano Quintet in Fmin	Richter	etc
PMA1043	Schumann: Cello Concerto, Shostakovich: Cello Sonata Op 40	Moscow PO	Samosud Rostropovitch / Rostropovitch D Shostakovich
PMA1044	Tchaikovsky: Piano Sonata Op 37, Schumann: Humoreske Op 20		Richter (piano)
PMA1045	Russian Folk Songs	various	
PMA1046	Tchaikovsky: The Months op 37a		Oborin (piano)
PMA1047-8	Borodin: Prince Igor (hlts), Mussorgsky: Boris Godunov (hlts)	Bolshoi	Nebolsin/Melik-Pashaev
PMA1049	Schubert: Piano Sonata D845		Richter
PMA1050-2	Tchaikovsky: Eugene Onegin	Bolshoi	Khaikin Vishnevskaya
PMA1053	Prokofiev: Symphony 4	USSR	Rozhdestvensky

PMA1054	Khachaturian: Piano Concerto, Rachmaninov: Etudes-Tableaux	USSR	Khachaturian Oborin (piano)
PMA1055	Mozart: Divertimento K334,	LenPO	Sanderling
PMA1056	Operatic Recital	Bolshoi	Nebolsin Reizen
PMA1057	Operatic Arias		Lehmann
PMA1058	Spanish Songs		Supervia
PMA1078	Haydn: Concerto Op 21,	LBE	Haas Scherzer(piano)
	Dittersdorf: Sinfonia Concertante,	LBE	Haas Riddle(viola)
	Schubert: Konzertstuck	LBE	Haas Eitler(violin)

Parlophone PMB series (10")

PMB1001	Dvorak: Serenade in Dmin op 44	LBE	Haas
PMB1002	Mozart: Serenade K375	LBE	Haas
PMB1003	V Williams: Song of Thanksgiving, Lark Ascending	LPO	Boult Pougnet
PMB1004	Bach,CPE: Sonatas for Wind, Telemann: Suite in D for Wind	LBE	Haas
PMB1005	Mozart:Serenata Notturna K239,Fux:Sonata in F for 2 Violins	LBE	Haas
PMB1006	Great Tauber Songs		Tauber
PMB1007	Songs of Old Vienna		Tauber
PMB1008	Mozart:6 Notturni for Voice&Woodwind,Dittersdorf: Partita in D	LBE	Haas
PMB1011	Operatic Recital (Mozart, Weber, Bizet, Lalo, Offenbach)		Tauber
PMB1012	Songs of Stage and Screen		Tauber
PMB1013	Bach,J.S: Brandenburg Concertos 3, 4	Chamber Orch	Barshai Oistrakh
PMB1014	Shostakovich: Violin Concerto op 99	LenPO	Mravinsky Oistrakh

Parlophone PMC series (classical only)

Note that there are many non classical LPs in the PMC series. These are listed as 'NC'.

PMC1001	Tchaikovsky: Nutcracker Suite	ROHCG	Irving
PMC1002	Ravel: Gaspard de la Nuit, Schubert: 3 Impromptus, 2 Moments Musicaux		Scherzer (piano)
PMC1003	Concert (Rimsky-Korsakov, Tchaikovsky, etc)	Philh	Schüchter
PMC1004	Poulenc: Les Biches, Faure: Dolly Suite op 56	LSO	Fistoulari
PMC1005	Dohnanyi: Variations on a Nursery Song, Strauss,R: Burleske	Philh	Fistoulari Jacquinot
PMC1006	Concert (Albeniz, Granados, Falla, Turina)	LSO	Poulet
PMC1007	Kabalevsky: Colas Breugnon suite, Prokofiev: The Gambler	Philh	Schüchter
PMC1008	Nights at the Ballet	ROHCG	Braithwaite
PMC1009	Balakirev: Thamar, Rimsky-Korsakov: Ivan the Terrible Suite	LSO	Fistoulari
PMC1010	Grieg: Sigurd Jorsalfar Suite, 2 Elegaic Melodies, Humperdinck	ROHCG	Hollingsworth
PMC1011	Dukas: La Péri, D'Indy: Istar Symphonic Variations	Westminster SO	Fistoulari
PMC1012	NC		
PMC1013	Massenet: Le Cid, Scènes Alsaciennes	ROHCG	Braithwaite
PMC1014	Tchaikovsky: Romeo and Juliet, Hamlet	Philh	Fistoulari
PMC1015	D'Indy: Symphony on a French Mt Song, St-Saens: Piano Concerto 5	Westminster SO	Fistoulari Jacquinot
PMC1016	Fauré: Pélleas and Mélisande Suite, Ravel: Alborada, Barque sur l'Ocean, Pavane	LSO	Poulet
PMC1017	Kodaly: Háry János, Dohnanyi: Ruralia Hungarica Suite	Philh	Schüchter
PMC1018	Moussorgsky: Orch Works	Philh	Susskind
PMC1019	Debussy: Fantaisie for Piano & Orch, Poulenc: Aubade for Piano & 18 Instruments	Westminster SO	Fistoulari Jacquinot
PMC1020	Chabrier: Suite Pastorale, Bizet: Jeux D'Enfants Suite	ROHCG	Braithwaite
PMC1021	Concert (Alfven, Svendsen, Nielsen, Sibelius)	ROHCG	Hollingsworth
PMC1022	Berlioz: Trojans (hlts), Overtures Carnaval Romain, Corsaire	Philh	Schüchter
PMC1023	Shostakovich: Concerto for Piano,Trumpet,Strings, Sonata op 64	Pressler (piano)	Glantz (trumpet)
PMC1024	Brahms: Overtures Acad Festival, Tragic, Schumann	LSO	Collingwood

PMC1025	Guilmant: Sonata op 42, Reubke: Sonata on 94th Psalm		Ellsasser (organ)
PMC1026	Gershwin: Piano Concerto in F, Rhapsody in Blue	Hamburg Pro Musica	Walther Bianca (piano)
PMC1027	Debussy: La Boîte à Joujoux Ballet, Ibert: Histoires		Pressler (piano)
PMC1028	Tchaikovsky: Mozartiana Suite op 51, The Slippers Suite	Philh	Fistoulari
PMC1029	Ballet Music from the Operas (William Tell, Aida, Faust, etc)	Philh	Braithwaite
PMC1030	Widor: Symphony 6		Elsasser (organ)
PMC1031	Orch concert (Glinka, Nicolai, Rimsky-Korsakov, Reznicek)	LSO/Philh	Fistoulari
PMC1032	Mozart: Transcriptions for Organ		Elsasser (organ)
PMC1033	NC		
PMC1034	Grieg: Piano Concerto, Tchaikovsky: Piano Concerto 1	Hamburg Pro Musica	Walther Bianca (piano)
PMC1035	Faure: Trio op 120, Ravel: Trio in Amin	Beaux Arts Trio	
PMC1036	Moussorgsky: Night on the Bare Mt, Tchaikovsky: Symphony 2	Hamburg Pro Musica	Winograd
PMC1037	Franck: Organ Concert		Elsasser (organ)
PMC1039	Beethoven: Symphony 5, Schubert: Symphony 8	Hamburg Pro Musica	Winograd
PMC1040	Haydn: Trio 1 in Gmaj, Mendelssohn: Trio op 49	Beaux Arts Trio	
PMC1041-2	Mozart: Sonatas for Organ and Orchestra	Hamburg CO	Winograd Elsasser
PMC1044	Haydn: Symphony 94, Mozart: Serenade 13 (Eine Kleine)	NWDR SO of Hamburg	Schmidt-Isserstedt
PMC1045	Bizet: Symphony in Cmaj, Jeux D'Enfants	LSO	Young
PMC1046	Tchaikovsky: Variations on a Rococo Theme, Bloch: Schelomo	LSO	Austin Navarra
PMC1048	Schubert: Symphony 5, Rosamunde (hlts)	NWDR SO of Hamburg	Schmidt-Isserstedt
PMC1050	Bruch: Kol Nidrei op 47, Khachaturian: Cello Concerto	Colonne Orch	Dervaux Navarra (cello)
PMC1051	Bizet: La Jolie Fille de Perth Suite, Massenet: Le Cid, Scènes Neopolitaines	PO	Le Conte
PMC1054	Sibelius: Symphony 2	NWDR SO of Hamburg	Schmidt-Isserstedt
PMC1055	NC		
PMC1056	Shostakovich: Preludes and Fugues op 87		Dimitri Shostakovich (piano)
PMC1058	Mendelssohn: Cello Sonata op 58, Strauss,R: Cello Sonata op 6	Navarra	Lush (piano)
PMC1061	NC		
PMC1062	NC		
PMC1064	NC		
PMC1065	NC		
PMC1066	NC		
PMC1069	NC		
PMC1074	NC		
PMC1075	NC		
PMC1077	NC		
PMC1078	Concert (Dittersdorff, Haydn, Schubert)	LBE	Haas Eitler (violin)

There are no further classical LPs in the PMC series.

Parlophone PMD series (10") (classical only)

Note that there are many non classical LPs in the PMD series. These are listed as 'NC'.

PMD1001	Schumann (arr Jacob): Carnaval Ballet Music	ROHCG	Rignold
PMD1002	Rossini (arr Respighi): La Boutique Fantasque	ROHCG	Rignold
PMD1003	Chopin (arr Jacob): Les Sylphides	ROHCG	Rignold
PMD1004	Coates: London Suite, London Again Suite	Philharmonic Prom Orch	Coates
PMD1005	Delibes: Sylvia, Gounod: Faust Ballet Music	ROHCG	Rignold
PMD1006	NC		
PMD1007	NC		
PMD1008	NC		
PMD1009	NC		
PMD1010	Schumann: Fantasie op 17		Scherzer (piano)
PMD1011	NC		
PMD1012	NC		
PMD1013	NC		
PMD1014	NC		
PMD1015	NC		
PMD1016	NC		
PMD1017	NC		
PMD1018	Turina: Danzas Fantasticas, Granados: Danzas Espanolas	Philh	Schüchter
PMD1019	Liszt: Les Préludes, Mazeppa	Philh	Fistoulari
PMD1020	Britten: Soirées Musicales op 9, Matinées Musicales op 24	ROHCG	Braithwaite
PMD1022	Operatic Intermezzi	Philh	Schüchter
PMD1023	Borodin: Prince Igor Suite, Polovtsian Dances act 2	Philh	Susskind
PMD1024	Berlioz: The Trojans Suite	Lamoureux	Martinon
PMD1025	Grieg: Norwegian Dances op 35, Peer Gynt Suite 1	Philh	Fistoulari
PMD1026	Liszt: Totentanz, Rimsky-Korsakov: Concerto in C#min op 30	Philh	Fistoulari Jacquinot (piano)
PMD1027	Schubert: Rosamunde (hlts)	ROHCG	Braithwaite
PMD1028	Rimsky-Korsakov: Skazka op 29, Snegourochka Suite	Philh	Fistoulari
PMD1031	Mendelssohn: Sextet op 110	Guilet String Quartet etc	
PMD1048	'O Come to Vienna'	Carl Loubé Orch Karas (zither)	
PMD1051	Beethoven: Piano Concerto 3	NWDR SO of Hamburg Schmidt-Isserstedt Yankoff	

Decca LXT

The LXT series was Decca's main label for mono classical material and was launched in June 1950 together with the 10" LX series. The label for both LXT and LX is orange with gold lettering, changing to silver lettering on later LXTs.

The original numbering sequence was LXT2501-2999 and the series was complete by early 1955. From then a new sequence began at LXT5000 and then continued to LXT5685 in late 1962. During this period stereo discs were introduced and this handbook shows the stereo numbers in the SXL series, cross-referenced where appropriate.

From September 1962 Decca introduced parallel numbering for LXT and SXL issues commencing at LXT/SXL6000. The mono discs were discontinued in early 1969, the last mono number used being LXT6376.

Number	Work	Orchestra	Performers
LXT2501	Bach: Brandenburg Concertos 4/6	StCO	Munchinger
LXT2502	Stravinsky: Petrushka	OSR	Ansermet
LXT2503-5	Bach,JS: The Art of Fugue	Radio Orch Beromunster	Scherchen
LXT2506	Beethoven: Piano Concerto 5	LPO	Szell Curzon
LXT2507	Opera Arias (Gounod, Puccini, Verdi)	OSR	Erede Tebaldi
LXT2508	Rimsky-Korsakov: Scheherazade	PCO	Ansermet
LXT2509	Tchaikovsky: Violin Concerto	NSO	Sargent Ricci
LXT2510	Bizet: L'Arlesienne Suite, Carmen Suite	LPO	Van Beinum/Collins
LXT2511	Tchaikovsky: Symphony 4	PCO	Kleiber
LXT2512	Berlioz: Romeo and Juliet, Royal Hunt & Storm (Trojans)	PCO	Munch
LXT2513	Beethoven: Symphony 5	OdeP	Schuricht
LXT2514	Opera Arias (Puccini, Verdi, Donizetti, Flotow, Bizet)	NSO	Erede Eugene Conley
LXT2515	Mozart: Quintet K516	Griller Quartet	
LXT2516	Bloch: "Sacred Service"	LPO	Bloch
LXT2517	Brahms: Symphony 4	LSO	Krips
LXT2518	Borodin: Polovtsian Dances, Falla: Love the Magician	LPO	Van Beinum/Collins
LXT2519	Dvorak: Piano Quintet in Amaj	Quintetto Chigiano	
LXT2520	Franck: Piano Quintet	Quintetto Chigiano	
LXT2521	Music from Spain (Granados/Falla/Turina/Albeniz)	PCO	Jorda
LXT2524	Debussy: Images	OSR	Ansermet
LXT2525	Elgar: Cockaigne Suite, Wand of Youth Suite 1	LPO	Van Beinum
LXT2527	Wagner: Orchestral hlts (Tristan, Parsifal)	LPO	Krauss
LXT2528	Opera Arias (Gounod, Offenbach, Thomas, Rossini, etc)	LSO	Matthieson Janine Micheau
LXT2529	Bartok: Concerto for Orchestra	Ccgbw	Van Beinum
LXT2530	Dvorak: String Qt in Fmaj	Griller Quartet	
LXT2531	Tchaikovsky: Romeo & Juliet Francesca da Rimini	LPO PCO	Van Beinum Jorda
LXT2532	Beethoven: Piano Sonatas Op 26, Op 53 ("Waldstein")		Backhaus
LXT2533	Schubert: Piano Quintet Op 114	Vienna Octet	Panhoffer
LXT2534	Mozart: Symphony 35, Handel-Harty: Water Music Suite	LPO	Beinum
LXT2535	Beethoven: Piano Sonata Op 109, Chopin: Piano Sonata Op 35		Backhaus
LXT2536-8	Mozart: Die Entfuhrung aus dem Serail	VPO	Krips Lipp W.Ludwig
LXT2539	Schubert: Lieder	Schlusnus	Peschko (piano)
LXT2540	Bach: Brandenburg Concertos 1, 5	StCO	Munchinger
LXT2542	Mozart: Divertimento K334	Vienna Octet	
LXT2543	Recital of Schubert and Faure	Souzay	Bonneau (piano)
LXT2544	Tchaikovsky: Symphony 6	OdeP	Munch
LXT2545	Tchaikovsky: Symphony 5	LPO	Celibidache

LXT2546	Beethoven: Symphony 3	Ccgbw	Kleiber
LXT2547	Beethoven: Symphony 7	Ccgbw	Kleiber
LXT2548	Strauss,R: Thus Spake Zarathustra	VPO	Krauss
LXT2549	Strauss,R: Till Eulenspiegel, Don Juan	VPO	Krauss
LXT2550-1	Strauss,J: Die Fledermaus	VPO	Krauss Gueden Patzak
LXT2553	Beethoven: Piano Concerto 3	VPO	Bohm Backhaus
LXT2554	Operatic recital (Mozart,Verdi,Wagner,etc)	VPO	Bohm Schoeffler
LXT2555	Rossini-Respighi: La Boutique Fantasque	LSO	Ansermet
LXT2556	Schumann: Frauenliebe und Leben, Brahms: 4 Serious Songs	Ferrier	Newmark (piano)
LXT2557	Opera Arias (Charpentier, Verdi, Bizet, Gluck, Massenet, etc)	OSR	Erede Suzanne Danco
LXT2558	Mozart: Symphony 25,	LPO	Celibidache
	Symphony 36	VPO	Bohm
LXT2559	Tchaikovsky: Piano Concerto 1	NSO	Szell Curzon
LXT2560-1	Wagner: Mastersingers Act 2	VPO	Knappertsbusch Schoeffler
LXT2562	Mozart: Symphony 29,	OSR	Maag
	Symphony 36	VPO	Bohm
LXT2563	Stravinsky: Rite of Spring	OSR	Ansermet
LXT2564	Beethoven: Symphony 4	LPO	Solti
LXT2565	Ravel: Concerto in Gmaj,	PCO	Munch Henriot
	Concerto for the Left Hand	OSR	Ansermet Blancard
LXT2566	Brahms: Violin Concerto	Ccgbw	Munch Renardy
LXT2567	Opera Recital (Tchaikovsky, Lehar, Verdi, Milloecker)	Vienna SO	Moralt Welitsch
LXT2568	Recital (Handel, Beethoven, Gluck, Lully, Debussy, Ravel)	PCO	Lindenburg Souzay
LXT2570	Loewe: Ballads	Wilhelm Strienz	Hausslein (piano)
LXT2571	Respighi: Ancient Airs & Dances, Pergolesi: Concertino in Fmin	StCO	Munchinger
LXT2572	Liszt: Annee de Pelerinage, Deux Legendes		Kempff
LXT2573	Beethoven: String Quartet Op 132	Griller Quartet	
LXT2574	Bartok: Violin Concerto	LSO	Sargent Rostal
LXT2575	Sibelius: String Quartet Op 65	Griller Quartet	
LXT2576	Strauss,J: Die Fledermaus (hlts)	VPO	Krauss Gueden Patzak
LXT2577	Schubert: Piano Sonata 21 in Bflat maj		Kempff
LXT2578	Organ Recital (Bach, Franck)		Demessieux
LXT2579-80	Rachmaninov: 24 Preludes		Lympany
LXT2581	Beethoven: Piano Sonatas op 27/2, op 110		Gulda
LXT2582-4	Offenbach: Tales of Hoffmann	RPO	Beecham Grandi Dargavel
LXT2585	Schubert: Symphony 6	LSO	Krips
LXT2586	Brahms: Symphony 2	LPO	Furtwangler
LXT2587	Beethoven: Symphony 6	LPO	Kleiber
LXT2588	Paganini: Caprices op 1		Ricci
LXT2589	Suppe: Overture (Poet&Peasant, Pique Dame, Light Cavalry, etc)	LPO	Solti
LXT2590	Offenbach: Overtures (Orpheus, Belle Helene, Bluebeard, etc)	LPO	Martinon
LXT2591	Schumann: String Quartet Op 41/2, Verdi: String Quartet	Italian Quartet	
LXT2592	Recital of opera and lieder	VPO	Bohm Dermota
LXT2593	Lehar: The Count of Luxembourg (hlts)	Reinshagen Tonhalle Orch Zurich	
LXT2594	Beethoven: Eroica Variations, Piano Sonata 26 ("Les Adieux")		Gulda
LXT2595	Rachmaninov: Piano Concerto 2	NSO	Fistoulari Katchen
LXT2596	Recital (Bruch, Bach)		Campoli
LXT2597-9	Weber: Der Freischutz	VPO	Ackermann Loose
LXT2600	Vivaldi: 4 Seasons	StCO	Munchinger
LXT2601	Dvorak: String Quartet	Boskowsky Quartet	
LXT2602	Schumann: Symphony 1	OSR	Ansermet
LXT2603	Beethoven: Piano Sonatas Op 10/1, Op 10/2, Op 79		Backhaus
LXT2604	Bach,JC: Sinfonia, Schubert: Symphony 3	Cincinatti SO	Johnson
LXT2605	Berlioz: Les Nuits D'été	Cincinatti SO	Johnson Danco
LXT2606	"Famous Overtures" (Adam, Boildieu, Herold)	LPO	Martinon
LXT2607	Lehar: The Merry Widow (hlts)	Zurich Tonhalle	Reinshagen

Catalog	Work	Orchestra	Conductor/Performers
LXT2608	Dvorak: Symphony 5 ("New World")	New SO	Jorda
LXT2609	Sullivan: Overtures	SO	Godfrey
LXT2610	Tchaikovsky: Sleeping Beauty, Ippolitov-Ivanov: Caucn Sketches	PCO	Desormiere
LXT2611	Tchaikovsky: Nutcracker Suite	PCO	Fistoulari
LXT2612-3	Strauss,J: The Gypsy Baron	VPO	Krauss Patzak Loose
LXT2614	Mozart: Symphonies 34, 38 ('Prague')	OSR	Maag/Ansermet
LXT2615-7	Bizet: Carmen	Paris Opera Comique	Wolff Juyol
LXT2618-20	Massenet: Manon	Opera Comique	Wolff Micheau
LXT2621	Falla: Nights in the Gardens of Spain, 3 Cornered Hat	LSO	Jorda Curzon
LXT2622-3	Puccini: La Boheme	AdSC	Erede Tebaldi
LXT2624	Beethoven: Piano Sonata op 106		Gulda
LXT2625	French Overtures (Berlioz, Lalo, Massenet, St-Saens)	Paris Opera Comique	Wolff
LXT2626	Bloch: Piano Quintet	Quintetto Chigiano	
LXT2627	Beethoven: Piano Concerto 1	VPO	Bohm Gulda
LXT2628	Conradin Kreutzer: Grand Septet	Vienna Octet	
LXT2629	Beethoven: Piano Concerto 4	VPO	Krauss Backhaus
LXT2630	Alfven: Midsmr Vigil op 19, Grieg: Suite Sigurd Jorsalfar op 56	Cincinatti SO	Johnson
LXT2631	Stravinsky: Fairy's Kiss, Martin: Petite Symphonie Concertante	OSR	Ansermet
LXT2632	Debussy: La Mer, Ravel: Mother Goose	OSR	Ansermet
LXT2633	Weber: Overtures (Euryanthe, Preciosa, Oberon, etc)	VPO	Bohm
LXT2634	Strauss,J: Fledermaus, Zigeunerbaron, Fruhlingstimmen, etc	VPO	Krauss
LXT2635	Mozart: Die Entfuhrung aus dem Serail (hlts)	VPO	Krips Lipp W.Ludwig
LXT2636	Schumann: Etudes Symphoniques op 13		Mewton-Wood
LXT2637	Ravel: Rhapsodie Espagnol, Debussy : Nocturnes	OSR	Ansermet
LXT2638-0	Puccini: Madama Butterfly	AdSC	Erede Tebaldi
LXT2641	Dvorak: Symphony 4	Ccgbw	Szell
LXT2642	Berlioz: Symphonie Fantastique	Ccgbw	Van Beinum
LXT2643	Strauss,R: Sinfonia Domestica	VPO	Krauss
LXT2644	Wagner: Scenes from Die Walkure, Siegfried, Parsifal	VPO	Knappertsbusch/Moralt Solosts
LXT2645	Vienna Philharmonic New Year Concert	VPO	Krauss
LXT2646-7	Wagner: Mastersingers Act 1	VPO	Knappertsbusch Schoeffler
LXT2648-50	Wagner: Mastersingers Act 3	VPO	Knappertsbusch Schoeffler
LXT2651-6	Wagner: Parsifal	Bayreuth	Knappertsbusch Windgassen
LXT2657	Grieg: Piano Concerto	LSO	Fistoulari Curzon
LXT2658	Concert of Contemporary Swiss Music	Instrumental Ensemble	
LXT2659-64	Wagner: Mastersingers of Nurnberg	VPO	Knappertsbusch Schoeffler
LXT2665	Rangstroem: Symphony 1	Stockholm Orch	Mann
LXT2666	Mozart: Piano Sonatas K281, K283, K545, K570		Blancard
LXT2667	Prokofiev: Symphony 6	OSR	Ansermet
LXT2668	Bach,JS: Fugues, Beethoven: Grosse Fuge	StCO	Munchinger
LXT2669	Wagner: Siegfried Idyll, Haydn: Symphony 45	StCO/OSR	Munchinger
LXT2670	Schumann: Arabesque, Liszt: Petrarch Sonnets		Kempff
LXT2671	Mozart: Serenade K320 ("Posthorn")	OSR	Maag
LXT2672	Opera Arias (Wagner, Beethoven, Cornelius, Verdi)	VPO	Moralt Edelmann
LXT2673	Bach,JS: Cello Suite 4		Mainardi
LXT2674	Beethoven: Violin Concerto	LSO	Krips Campoli
LXT2675	Brahms: Symphony 1	Ccgbw	Van Beinum
LXT2676	Brahms: Symphony 3	Ccgbw	Szell
LXT2677	Berlioz: Corsair Ov, Benvenuto Cellini Ov, Ravel: Bolero	PCO	Munch
LXT2678	Semenoff: Double Concerto, Rodrigo: Concerto d'ete	PCO	Barbizet Ferras
LXT2679	Beethoven: String Quartet op 59/3,Schubert: String Quartet D703	New Italian Quartet	
LXT2680	Haydn: String Quartet 69, Boccherini: String Quartet Op 6/1	Italian Quartet	
LXT2681-2	Tchaikovsky: Swan Lake	LSO	Fistoulari Campoli
LXT2683	Haydn: Symphonies 100, 104	LPO	Van Beinum/Krips
LXT2684	Mozart: Ovs Magic Flute, Cosi, Figaro, Giovanni, Impressario,etc	LSO	Krips
LXT2685	Mozart: Arias (Figaro, Don Giovanni, Zauberflote)	Dermota	Della Casa Schoeffler

LXT2686	Mozart: Symphony 33, Haydn: Symphony 94	Ccgbw	Van Beinum
LXT2687	Brahms: Quintet in Fmin for Piano and Strings	Quintetto Chigiano	
LXT2688	Operatic hlts (Donizetti, Ponchielli, Gounod, Rossini, etc)	Various	
LXT2689	Mozart: Symphonies 31/39	LSO	Krips
LXT2690	Shakespeare: Henry VIII (hlts)	Sybil Thorndike	Lewis Casson
LXT2691	Prokofiev: Piano Sonatas 2, 5		Robert Cornman
LXT2692	Franck: Symphony, Symphonic Variations	PCO	Munch E.Joyce
LXT2693	V Williams: A London Symphony	LPO	Boult
LXT2694	Sibelius: Symphony 1	LSO	Collins
LXT2695	Test Record		
LXT2696	Tchaikovsky: 1812 Overture, Hamlet Overture	LPO	Boult
LXT2697	Nielsen: Symphony 3 (Sinfonia Espansiva)	Copenhagen RSO	Tuxen
LXT2698	Mozart: Quintet for Strings and Clarinet	Italian Quartet	Bavier
LXT2699	Elgar: Intro & Allegro Op 47, Serenade Op 20, V-Williams	LSO	Collins
LXT2701	Rachmaninov: Piano Concerto 3	LSO	Collins Lympany
LXT2702	Burkhard: Toccata, Mueller: Sinfonia	Zurich Collegium Musicum	Sacher
LXT2703	C Beck: Viola Concerto, Reichel	OSR	Meylan Kägi
LXT2704-8	Gregorian Chant	Monks of Abbey of St Pierre de Solesmes	
LXT2709	Schubert: String Quartet in Amin Op 29	Vegh Quartet	
LXT2710	Brahms: String Quartet 1 op 51	Vegh Quartet	
LXT2711-4	Debussy: Pelleas and Melisande	OSR	Ansermet Danco
LXT2715	Beethoven: Piano Sonatas Op 57 (Appassionata), Op 101		Backhaus
LXT2716	Falla: 3 Cornered Hat	OSR	Ansermet
LXT2717	Beethoven: Trio Op 97 ("Archduke")	Trio di Trieste	
LXT2718	Mahler: Symphony 4	Ccgbw	Van Beinum Ritchie
LXT2719	Schubert: Symphony 9	Ccgbw	Krips
LXT2720	Poulenc: Les Biches, Scarlatti: Good Humoured Ladies	PCO	Desormiere
LXT2721-2	Mahler: Das Lied von der Erde, Rückert Songs	VPO	Walter Ferrier
LXT2723	Brahms: Piano Concerto 2	VPO	Schuricht Backhaus
LXT2724	Beethoven: Symphony 2	VPO	Schuricht
LXT2725-6	Beethoven: Symphony 9	VPO	Kleiber Gueden Dermota
LXT2727	Dvorak: Cello Concerto	LSO	Krips Nelsova
LXT2728	Mozart: String Quartets K168, K458 ("The Hunt")	Griller Quartet	
LXT2729	Strauss,R: Ein Heldenleben	VPO	Krauss
LXT2730-1	Puccini: Tosca	AdSC	Erede Tebaldi
LXT2732	Beethoven: Violin Sonata 9 ("Kreutzer")	Rostal	Osborn
LXT2733	Rossini: Overtures Semiramide, William Tell, Silken Ladder	Ccgbw	Van Beinum
LXT2734	Schumann: Dichterliebe	Souzay	Bonneau
LXT2735-7	Verdi: Aida	AdSC	Erede Tebaldi Del Monaco
LXT2738-40	Delibes: Lakme	Paris Opera Comique	Sebastian Robin
LXT2741	Beethoven: Creatures of Prometheus Ballet Music	LPO	Van Beinum
LXT2743	Debussy: La Damoiselle Elue, Chabrier: Ode a la Musique	OdeP	Fournet etc
LXT2744	Sibelius: Symphony 5, Karelia Suite	DSRO	Tuxen
LXT2745	Schumann: Symphony 2	PCO	Schuricht
LXT2746	Massenet: Le Cid, Meyerbeer: Les Patineurs	LSO	Irving
LXT2747	Beethoven: Piano Sonatas op 2, op 31		Backhaus
LXT2748	Nielsen: Symphony 1	DSRO	Jensen
LXT2749	Shostakovich: Piano Quintet	Quintetto Chigiano	
LXT2750	Beethoven: Violin Concerto	LPO	Boult Ricci
LXT2751	Handel: 6 Sonatas for Harpsichord and Violin Op 1	Malcolm	Campoli
LXT2752	Beethoven: Violin Sonatas Op 23, Op 30/3	Rostal	Osborn
LXT2753	Mozart: Divertimento 2 in Dmaj, Haydn: Symphony 49	LMP	Blech
LXT2755	New Year's Concert (Johann & Josef Strauss)	VPO	Krauss
LXT2756	Strauss,R: Incidental Music for Le Bourgeois Gentilhomme	VPO	Krauss
LXT2757	Recital of Bach and Handel Arias	LPO	Boult Ferrier
LXT2758	Tchaikovsky: Symphony 5	Hamburg RSO	Issersdedt

Catalog	Work	Orchestra	Artists
LXT2759	Handel: Organ Concerto op 4/1-2	OSR	Ansermet Demessieux
LXT2760	St-Saens: Danse Macabre, Rouet D'Omphale, Chabrier, Ravel	OSR	Ansermet
LXT2761	Tchaikovsky: Capriccio Italien, Suite 3	PCO	Schuricht
LXT2762-3	Tchaikovsky: The Sleeping Princess (complete)	PCO	Fistoulari
LXT2764	Prokofiev: Symphony 5	DSRO	Tuxen
LXT2765	Vivaldi: Concerto for Cello and Strings, Couperin, Boccherini	StCO	Munchinger Fournier
LXT2766	Recital		Fournier
LXT2767	Khachaturian: Piano Concerto	LPO	Fistoulari Lympany
LXT2768	Mendelssohn: Symphony 3	LSO	Solti
LXT2769	Rimsky-Korsakov: Golden Cockerel Suite, Capriccio Espagnol	OSR	Ansermet
LXT2770	Schubert: Rosamunde, Mendelssohn: Midsummer Nights Drm	Ccgbw	Van Beinum
LXT2771	Bartok: Dance Suite, Kodaly: Dances of Galanta	LPO	Solti
LXT2772	Mozart: Piano Quartets K478, K493		Amadeus Quartet Curzon
LXT2773	Organ Recital (Liszt, Widor)		Demessieux
LXT2774	French Songs (Debussy, Chabrier, Ravel)		Jacques Jansen (baritone) Bonneau (piano)
LXT2775	Ravel: Daphnis & Chloe	OSR	Ansermet
LXT2776	Sibelius: En Saga, Tapiola	Ccgbw	Van Beinum
LXT2777	Beethoven: Piano Sonatas Op 106 (Hammerklavier)		Backhaus
LXT2778	Brahms: Variations on a theme of Haydn, Tragic Ov	Ccgbw	Van Beinum
LXT2779	Schubert: Symphony 4 ("Tragic")	Ccgbw	Van Beinum
LXT2780	Beethoven: Piano Sonatas Op 27/1 Op 27/2, Op 49/1, Op 49/2		Backhaus
LXT2781	Schubert: 4 Impromptus Op 142		Curzon
LXT2782	Spohr: Nonet Op 31		Vienna Octet
LXT2786	Elgar: Enigma Variations, Suite from Dramatic Music of Purcell	LSO	Sargent
LXT2787	V-Williams: Pastoral Symphony	LPO	Boult Ritchie
LXT2788	Delius: Brigg Fair, Walk to the Paradise Garden, etc	LSO	Collins
LXT2789	Bizet: Pearl Fishers (hlts), Gounod: Mireille (hlts)	Paris Opera	Erede Micheau Giannotti
LXT2790	Britten: Vns on a Theme of Frank Bridge, Warlock: Capriol Suite	Boyd Neel Orchestra	
LXT2791	Walton: Facade, Lambert: Horoscope	LSO	Irving
LXT2792	Handel: Water Music, Royal Fireworls Music	Ccgbw	Van Beinum [LXT5379]
LXT2793	Marches (Bax, Walton, Elgar)	LSO	Sargent
LXT2794	V Williams, Rubbra: Masses		Fleet Street Choir Lawrence
LXT2795-6	English Keyboard Music		Dart (harpsichord) Jones (organ)
LXT2797	"The Songs of England"		Vyvyan Lush
LXT2798	Aldeburgh Fest 1953: British Music to Celebrate the Coronation		Aldeburgh Britten Pears Deller
LXT2799-2800	Schubert: Die Winterreisse		Schmitt-Walter (baritone) Giesen (piano)
LXT2801	Lalo: Symphonie Espagnole	LPO	Van Beinum Campoli
LXT2802	Mozart: Violin Sonatas K454, K526		Frederick Grinke Taylor
LXT2803	Nielsen: Quintet for Wind Instruments, Bozza: Variations, Ibert		Copenhagen Wind Quintet
LXT2804	Beethoven: Diabelli Vns		Katchen
LXT2805	"Spanish and Portuguese Keyboard Music"		Felicja Blumental (piano)
LXT2806	Schumann: Piano Concerto	LSO	Krips Curzon
LXT2807	Dvorak: Symphony 2		Hamburg RSO Scmidt-Isserstedt
LXT2808	Paganini: Recital		Ricci
LXT2809	Beethoven: Piano Sonatas Op 7, op 10/3		Backhaus
LXT2810	Debussy: Violin Sonata, Faure: Violin Sonata		Ferras Barbizet
LXT2811	Beethoven: String Quartet op 18/6		Italian Quartet
LXT2812	Bartok: Mikrokosmos Sonata, Rorem: Sonata		Katchen
LXT2813	Sibelius: Violin Concerto	LPO	Van Beinum Damen
LXT2814	Brahms: Hungarian Dances 1,2,3,5,6,7,10, Dvorak: Slav Dances		Hamburg RSO Schmidt-Isserstedt
LXT2815	Sibelius: Symphony 2	LSO	Collins
LXT2816	Ravel: Piano Concerto in Gmaj, Concerto for Left Hand	OSR	Ansermet Blancard
LXT2817	Debussy: Suite Bergamasque, Ravel: Gaspard de la Nuit		Gulda
LXT2818	Strauss,R: Violin Sonata, Prokofiev: Violin Sonata	Ricci	Bussotti
LXT2819	Mozart: Symphony 40, Haydn: Symphony 92	LSO	Krips
LXT2820	Bach,JS: Recital		Kempff

Catalog	Work	Orchestra/Ensemble	Conductor/Soloist
LXT2821	Ravel: Valses Nobles et Sentimentale, Tombeau de Couperin	OSR	Ansermet
LXT2822	Wagner: Flying Dutchman, Ride of the Valkyries, Tannhauser	VPO	Knapperstbusch
LXT2823	Songs of Duparc		Gerard Souzay Bonneau (piano)
LXT2824	Beethoven: Symphonies 1, 8	VPO	Schuricht/Bohm
LXT2825	Brahms: Piano Concerto 1	Ccgbw	Van Beinum Curzon
LXT2826	Mozart: Piano Sonata K310, Bach,JS: English Suite 3		Gulda
LXT2827	Chausson: Poeme, Ravel: Tzigane, Honegger: Sonata	Belgian NO	Sebastian Ferras
LXT2828	Ravel: L'Heure Espagnole	OSR	Ansermet Danco
LXT2829-30	Bruckner: Symphony 7, Franck: Psyche	Ccgbw	Van Beinum
LXT2831	Sibelius: 4 Legends	DSRO	Jensen
LXT2832	Haydn: Symphonies 44, 48	DSRO	Woldike
LXT2833	Prokofiev: Classical Symphony, Glinka, Borodin, Mussorgsky	OSR	Ansermet
LXT2834	Schubert: Piano Sonata 16 in Amin		Kempff
LXT2835	Dorumsgaard: Canzone Scordate, 5 Scarlatti Songs, etc	Souzay	Bonneau (piano)
LXT2836	Prokofiev: Piano Sonatas 3, 4, 8		Cornman
LXT2837	Chopin: 24 Preludes op 28		Gulda
LXT2838	Liszt: Mephisto Waltz, Funerailles, Mendelssohn		Katchen
LXT2839	Beethoven: Piano Concerto 5 (Emperor)	VPO	Krauss Backhaus
LXT2840	Mozart: Symphonies 28, 29	OSR	Maag
LXT2841	Boccherini: Quintet in Amaj, Quintet in Amin	Quintetto Chigiano	
LXT2842	Strauss,R: Don Quixote	VPO	Krauss Fournier
LXT2843	Brahms: Symphony 3	VPO	Bohm
LXT2844	Adam: Giselle	Paris Opera	Blareau
LXT2845-6	Leoncavallo: Pagliacci	AdSC	Erede Del Monaco
LXT2847	Haydn: Symphonies 96,97	Ccgbw	Van Beinum
LXT2848	Strauss,J: Graduation Ball	New SO	Fistoulari
LXT2849	Regamey: String Quintet 1	Winterthur String Quartet (violin: P.Rybar)	
	Honegger: Petite Suite for Violin, Clarinet & Piano		
	Moeshinger: Violin Sonata 1 op 62		Schneeberger Souvairan etc
LXT2850	Brahms: Rhapsody for Orch & Contralto, 4 Songs	LPO	Krauss Ferrier
LXT2851	Beethoven: Symphony 5	LPO	Kleiber
LXT2852	Mozart: String Quartets K155, K590	Italian Quartet	
LXT2853	Mozart: String Quartets K465, K546	Italian Quartet	
LXT2854	Schubert: String Quartet 13 in Amin	Italian Quartet	
LXT2855	Schubert: String Quartet 8 in Bflat maj	Italian Quartet	
LXT2856	Beethoven: String Quartet Op 59/1 ("Rasumovsky")	Italian Quartet	
LXT2857	Schubert: Arpeggione Sonata, Schumann: Fantasiestucke	Gendron	Francaix
LXT2858	Brahms: Quintet in Bmin for Clarinet and Strings	Vienna Octet	Boskowsky
LXT2859	Brahms: Symphony 2	VPO	Schuricht
LXT2860	Bizet: Jeux D'Enfants, Chabrier: Suite Pastorale	PCO	Lindenburg
LXT2861	Mozart: Piano Concertos K271, K450	StCO	Munchinger Kempff
LXT2862	Rachmaninov: Rhapsody on Paganini, Dohnanyi	LPO	Boult Katchen
LXT2863-4	Strauss,R: Salome	VPO	Krauss Goltz Patzak
LXT2865	Strauss,R: Duets from Arabella	VPO	Moralt Gueden Della Casa
LXT2866	Brahms: Piano Concerto 1	VPO	Bohm Backhaus
LXT2867	Mozart: Piano Concertos K488, K491	LSO	Krips Curzon
LXT2868	Chopin: Les Sylphides	PCO	Desormiere
LXT2869	Franck: Prelude,Chorale&Fugue,Schumann:Etudes Symphoniques		Katchen
LXT2870	Mendelssohn: Octet in Eflat maj Op 20	Vienna Octet	
LXT2871	Holst: The Planets	LSO	Sargent
LXT2872	Beethoven: Symphony 6	CgbW	Kleiber
LXT2873	Pijper: Symphony 3, Diepenbrock: Marsyas Suite	CgbW	Van Beinum
LXT2874	Beethoven: Symphony 4	Ccgbw	Krips
LXT2875	Schumann: Dichterliebe, 4 Songs	Souzay	Bonneau
LXT2876	Smetana: String Quartet 1, Kodaly: String Quartet 2	Vegh Quartet	
LXT2877	Liszt: Dante Sonata, Polonaise 2/6, Consolations		Peter Katin

Catalog	Work	Orchestra	Performers
LXT2878	Kodaly: Psalmus Hungaricus, Peacock Variations	LPO	Solti
LXT2879	Italian Song Recital		Poggi (tenor)
LXT2880-4	Wagner: Lohengrin	Bayreuth	Keilberth Windgassen Varnay etc
LXT2885	Rosenberg: Symphony 2	Stockholm RSO	Mann
LXT2886	Britten: 4 Sea Interludes, Young Persons Guide to the Orch	Ccgbw	Van Beinum
LXT2887	Mendelssohn: Symphony 4, Schumann: Symphony 4	LSO	Krips
LXT2888	Tchaikovsky: Symphony 6	OdeP	Kleiber
LXT2889	Albeniz: Iberia, Turina: Danzas Fantasticas	OdeP	Argenta
LXT2890-2	Gounod: Romeo and Juliet	OdeP	Erede Jobin Micheau
LXT2893	Gluck: Orfeo ed Euridice	Glyndebourne	Stiedry Ferrier
LXT2894	Prokofiev: Piano Concerto 3, Bartok: Piano Concerto 3	OSR	Ansermet Katchen
LXT2895	Tchaikovsky: Rococo Vns, Schumann: Cello Concerto	OSR	Ansermet Gendron
LXT2896	Mussorgsky: Pictures at an Exhibition, Ravel: La Valse	PCO	Ansermet
LXT2897	Song Recital (Faure, Milhaud)		Irma Kolassi Collard (piano)
LXT2898	Opera Arias (Donizetti, Gounod)	PCO	Blareau Mado Robin (sop)
LXT2899	Delius: Paris, In a Summer Garden, Summer Night on the River	LSO	Collins
LXT2900	Granados: Goyescas		Magaloff
LXT2901	Brahms: Trio 1 op 8		Trio di Trieste
LXT2902	Beethoven: Piano Sonatas Op 2/1, 81a, 90		Backhaus
LXT2903	Beethoven: Piano Sonatas Op 13 (Pathetique), Op 14, Op 15		Backhaus
LXT2904	Bruch: Violin Concerto, Mendelssohn: Violin Concerto	LPO	Van Beinum Campoli
LXT2905	Franck: Symphony in Dmin	VPO	Furtwangler
LXT2906	St-Saens: Cello Concerto 1, Lalo: Cello Concerto	LPO	Boult Nelsova
LXT2907-8	V Williams: A Sea Symphony, Wasps	LPO	Boult Baillie Cameron
LXT2909	V Williams: Symphony 4	LPO	Boult
LXT2910	V Williams: Symphony 5	LPO	Boult
LXT2911	V Williams: Symphony 6	LPO	Boult
LXT2912	V Williams: Sinfonia Antartica	LPO	Boult Gielgud
LXT2913	"3rd New Year Concert"	VPO	Krauss
LXT2914	Brahms: Ballades Op 10/1-4, Capricci & Intermezzi Op 76/1-8		Kempff
LXT2915	Bach,JS: Organ recital		Demessieux
LXT2916	Stravinsky: Symphony of Psalms, Firebird	LPO/OSR	Ansermet
LXT2917	Strauss,R: Aus Italien	VPO	Krauss
LXT2918	Scarlatti: Sonatas		George Malcolm (hpsd)
LXT2919	Byrd: Mass for 4 Voices, Mass for 5 Voices		Fleet Street Choir Lawrence
LXT2920	Beethoven: Piano Sonatas Op 2, Op 22, Op 78		Backhaus
LXT2921-4	Handel: Messiah	LPO	Boult Procter Vyvyan
LXT2925	Chopin: Piano Concerto 1	LPO	Boult Gulda
LXT2926	Bach,JS: Cantatas 51,202	StCO	Munchinger Danco
LXT2927	Debussy: Jeux, 6 Antique Epigraphes	OSR	Ansermet
LXT2928-9	Mascagni: Cavalleria Rusticana	orch cond	Ghione del Monaco Milanov Protti
LXT2930	Sarasate: Violin Recital		Ricci
LXT2931	Beethoven: Piano Sonatas Op 14, Op 54		Backhaus
LXT2932	Liszt: Totentanz, Mendelssohn: Capriccio	LPO	Martinon Katin
LXT2933	Schumann: Fantasia in Cmaj, Kinderscenen		Curzon
LXT2934	Nielsen: Three Motets op 55,		Danish State Radio Madrigal Ch Wöldike
LXT2935	Brahms: Piano Recital vol 2		Kempff
LXT2937	Vaughan Williams: Job, A Masque for Dancing	LPO	Boult
LXT2938	Beethoven: Piano Sonatas Op 2/3, Op 49/1, Op 49/2		Gulda
LXT2939	Beethoven: Piano Sonatas Op 110, Op 111		Backhaus
LXT2940	Elgar: Falstaff Symphonic Study Op 68	LSO	Collins
LXT2941	Britten: Les Illuminations, Sernd for Tenor,Horn, and Strings	NSO	Pears Brain Goossens
LXT2942	Beethoven: Violin Sonatas Op 30/2, Op 96		Ricci Gulda
LXT2943	Recorder recital		Dolmetsch Saxby (harpsichord)
LXT2944	Mozart: Violin Sonatas K304, K378, K481		Langbein Jones
LXT2945	Palestrina: 4 Choral Works, Victoria: 2 Responsories		Quartetto Polifonico

Cat. No.	Work	Orch.	Performers
LXT2946	Mozart: Symphonies 25, 38	LSO	Solti
LXT2947	Spanish Music Recital		Paolo Spagnolo
LXT2948	Beethoven: Piano Concerto 4	VPO	Knappertsbusch Curzon
LXT2949	Brahms: Violin Concerto	VPO	Schuricht Ferras
LXT2950	Beethoven: Piano Sonatas Op 31/1, Op 31/3		Backhaus
LXT2951-3	Bach,JS: Violin Sonatas and Partitas		Telmanyi
LXT2954-7	Strauss,R: Der Rosenkavalier	VPO	Kleiber Reining Jurinac Weber
LXT2958	Beethoven: Piano Sonatas Op 2/1, Op 2/2		Gulda
LXT2959	Weber: Six Sonatas for Violin and Piano	Ricci	Bussotti
LXT2960	Sibelius: Symphonies 3, 7	LSO	Collins
LXT2961	Mendelssohn: Ovs Fingal's Cave, Fair Melusina, Ruy Blas, etc	VPO	Schuricht
LXT2962	Sibelius: Symphony 4, Pohjola's Daughter	LSO	Collins
LXT2963	Faure: Ballades & Nocturnes, Francaix: Conc for Piano & Orch	LPO	Martinon Kathleen Long
LXT2964	Opera Recital (Verdi, Ponchielli, Halevy, Leoncavallo)	AdSC	Erede Del Monaco
LXT2965	Strauss: Blue Danube, Tales from the Vienna Woods, etc	VPO	Krauss
LXT2966	Balakirev: Thamar Symphonic Poem, Liadov: Orch Music	OSR	Ansermet
LXT2967	Bruckner: Symphony 3	VPO	Knappertsbusch
LXT2968	Haydn: Cello Concerto, Boccherini: Cello Concerto	StCO	Munchinger Fournier
LXT2969	Piano Recital (Granados, Albeniz, St-Saens, etc)		Raucea
LXT2970	Tchaikovsky: Violin Concerto	LPO	Boult Elman
LXT2971	Liszt: Piano Recital		Katin
LXT2973	Mahler: Symphony 1	VPO	Kubelik
LXT2974	Guitar Recital		Narciso Yepes
LXT2975	Paderewski: Fantaisie Polonaise op 19, Tavares: Concerto in Brazilian Forms op 105	LSO	Fistoulari Felicia Blumenthal
LXT2976	The Trumpet vol 2 (Selmer demo record)		Louis Menardi
LXT2977	Walton: Facade	English Opera	Collins Pears
LXT2978	Berkeley: Violin Sonata, Theme & Vns	Grinke	Berkeley (piano)
LXT2979	Nielsen: Flute Concerto, Clarinet Concerto	DSRO	Jensen Jespersen Erikson
LXT2980	Nielsen: Symphony 5, Maskarade Overture	DSRO	Jensen
LXT2981	Britten: Sinfonia da Requiem, Diversions	LSO	Britten Katchen
LXT2982	Rimsky-Korsakov: Antar Sym Suite, Glazunov Stenka Razin	OSR	Ansermet
LXT2983	Schubert: Octet Op 166	Vienna Octet	
LXT2984	Haydn: Symphonies 100, 102	LPO	Solti
LXT2985	Schumann: Symphony 3, Overture Scherzo and Finale	PCO	Schuricht
LXT2988	Handel: Water Music	Boyd Neel Orchestra	
LXT2989	Handel: Messiah (hlts)	LPO	Boult Vyvyan Procter
LXT2990	Mozart: Clarinet Concerto K622, Bassoon Concerto K191	LSO	Collins De Peyer/Helaerts
LXT2991	Strauss,J: Waltzes	VPO	Krauss
LXT2992-4	Verdi: La Traviata	AdSC	Molinari-Pradelli Tebaldi
LXT2995-7	Puccini: Manon Lescaut	AdSC	Molinari-Pradelli Tebaldi
LXT2998	Schubert: Symphonies 5, 8	VPO	Bohm
LXT2999	Dvorak: Cello Concerto	VPO	Kubelik Fournier
LXT5000-2	Mendelssohn: Elijah	LPO	Krips Delman Procter
LXT5003	Rachmaninov: Isle of the Dead, Dukas: La Peri	PCO	Ansermet
LXT5004	Ravel: Bolero, La Valse, Honegger: Pacific 231, Dukas	PCO	Ansermet
LXT5005	Auber: Overtures Bronze Horse, Crown Diamonds, Fra Diavolo	PCO	Wolff
LXT5006-8	Verdi: Rigoletto	AdSC	Erede Protti Del Monaco
LXT5009-11	Verdi: Otello	AdSC	Erede Del Monaco Tebaldi
LXT5012	"Homage to Fritz Kreisler"		Campoli
LXT5013	Mozart: Piano Concerto K449, Strauss,R: Burleske	LSO	Collins Gulda
LXT5014	Elgar: Violin Concerto	LPO	Boult Campoli
LXT5015	Holst: Perfect Fool, Butterworth: Shropshire Lad, Bax: Tintagel	LPO	Boult
LXT5016	Beethoven: Diabelli Variations op 120		Backhaus
LXT5017	Strauss,R: Operatic Recital (Ariadne, Arabella, Capriccio)	VPO	Hollreiser Della Casa
LXT5018	Delibes: Lakmé (hlts)	Opera Comique	Sebastian Robin

Cat. No.	Work	Performers	[Stereo]
LXT5019	Ravel: L'Enfant et les Sortilèges	OSR Ansermet	[SXL2212]
LXT5020	Handel: 6 Concerti Grossi op 3	Boyd Neel Orchestra	
LXT5021	Gounod: Romeo and Juliette (hlts)	Paris Opera Erede Micheau	
LXT5022	Borodin: Symphonies 2, 3	OSR Ansermet	
LXT5023	Schubert: Recital	Souzay Baldwin	
LXT5024	Debussy: The Martyrdom of St Sebastian	OSR Ansermet Danco	
LXT5025	Liszt: Piano Concertos 1, 2	LSO Fistoulari Kempff	
LXT5026	Wagner: Gotterdammerung, Tristan (orch hlts)	PCO Schuricht	
LXT5027	Brahms: String Quartets 2, 3	Vegh Quartet	
LXT5028	Walton: Portsmouth Point, Wise Virgins, Scapino, Siesta	LPO Boult	
LXT5029	Bach,JS: Organ Recital	Richter	[SXL2219]
LXT5030	Bizet: Symphony 1, Patrie Ov Op 19	OSR Ansermet	
LXT5031	Ravel: Scheherazade	OSR Ansermet Danco	
LXT5032	Mozart: Quintet in Amaj K581	Vienna Octet	
LXT5033	Operetta Recital (Strauss, Kalman, etc)	Vienna State Opera Schonherr Gueden	
LXT5034	Berlioz: Damnation of Faust (hlts), Massenet: Werther (hlts)	LSO Fistoulari Kolassi	
LXT5035	Roussel: Le Festin de L'Araignée op 17, Petite Suite op 39	OSR Ansermet	
LXT5036	Bach,J.S: The Musical Offering	StCO Munchinger	[SXL2204]
LXT5037	Chopin: Sonata 3, Impromptus	Magaloff	
LXT5038-9	Britten: The Turn of the Screw	English Opera Group Orch Britten Pears	
LXT5040	Haydn: Symphonies 88, 101	VPO Munchinger	
LXT5041-3	Handel: Concerti Grossi Op 6	Boyd Neel Orchestra	
LXT5044	Mozart: Violin Concertos K216, K268	StCO Munchinger Ferras	
LXT5045-8	Mussorgsky: Khovanschina	Belgrade National Orch Baranovich	
LXT5049-53	Borodin: Prince Igor	Belgrade National Orch Danon	
LXT5054-6	Mussorgsky: Boris Godunov	Belgrade National Orch Baranovich	
LXT5057	Slavenski: Sinfonia Orienta	Belgrade PO Zdravkovich	
LXT5058	Baranovich: Gingerbread Heart, Lhotka: The Devil in the Village	Orch cond by the composers	
LXT5059	Bartok: Music for Strings Perc & Celeste, Kodaly: Hary Janos	LPO Solti	
LXT5060	Britten: St Nicolas Op 42	Aldeburgh Britten Pears Hemmings	
LXT5061	Holmboe: String Quartet op 47, Nielsen: String Quartet op 5	Musica-Vitalis Quartet	
LXT5062	Bloch: Schelomo, Voice in the Wilderness	LPO Ansermet Nelsova	
LXT5063	Gluck: Ballet Suite 1, Gretry: Ballet Suite	NSOL Irving	
LXT5065-6	Bruckner: Symphony 4, Wagner: Siegfried Idyll	VPO Knappertsbusch	
LXT5067	Duets (Puccini: Manon-Lescaut, Verdi: Otello, Aida)	AdSC Erede Tebaldi Del Monaco	
LXT5068	Beethoven: Violin Concerto	LPO Solti Elman	
LXT5069	Gershwin: Rhapsody in Blue, Concerto in F	Mantovani Katchen	
LXT5070	Diabelli: Trio for Flute, Viola, Guitar, Furstenau, Matiegka	Birkelund Eriksen Neumann Friisholm	
LXT5071	Bloch: String Quartet 1	Griller Quartet	
LXT5072	Bloch: String Quartet 2	Griller Quartet	
LXT5073	Bloch: String Quartets 3, 4	Griller Quartet	
LXT5074	Mozart: Serenade K203	NSOL Maag	
LXT5075	Paganini: Violin Concertos 1-2	LSO Collins Ricci	
LXT5076	Operatic Recital (Boheme,Lescaut,Butterfly,Traviata,Aida,Otello)	Tebaldi	
LXT5077	Brahms: Cello Sonatas in Emin, Fmaj	Backhaus Fournier	
LXT5078	Mozart: Violin Concertos K218, K219	New SO Krips Elman	
LXT5079-0	Dvorak: Slavonic Dances, Tchaikovsky: Romeo & Juliet	VPO Kubelik	
LXT5081	Bartok:Div for Strings,Muller:Sinfonia 2 for Strings&Flute op 53	Zurich CO de Stoutz Jaunet (flute)	
LXT5082	Rimsky-Korsakov: Scheherazade	OSR Ansermet	[SXL2086]
LXT5083	Sibelius: Symphony 5, Night Ride and Sunrise	LSO Collins	
LXT5084	Sibelius: Symphony 6, Pelleas et Melisande Suite	LSO Collins	
LXT5085-7	Mozart: Magic Flute	VPO Bohm	[SXL2215-7]
LXT5088-91	Mozart: Marriage of Figaro	VPO Kleiber	[SXL2087-90]
LXT5092	Holmboe: String Quartet op 48, Nielsen: String Quartet op 44	Koppel Quartet	
LXT5093	Chopin: Piano Sonatas Op 35 ("Funeral March"), Op 58	Katchen	
LXT5094	Beethoven: Septet Op 20	Vienna Octet	

LXT5095	Britten: Winter Words op 52, 7 Sonnets of Michelangelo op 22	Britten	Pears
LXT5096	Operatic Recital (Halevy, Meyerbeer, Verdi)	AdSC	Erede Siepi
LXT5097	Geiser: Symphony op 44, Oboussier: Antigone for Alto & Orch	OSR	Ansermet Cavelti (alto)
LXT5098	Stravinsky: Oedipus Rex	OSR	Ansermet Bouvier Haefliger
LXT5099	Tchaikovsky: Suite 3	PCO	Boult
LXT5100	Massenet: Scenes Pittoresques, Scenes Alsaciennes	PCO	Wolff
LXT5101-2	Liszt : A Faust Symphony, Les Preludes	PCO/OSR	Argenta
LXT5103-6	Mozart: Don Giovanni	VPO	Krips [SXL2117-20]
LXT5107-9	Mozart: Cosi fan Tutte	VPO	Bohm Della Casa Ludwig
LXT5110	Bach: Toccata&Fugue in Dmin, Liszt : Prelude&Fugue on BACH		Karl Richter [SXL2219]
LXT5111	Mozart: Symphonies 34, 38	VPO	Bohm
LXT5112	Mozart: Divertimento K287	Members of Vienna Octet	
LXT5113	Grieg: Violin Sonatas 1, 3	Elman	Seiger
LXT5114	Lalo: Namouna Ballet Suites 1, 2	LPO	Martinon
LXT5115	Stravinsky: The Firebird	OSR	Ansermet [SXL2017]
LXT5116	Debussy: Preludes Book 1		Gulda
LXT5117	Debussy : Preludes book 2		Gulda
LXT5118	Honegger : Symphony 3, Chant de Joie	PCO	Denzler
LXT5119	Prokofiev: Love of 3 Oranges, Lt Kije Suite	LPO	Boult
LXT5120	Schumann : Noveletten op 21		Blancard (piano)
LXT5121	Mozart: Serenade for 13 Wind Instruments K361	OSR	Ansermet
LXT5122	Chopin: Nocturnes 1-10		Katin
LXT5123	Mozart: Piano Concerto K595, Piano sonata K331	VPO	Bohm Backhaus [SXL2214]
LXT5124	Mozart: Symphonies 33, 40	VPO	Munchinger
LXT5125	Tchaikovsky: Symphony 4	OSR	Argenta [SXL2015]
LXT5126	Beethoven : Violin Sonatas op 74 (Kreutzer), op 24 (Spring)	Elman	Sieger
LXT5127	Operatic recital (Verdi, Puccini, Leoncavallo, Mascagni)	AdSC	Erede Del Monaco
LXT5128-0	Puccini: Turandot	AdSC	Erede Borkh [SXL2078-80]
LXT5131-4	Verdi: The Force of Destiny	AdSC	Pradelli Tebaldi [SXL2069-72]
LXT5135	Mozart : Symphony 14 K114, Bach,JC : Sinfonia in B$_b$maj, etc	DSRO	Wöldike
LXT5136	Operatic Choruses (Verdi, Leoncavallo, Puccini)	AdSC	Erede/Molinari-Pradelli
LXT5137	Rossini : Overtures (Tell, Tancredi, Cinderella, Corinth, etc)	LSO	Gamba
LXT5138	Mozart : Piano Concertos K503, K537	NSOL	Collins Gulda
LXT5142	Liszt: Mephisto Waltz 1, Sym Poems Mazeppa, Hamlet, Prometheus	PCO	Munchinger
LXT5143	Benjamin: Sonatina for Violin & Piano	Grinke (violin) Benjamin	
LXT5144	Haydn: Piano Sonatas 20, 31, 40, 46		Kathleen Long
LXT5145	Mozart : Piano Concertos K415, K466	NSOL	Maag Katchen
LXT5146-8	Donizetti: La Favorita	MMF	Erede Simionato Bastianini
LXT5149	Strauss,J: Le Beautiful Danube, William Tell Ballet Music	LPO	Martinon
LXT5150-2	Wagner: Flying Dutchman	Bayreuth 1955 Keilberth Uhde Varnay	
LXT5153	Martin: Passacaille for String Orch, Hindemith: 5 Pieces	StCO	Munchinger
LXT5154	Stravinsky: Conc for Piano & Orch, Conc for Piano & Wind	OSR	Ansermet Magaloff
LXT5155-7	Donizetti: L'Elisir D'Amore	Pradelli	Gueden Di Stefano
LXT5158	Faure: Requiem	OSR	Ansermet [SXL2211]
LXT5159-61	Tchaikovsky: Eugene Onegin	Belgrade Nat Opera Danon	
LXT5162	Berlioz: Overtures Corsaire, King Lear, Francs-Juges, etc	PCO	Wolff
LXT5163	Britten: The Little Sweep	English Opera Group Britten Pears Vyvyan	
LXT5164	Tchaikovsky: Piano Concerto 1, Liszt: Hungarian Fantasia	LSO	Gamba Katchen
LXT5165	Grieg: Piano Concerto, Falla: Nights in the Gardens of Spain	LSO	Fistoulari Curzon
LXT5166	Bliss: Concerto for Violin and Orch	LPO	Bliss Campoli
LXT5167	Mozart: Piano Sonatas K330, K511, K457, K475		Backhaus
LXT5169	Stravinsky: Apollon Musagetes, Renard	OSR	Ansermet
LXT5170	Bliss: A Colour Symphony, Introduction & Allegro	LSO	Bliss
LXT5171	Gregorian Chant – Easter	Abbey of St Pierre de Solesmes	
LXT5172	Gounod: Little Symphony in Bflat for Wind, Schubert	Ensemble d'Instruments a Vent Pierre Poulteau	
LXT5173-6	Glinka: A Life for the Tsar	Belgrade Nat Op Danon	

LXT5177	Mozart: Div K251, Schubert: 5 Minuets, 5 German Dances	StCO	Munchinger
LXT5178	Rachmaninov: Piano Concerto 2	LPO	Boult Curzon
LXT5180-4	Strauss,R: Die Frau Ohne Schatten	VPO	Bohm Rysanek Goltz
LXT5185	Franck: Chorales 1,2,3, Vivaldi-Bach: Concerto BWV593		Demessieux (organ)
LXT5186	Tchaikovsky: Capriccio Italien, Francesca di Rimini	LSO	Collins
LXT5187	Beethoven: Sonatas Op 57("Appassionata"), Op 111		Katchen
LXT5188	SELMER demonstration disc - The Saxophone vol 5	Marcel Mule Saxophone Quartet	
LXT5189-92	Tchaikovsky: The Queen of Spades	Belgrade National Opera Baranovich	
LXT5193-7	Rimsky-Korsakov : The Snow Maiden	Belgrade Nat Op Baranovich	
LXT5198-9	Bach,J.S: Brandenburg Concertos	StCO	Munchinger
LXT5200	Boccherini: Quartet op 39/8, Trio op 38/2, etc	Carmirelli Quartet	
LXT5201	Mendelssohn: Piano Concertos 1, 2	LSO	Collins Katin
LXT5202	Operatic Recital (Verdi, Puccini, Massenet, Bizet, Meyerbeer, etc)	NSOL	Erede Del Monaco [SXL2122]
LXT5203	Bach,JS: Hpsd Concerto BWV1052, Conc for 2 Hpsds BWV1061	Ansbach Festival Richter Muller	
LXT5204	Brahms: Trio op 87, Haydn: Trio Op 73/2	Trio di Trieste	
LXT5205-10	Wagner: Gotterdammerung	Fjelstad	Flagstad Svanholm
LXT5211-3	Moliere: Le Bourgeois Gentilhomme (music by Lully)	Collegium Musicum de Paris Douatte	
LXT5214	Brahms: Symphony 4	VPO	Kubelik [SXL2206]
LXT5215	Beethoven: Symphony 3	Ccgbw	Kleiber
LXT5216	Schumann: Liederkreis op 24, Wolf: Mörike Lieder	Souzay	Baldwin
LXT5217	Delibes: Coppelia & Sylvia Ballet Suites	PCO	Desormiere Nerini (violin)
LXT5218	Spanish and Portuguese Keyboard Music vol 2		Blumental (piano)
LXT5219	Mozart: Piano Sonatas K309, K282, K332, K135		Spagnolo (piano)
LXT5220	Operatic recital (Mozart, Rossini, Mascagni, etc)	AdSC	Erede Tebaldi [SXL2043]
LXT5221	SELMER demonstration disc - The Saxophone vol 6	Marcel Mule (sax) Robin (piano)	
LXT5222	Bruch: Violin Concerto 1,Wieniawski: Violin Concerto 2	LPO	Boult Elman
LXT5223-5	Leoncavallo: I Pagliacci, Mascagni: Cavalleria Rusticana	AdSC	Erede/Ghione Del Monaco
LXT5226	Gregorian Chant (Masses for Pentecost and Corpus Christi)	Abbey of St Pierre de Solesmes	
LXT5227	Gregorian Chant (Ascension and Assumption)	Abbey of St Pierre de Solesmes	
LXT5228	Rachmaninov: Cello Sonata Op 19	Nelsova	Balsam
LXT5229-0	Bizet: L'Arlesienne (perf of play by Daudet with Bizet's music)		Wolff
LXT5232	Beethoven: Symphonies 1, 8	OSR	Ansermet
LXT5233	Stravinsky: Pulcinella Suite, Song of the Nightingale	OSR	Ansermet [SXL2188]
LXT5234	Roussel: Symphonies 3, 4	OSR	Ansermet
LXT5238	Chopin: Nocturnes 11-20		Katin
LXT5239	Strauss,R: Don Juan, Death & Transfiguration	OdeP	Knappertsbusch
LXT5240	Glazunov: The Seasons	OdeP	Wolff [SXL2141]
LXT5241	Tchaikovsky: Symphony 5	PCO	Solti
LXT5242	Mozart: Operatic Recital (Figaro, Giovanni, Idomeneo, etc)		Gueden
LXT5244	Berlioz: Ov Benvenuto Cellini, Chausson: Symphony op 20	OSR/PCO	Denzler
LXT5245	Tchaikovsky: Symphony 2 (Little Russian)	PCO	Solti
LXT5246	Charpentier: Impressions D'Italie	OdeP	Wolff
LXT5247	"Favourite Ballads"	Thomas (bar) Newton (piano)	
LXT5248	"Scottish Songs"	Thomas (bar) Newton (piano)	
LXT5249	Wagner Recital: Wesendonck Lieder, Parsifal, Walkure, etc	VPO	Knappertsbusch Flagstad
LXT5250	Recital (R Strauss, Salome, Beethoven, Weber, etc)	VPO	Krips Borkh
LXT5251	Gregorian Chant – Xmas	Abbey of St Pierre de Solesmes	
LXT5252	Cello Recital (Bach, Kodaly, Reger)		Nelsova
LXT5253	Beethoven: Trio op 70/1 (Geister), Mozart: Trio K542	Trio di Trieste	
LXT5254	Poetry Readings (Shakespeare, Browning, Blake, Tennyson, etc)		Peggy Ashcroft
LXT5255-6	Bruckner: Symphony 5	VPO	Knappertsbusch
LXT5257	Mozart: Symphony 35, Schubert: Symphony 8	VPO	Schuricht
LXT5258	Lieder Recital (Schubert, Brahms, Wolf, R Strauss, etc)	Della Casa	Hudez (piano)
LXT5259	Khachaturian: Violin Concerto	LPO	Fistoulari Ricci
LXT5260-2	Verdi: Il Trovatore	Geneva	Erede Tebaldi [SXL2129-31]
LXT5263	Recital of Lieder by Schubert and Schumann	Flagstad	McArthur (piano)

Cat. No.	Work	Orch	Artists	Stereo
LXT5264	Grieg: Recital	Flagstad	McArthur (piano)	
LXT5265	Poetry Readings vol 2 (Byron, Blake, Pope, Wordsworth, etc)		Peggy Ashcroft	
LXT5268	Beethoven: Cello Sonata Op 69, 12 Vns on "The Magic Flute"	Nelsova	Balsam	
LXT5269	French Operatic Arias	Souzay	Bonneau	
LXT5270	Brahms: Violin Sonatas 2, 3	Ricci	Katchen	
LXT5271	Frescobaldi: Quattro Pezzi, Petrassi: Concerto 1 for Orch	AdSC	Previtali	
LXT5272	Recital of Songs and Arias	Tebaldi	Favaretto	
LXT5273-6	Gluck: Alceste	Orch	Jones Flagstad	
LXT5277	Recital (Handel, Mozart)	VPO	Kleiber Della Casa	
LXT5278	Casella: La Giara – Suite Sinfonica, Respighi: Pines of Rome	AdSC	Previtali Luzi (tenor)	
LXT5279	Elgar: The Wand of Youth (suites 1 & 2)	LPO	Van Beinum	
LXT5280	Schumann: Piano Concerto op 54, Weber: Konzertstuck op 79	VPO	Andreae Gulda	
LXT5283-5	Rossini: The Barber of Seville	MMF	Erede Bastianini Simionato	
LXT5287	SELMER demonstration disc - The Trumpet vol 3	various		
LXT5288	"Orch hlts from the Operas" (Mascagni, Puccini, Rossini, etc)	MMF	Gavazzeni	
LXT5289	Operatic Recital (Verdi, Bellini, Spontini, Puccini, etc)	MMF	Gavazzeni Cerquetti (sop)	
LXT5290	Dvorak: Symphony 8	VPO	Kubelik	
LXT5291	Dvorak: Symphony 9	VPO	Kubelik	[SXL2005]
LXT5292	Brahms: Symphony 1	VPO	Krips	
LXT5293	Mozart: Wind Quintet K452, Clarinet Trio K498	Vienna Octet		
LXT5294	Spohr: Octet/etc	Vienna Octet		
LXT5295-6	Readings from Charles Dickens (Pickwick, Dombey & Sons)		Emlyn Williams	
LXT5297	Tchaikovsky: Symphony 3	LPO	Boult	
LXT5301	SELMER demonstration disc - The Clarinet vol 6	Ulysse Delecluse (clarinet)		
LXT5302	Paganini: Violin Concerto, Saint-Saens Violin Concerto	LSO	Gamba Campoli	
LXT5303	Violin Recital (Sammartini, Vitali, Handel, Bach)	Elman	Seiger	
LXT5304	Recital (Dvorak, Kreisler, Wieniawski, Smetana, etc)	Elman	Seiger	
LXT5305	Bartok: Concerto for Orchestra	OSR	Ansermet	
LXT5306	Tchaikovsky: Symphony 6	OSR	Ansermet	
LXT5307	Operatic Recital (Rossini, Cimarosa, Gounod, etc)	OSR	Walker Corena	
LXT5308	Brahms: Recital (6 Pieces Op 118, Capriccio, Intermezzos, etc)		Backhaus	[SXL2222]
LXT5309	Bach,JS: English Suite 6, French Suite 5, etc		Backhaus	[SXL2205]
LXT5311	Rimsky-Korsakov: Tsar Saltan, May Night, Russian Easter	OSR	Ansermet	[SXL2221]
LXT5312	Haydn: Symphonies 45, 55	Aldeburgh	Britten	
LXT5313	Tchaikovsky: Violin Concerto	LSO	Argenta Campoli	[SXL2029]
LXT5314	V Williams: Symphony 8, Partita for Double String Orch	LPO	Boult	[SXL2207]
LXT5316	Recital of Bach and Handel	LPO	Boult Flagstad	
LXT5317	Operatic Recital (Verdi, Bellini, Donizetti, Puccini)	MMF	Gavazzeni Zeani (sop)	
LXT5318-0	Chopin: Mazurkas (complete)		Magaloff	
LXT5321-2	Honegger: King David, Stravinsky: The Soldier's Tale	OSR	Ansermet	
LXT5323	Mozart: Piano Sonatas K331, K333, K545		Katchen	
LXT5324	Recital (Wolf, Purcell, etc)	Ferrier	Spurr (piano)	
LXT5325	"Adventure in Sound" (Traviata, Cleopatra, Gioconda,etc)	LSO	Gamba	
LXT5326	"An Evening at the Chicago Lyric Opera"	Chicago Lyric Opera	Solti Tebaldi Simionato	
LXT5327	Grieg: Recital	Flagstad	McArthur (piano)	
LXT5329	Recital of Wolf and R Strauss	Flagstad	McArthur (piano)	
LXT5330	Liszt: Piano Concertos 1, 2	LPO	Argenta Katchen	[SXL2097]
LXT5331	Lieder Recital (Brahms, Wolf)	Cavelti (alto)	Haeusslein (piano)	
LXT5332	SELMER demonstration disc - The Bassoon vol 1	various		
LXT5333	Espana (Chabrier, Rimsky-Korsakov, Granados, Moszkowski)	LSO	Argenta	[SXL2020]
LXT5334	Mendelssohn: Violin Concerto, Bruch: Violin Concerto 1	LSO	Gamba Ricci	[SXL2006]
LXT5336-7	Britten: Prince of the Pagodas	ROHCG	Britten	
LXT5338	Granados: Goyescas	NOS	Argenta	
LXT5339	Brahms: Symphony 2	VPO	Kubelik	[SXL2059]
LXT5341	Rossini-Respighi: La Boutique Fantasque, Dukas	IPO	Solti	[SXL2007]
LXT5342-3	Delibes: Coppelia	OSR	Ansermet	[SXL2084-5]

LXT5344	Mendelssohn: A Midsummer Night's Dream	LSO	Maag	[SXL2060]
LXT5345	Brahms: Recital	Flagstad	McArthur (piano)	
LXT5346	Microgroove Frequency Test Record			
LXT5347	Schumann: Symphonies 1, 4	LSO	Krips	[SXL2223]
LXT5348	Debussy: Images Pour Orchestre	OSR	Argenta	
LXT5351	Debussy: La Boite a JouJoux, Printemps, etc	OSR	Ansermet	[SXL2136]
LXT5352	Beethoven: Violin Concerto	LSO	Krips Campoli	
LXT5353	Beethoven: Piano Concerto 3	VPO	Bohm Backhaus	
LXT5354	Beethoven: Piano Concerto 4	VPO	Krauss Backhaus	
LXT5355	Beethoven: Piano Concerto 5	VPO	Krauss Backhaus	
LXT5356	Mozart: Symphonies 39, 40	LSO	Krips	
LXT5357	Falla: Three Cornered Hat	OSR	Ansermet	
LXT5358	Beethoven: Symphony 5	CgbW	Kleiber	
LXT5359	Beethoven: Symphony 6	CgbW	Kleiber	
LXT5360	Beethoven: Symphony 7	Ccgbw	Kleiber	
LXT5361	Beethoven: Symphony 8	VPO	Bohm	
	Mendelssohn: Symphony 4	LSO	Krips	
LXT5362-3	Beethoven: Symphony 9	VPO	Kleiber Gueden Dermota	
LXT5364	Brahms: Piano Concerto 1	VPO	Bohm Backhaus	
LXT5365	Brahms: Piano Concerto 2	VPO	Schuricht Backhaus	
LXT5366	Brahms: Symphony 1	Ccgbw	Van Beinum	
LXT5367	Brahms: Symphony 3	Ccgbw	Szell	
LXT5368	Brahms: Symphony 4	LSO	Krips	
LXT5369	Haydn: Symphonies 96, 104	VPO	Munchinger	
LXT5370	Tchaikovsky: Symphony 6	PCO	Kleiber	
LXT5371	Tchaikovsky: Nutcracker Suites 1, 2	PCO	Fistoulari	
LXT5372	Strauss,J: Ballet: Graduation Ball	NSOL	Fistoulari	
LXT5373	Tchaikovsky: Violin Concerto	NSOL	Sargent Ricci	
LXT5374	Rachmaninov: Paganini Vns/Dohnanyi: Nursery Song Vns	LPO	Boult Katchen	
LXT5375	Stravinsky: Petrushka	OSR	Ansermet	
LXT5376	Mozart: Overtures Magic Flute, Cosi, Figaro, Giovanni, etc	LSO	Krips	
LXT5377	Vivaldi: The Four Seasons	StCO	Munchinger Barchet	
LXT5378	Adam: Giselle (hlts)	Paris Op	Blareau	
LXT5379	Handel: Royal Fireworks Music, Water Music	LPO	Van Beinum	[LXT2792]
LXT5380	Prokofiev: Classical Symphony, Bizet: Symphony 1	OSR	Ansermet	
LXT5381	Schubert: Symphonies 5, 8 ("Unfinished")	VPO	Bohm	
LXT5382	Recital of Bach & Handel Arias	LPO	Boult Ferrier	[SXL2234]
LXT5383	Handel: Messiah (arias and choruses)	LPO	Boult Vyvyan Procter	
LXT5384	Puccini: Madama Butterfly (hlts)	AdSC	Erede Tebaldi Campora	
LXT5385	Verdi: Aida (hlts)	AdSC	Erede Tebaldi Del Monaco	
LXT5386	Puccini: Tosca (hlts)	AdSC	Erede Tebaldi Campora	
LXT5387	Puccini: La Boheme (hlts)	AdSC	Erede Tebaldi Prandelli	
LXT5388	Stravinsky: Rite of Spring	OSR	Ansermet	[SXL2042]
LXT5389-0	Wagner: Die Walkure Act 3	VPO	Solti Flagstad	[SXL2031-2]
LXT5391	Beethoven: Piano Concerto 5	VPO	Knappertsbusch Curzon	[SXL2002]
LXT5392	Sacred Songs	LPO	Boult Flagstad	[SXL2049]
LXT5394	Brahms: Ovs Acad Festival, Tragic, Alto Rhapsody, Haydn Vns	VPO	Knappertsbusch West (alto)	
LXT5395	Mahler: Kindertotenlieder, Lieder eines Fahrenden Gesellen	VPO	Boult Flagstad	[SXL2224]
LXT5397	Verdi: Rigoletto (hlts)	AdSC	Erede Del Monaco Gueden	
LXT5398	Rimsky Korsakov: Xmas Eve, Sadko, Dubinushka, etc	OSR	Ansermet	[SXL2113]
LXT5399	Verdi: La Traviata (hlts)	AdSC	Molinari-Pradelli Tebaldi	
LXT5400-2	Ponchielli: La Gioconda	MMF	Gavazzeni	[SXL2225-7]
LXT5403-6	Strauss,R: Arabella	VPO	Solti Della Casa	[SXL2050-3]
LXT5407	Operatic Recital (Aida, Luisa Miller, Forza, Ballo,etc)		Bergonzi	[SXL2048]
LXT5409	Tchaikovsky: Swan Lake hlts	LSO	Fistoulari	
LXT5410	Recital of Songs and Arias no. 2 (Mozart, Bellini, Rossini)	Tebaldi	Favaretto (piano)	

LXT5411-12 Giordano: Andrea Chenier	AdSC	Gavazzeni Tebaldi	[SXL2208-10]
LXT5413 Schubert: Moments Musicaux, Schumann: Waldscenen		Backhaus	
LXT5414 Mozart: Symphonies 35, 41	IPO	Krips	[SXL2220]
LXT5415 Debussy: Pour le Piano, Estampes 2, Ravel: Sonatina, Valses		Gulda	
LXT5416 Britten: A Boy was Born op 3, Rejoice in the Lamb op 30	English Opera Gp	Purcell Singers Britten	
LXT5417 Brahms: Symphony 1	VPO	Kubelik	[SXL2013]
LXT5418 Haydn: Symphonies 94, 99	VPO	Krips	[SXL2098]
LXT5419 Brahms: Symphony 3	VPO	Kubelik	[SXL2104]
LXT5420 "Vienna Holiday" (Radetzky March, Vienna Woods,etc)	VPO	Knappertsbusch	[SXL2016]
LXT5421 Overtures (Adam, Auber, Herold, Reznicek, Suppe, Nicolai)	PCO	Wolff	[SXL2008]
LXT5422 Chopin: Les Sylphides, Delibes: La Source	PCO	Maag	[SXL2044]
LXT5423 Berlioz: Symphonie Fantastique	PCO	Argenta	[SXL2009]
LXT5424 Debussy: La Mer, L'Apres Midi, Ravel: Rapsodie Espagnole	OSR	Ansermet	
LXT5425 Stravinsky: Petrushka	OSR	Ansermet	[SXL2011]
LXT5426 Ravel: Mother Goose Suite, Debussy: Nocturnes	OSR	Ansermet	[SXL2062]
LXT5429-30 Wagner: Die Walkure Act 1, Gotterdammerung highlights	VPO	Knappertsbusch	[SXL2074-5]
LXT5431 Strauss Waltzes (Blue Danube, Acceleration, Emperor,etc)	VPO	Krips	[SXL2047]
LXT5432 Johann Strauss Concert	VPO	Boskowsky	[SXL2082]
LXT5433 Schubert: Trout Quintet	Vienna Octet	Curzon	[SXL2110]
LXT5434 Brahms: Piano Concerto 2	VPO	Knappertsbusch Curzon	
LXT5438 Schumann: Fantasia in C, Toccata, Arabeske		Katchen	
LXT5439 Schubert: Wanderer Fantasia, Schumann: Carnaval op 9		Katchen	
LXT5441 Grieg: Peer Gynt Incidental Music	LSO	Fjeldstad	[SXL2012]
LXT5443 Mozart: Don Giovanni (hlts)	VPO	Krips Siepi Della Casa	
LXT5444 Sibelius: Song Recital	LSO	Fjelstad Flagstad	[SXL2030]
LXT5445 Chopin: Ballade op 47, Polonaise op 22, Fantaisie op 49, etc		Kempff	[SXL2081]
LXT5446 Prokofiev: Violin Concertos 1, 2	OSR	Ansermet Ricci	
LXT5447 Rachmaninov:Piano Conc 1,Tchaikovsky: Concert Fantasia op 56	LPO	Boult Katin	[SXL2034]
LXT5448-9 Lehar: Merry Widow	Vienna State Opera	Stolz	[SXL2022-3]
LXT5450 Verdi: Otello (hlts)	AdSC	Erede Tebaldi Del Monaco	
LXT5451 Chopin: Piano Recital		Kempff	[SXL2024]
LXT5452 Chopin: Piano Sonatas op 35, op 58		Kempff	[SXL2025]
LXT5453 Bruch: Scottish Fantasia op 46, Mendelssohn: Violin Conc op 64	LPO	Boult Campoli	[SXL2026]
LXT5454 Debussy: Jeux, Dukas: La Peri	OSR	Ansermet	[SXL2027]
LXT5455 Schubert: Octet op 166	Vienna Octet		[SXL2028]
LXT5456 Massenet: Le Cid, Meyerbeer	IPO	Martinon	[SXL2021]
LXT5457 Haydn: Recital (Piano sonatas 34, 48, 52, Fantasia, etc)		Backhaus	
LXT5458 Opera Recital (St-Saens, Massenet, Bizet, Verdi)	AdSC	Previtali Simionato	
LXT5459 Mozart: Figaro (hlts)	VPO	Kleiber	[SXL2035]
LXT5460 Virtuoso Showpieces		Ricci	
LXT5461 Bizet: Carmen Suite, L'Arlesienne Suite	OSR	Ansermet	[SXL2037]
LXT5463-5 Puccini: La Fanciulla del West	AdSC	Capuana Tebaldi	[SXL2039-41]
LXT5468-70 Puccini: Madama Butterfly	AdSC	Serafin Tebaldi	[SXL2054-6]
LXT5471 Schubert: Symphony 9	LSO	Krips	[SXL2045]
LXT5472 Mozart: Serenade K525, Tchaikovsky: Serenade for Strings op 48	IPO	Solti	[SXL2046]
LXT5474-5 Smetana: Ma Vlast	VPO	Kubelik	[SXL2064-5]
LXT5477 Mendelssohn: Symphony 4, Schubert: Symphony 5	IPO	Solti	[SXL2067]
LXT5478 Wagner: Hlts from Dutchman, Mastersingers, Die Walkure	VPO	Knappertsbusch	[SXL2068]
LXT5480 Rossini: Barber of Seville (hlts)	MMF	Erede Simionato	
LXT5481 Verdi: The Force of Destiny (hlts)	AdSC	Molinari-Pradelli Tebaldi	
LXT5482 Beethoven: Piano Concerto 4	VPO	Schmidt-Isserstedt Backhaus	[SXL2010]
LXT5483 Tchaikovsky: Symphony 6	VPO	Martinon	[SXL2004]
LXT5484 Brahms: Handel Variations, Paganini Variations		Katchen	
LXT5485 "Italy" (Recital of Italian Songs)		di Stefano	[SXL2083]
LXT5487-9 Boito: Mefistofele	AdSC	Serafin Tebaldi	[SXL2094-6]
LXT5490 Rachmaninov: Piano Concerto 2, Balakirev: Islamey	LSO	Solti Katchen	[SXL2076]

LXT5492	Falla: Gardens of Spain, Rodrigo: Guitar Concerto	NOS	Argenta Yepes	[SXL2091]
LXT5493-4	Tchaikovsky: The Nutcracker (complete)	OSR	Ansermet	[SXL2092-3]
LXT5495-7	Wagner: Das Rheingold	VPO	Solti	[SXL2101-3]
LXT5498	Donizetti: L'Elisir d'Amore (hlts)	Florence May Festival	Molinari-Pradelli	
LXT5499	Falla: 3 Cornered Hat, Ravel: Bolero, Alborada, Weber	PCO	Wolff	[SXL2105]
LXT5500	Beethoven: Piano Concerto 3	LSO	Gamba Katchen	[SXL2106]
LXT5501-2	Tchaikovsky: Swan Lake	OSR	Ansermet	[SXL2107-8]
LXT5503	Tchaikovsky: Symphony 5	VPO	Krips	[SXL2109]
LXT5504	Operatic Recital (Puccini, Massenet, Gounod, etc)	AdSC	Patané Di Stefano	[SXL2111]
LXT5505	Weber: Overtures (Freischutz, Preciosa, Oberon, Euryanthe, etc)	OSR	Ansermet	[SXL2112]
LXT5507	Beethoven: Symphony 4, Coriolan Overture	OSR	Ansermet	[SXL2116]
LXT5508	Beethoven: Symphony 7	VPO	Solti	[SXL2121]
LXT5509	Puccini: Operatic Recital	AdSC	Patané Zeani	[SXL2123]
LXT5510	Beethoven: Symphony 5	VPO	Solti	[SXL2124]
LXT5511	Mozart: Cosi fan Tutte (hlts)	VPO	Bohm Della Casa	[SXL2058]
LXT5512-3	Bach,JS: Brandenburg Concertos 1-6, Suite 3, Musical Offering	StCO	Munchinger	[SXL2125-7]
LXT5514	Rossini: Operatic Recital	LSO	Gibson Berganza	[SXL2132]
LXT5515	Adam: Giselle	PCO	Martinon	[SXL2128]
LXT5516	Recital: Bach, Scarlatti, Schumann, Brahms, etc		Katin	[CS6085]
LXT5517	Berlioz: Overtures (Corsair, Beatrice, Benvenuto, etc)	PCO	Martinon	[SXL2134]
LXT5518	Mozart: Symphonies 32, 38 ("Prague")	LSO	Maag	[SXL2135]
LXT5519	Vivaldi: Four Seasons	StCO	Munchinger	[SXL2019]
LXT5520	Lehar: Merry Widow (hlts)	Vienna Op	Stolz Gueden	[SXL2133]
LXT5521-3	Britten: Peter Grimes	ROHCG	Britten Pears	[SXL2150-2]
LXT5524	Strauss,R: Also Sprach Zarathustra	VPO	Karajan	[SXL2154]
LXT5525	Beethoven: Symphony 5, Egmont Ov	OSR	Ansermet	[SXL2003]
LXT5527	Lalo: Symphonie Espagnole, Ravel: Tzigane	OSR	Ansermet Ricci	[SXL2155]
LXT5528	Schubert: Symphonies 2, 8	VPO	Munchinger	[SXL2156]
LXT5529	Beethoven: Septet	Vienna Octet		[SXL2157]
LXT5530	Beethoven: Quintet op 16, Spohr: Octet op 32	Vienna Octet		[SXL2158]
LXT5531	Operatic Arias from Lucia, Ernani, Sicilian Vespers, etc	PCO	Santi Sutherland	[SXL2159]
LXT5532-4	Tchaikovsky: Sleeping Beauty	OSR	Ansermet	[SXL2160-2]
LXT5535	Strauss, Johann & Strauss, Josef: Waltzes and Polkas	VPO	Boskowsky	[SXL2163]
LXT5536	Ravel: Daphnis & Chloe	LSO	Monteux	[SXL2164]
LXT5537	Beethoven: Symphony 3	VPO	Solti	[SXL2165]
LXT5538	Tchaikovsky: Symphony 4	PCO	Wolff	[SXL2166]
LXT5539-41	Verdi: Aida	VPO	Karajan Tebaldi	[SXL2167-9]
LXT5542-3	Puccini: La Boheme	AdSC	Serafin Tebaldi	[SXL2170-1]
LXT5544	Wagner: Mastersingers (hlts)	VPO	Knappertsbusch Schoeffler	
LXT5546	Brahms: Piano Concerto 1	LSO	Monteux Katchen	[SXL2172]
LXT5547	Grieg: Piano Concerto in Amin, Franck: Symphonic Vns	LSO	Fjeldstad Curzon	[SXL2173]
LXT5548	Suppé: Overtures (Light Cavalry,Poet & Peasant,Pique Dame,etc)	VPO	Solti	[SXL2174]
LXT5549	Puccini: Turandot (hlts)	AdSC	Erede Borkh	[SXL2175]
LXT5550	Dohnanyi: Vns on Nursery Song, Rachmaninov: Paganini Vns	LPO	Boult Katchen	[SXL2176]
LXT5551	Wolf-Ferrari: Orch hlts from the Operas	PCO	Nello Santi	[SXL2177]
LXT5552	Beethoven: Piano Concertos 1, 2	VPO	Schmidt-Isserstedt Backhaus	[SXL2178]
LXT5553	Beethoven: Piano Concerto 5 (Emperor)	VPO	Schmidt-Isserstedt Backhaus	[SXL2179]
LXT5554-5	Puccini: Tosca		Molinari-Pradelli Tebaldi	[SXL2180-1]
LXT5556	Rossini: Overtures (Tell, Cenerentola, Semiramide, etc)	PCO	Maag	[SXL2182]
LXT5557	Liszt: Piano Recital (Polonaises 1,2, Dante Sonata, etc)		Katin	[SXL2183]
LXT5558	Norwegian Songs	LSO	Fjeldstad Flagstad	[SXL2145]
LXT5559	Wagner: Tristan & Isolde (hlts)	VPO	Knappertsbusch	[SXL2184]
LXT5560-1	Leoncavallo: Pagliacci, Recital of Italian Songs	AdSC	Molinari-Pradelli	[SXL2185-6]
LXT5563	Schubert: Lieder	Lichtegg (tenor) Haeusslein (piano)		
LXT5564	Britten: Nocturne op 60, Peter Grimes – Sea Interludes	LSO	Britten Pears	[SXL2189]
LXT5565	Mussorgsky: Pictures, Liszt: Symphonic Poem The Huns	OSR	Ansermet	[SXL2195]

LXT5566	Beethoven: Symphony 6, Prometheus Overture	OSR	Ansermet	[SXL2193]
LXT5567	Lute Songs (Dowland, Morley, Campian, etc)	Bream	Pears	[SXL2191]
LXT5568	Boito: Mefistofele (hlts)	AdSC	Serafin Tebaldi	[SXL2192]
LXT5569	Paganini: Caprices op 1		Ricci	[SXL2194]
LXT5570	Mozart: Serenata Notturna, etc	LSO	Maag	[SXL2196]
LXT5571	Bizet:Carmen Fantasie, Sarasate: Zigeunerweisen, St-Saens	LSO	Gamba Ricci	[SXL2197]
LXT5572	Waltzes and Polkas by the Strauss Family	VPO	Boskovsky	[SXL2198]
LXT5573	Instruments of the Orchestra	Presented by Sargent		[SXL2199]
LXT5574	Schubert: Die Schöne Müllerin	Pears	Britten	[SXL2200]
LXT5575	Puccini: Madama Butterfly (hlts)	AdSC	Serafin Tebaldi	[SXL2202]
LXT5576	Mahler: Das Lied Von Der Erde	VPO	Walter Ferrier Patzak	
LXT5577	Prokofiev: Peter and the Wolf, St-Saens: Carnival of the Animals	LSO	Katchen Lillie	[SXL2218]
LXT5578	Handel: Organ Concertos vol 1: op 4/1-4		Karl Richter	[SXL2115]
LXT5579	Handel: Organ Concertos vol 2: op 4, op 5, op 6, op 7/1-2		Karl Richter	[SXL2187]
LXT5580	Handel: Organ Concertos vol 3: op 7/3-6		Karl Richter	[SXL2201]
LXT5581	Tchaikovsky: Swan Lake (hlts)	OSR	Ansermet	[SXL2153]
LXT5584	Beethoven: Symphony 2, Leonora 2 Ov	OSR	Ansermet	[SXL2228]
LXT5585	Mendelsshohn: Midsmr Nights Dream, Schubert: Rosamunde	OSR	Ansermet	[SXL2229]
LXT5586	Wagner: Das Rheingold, Die Walkure (hlts)	VPO	Solti Flagstad	[SXL2230]
LXT5587	Ravel: String Quartet, Prokofiev: String Quartet	Carmirelli Quartet		[SXL2231]
LXT5588	Searle: Symphony 1, Seiber: Elegy etc	LPO	Boult Seiber	[SXL2232]
LXT5589	Mozart: Concert Arias, Haydn: Scena di Berenice	Haydn Orch	Newstone Vyvyan	[SXL2233]
LXT5590	Beethoven: Symphony 7, Fidelio Ov	OSR	Ansermet	[SXL2235]
LXT5591	Brahms: Piano Concerto 2	LSO	Ferencsik Katchen	[SXL2236]
LXT5592	Stravinsky: Symphony in C, Symphony in 3 mvmts	OSR	Ansermet	[SXL2237]
LXT5593	Mozart: Clarinet Concerto, Horn Concertos 1&3	LSO	Maag Tuckwell	[SXL2238]
LXT5594	All Time Popular Favourites	VPO	Knappertsbusch	[SXL2239]
LXT5595	Recital (Bartok, Stravinsky, Prokofiev, Hindemith)		Ricci	[SXL2240]
LXT5596	Beethoven: Waldstein and Appassionata Sonatas		Backhaus	[SXL2241]
LXT5597	Verdi: Aida excerpts	VPO	Karajan Tebaldi	[SXL2242]
LXT5598	Albeniz: Iberia, Turina: Danzas Fantasticas	OSR	Ansermet	[SXL2243]
LXT5599	Beethoven: Symphony 3	OSR	Ansermet	[SXL2244]
LXT5600	Classical Indian Music	Introduced by Menuhin		[SXL2245]
LXT5601	Mendelssohn: Symphony 3, Fingal's Cave	LSO	Maag	[SXL2246]
LXT5602	Cimarosa: Il Maestro di Capella/other arias		Corena (bass)	[SXL2247]
LXT5608	Puccini: La Boheme (hlts)	AdSC	Serafin Tebaldi	[SXL2248]
LXT5609	Hungarian/Slavonic Dances (Brahms/Dvorak)	VPO	Reiner	[SXL2249]
LXT5610	Strauss (arr Dorati) Graduation Ball, etc	VPO	Boskovsky	[SXL2250]
LXT5611	Arias of the 18th Century (Gluck, Cherubini, Handel)	ROHCG	Gibson Berganza	[SXL2251]
LXT5612	Bizet: Jeux D'Enfants, Ibert: Divertissement, etc	PCO	Martinon	[SXL2252]
LXT5613-5	Mascagni: Cavalleria Rusticana, Leoncavallo: Pagliacci	Serafin Del Monaco		[SXL2253-5]
LXT5616-7	The Art of the Prima Donna	ROHCG	Pradelli Sutherland	[SXL2256-7]
LXT5618	Puccini: Tosca (hlts)	AdSC	Pradelli Tebaldi	[SXL2258]
LXT5619	Bach,J.S: Italian Concerto, etc		George Malcolm	[SXL2259]
LXT5620	Strauss,R: Till Eulenspiegel, Death & Transfiguration	VPO	Karajan	[SXL2261]
LXT5621	Beethoven: Diabelli Variations		Katchen	[SXL2262]
LXT5622	"French Overtures" (Lalo/Herold/Offenbach/Auber)	OSR	Ansermet	[SXL2263]
LXT5623	Strauss,R: Der Rosenkavalier (hlts)	VPO	Kleiber Reining	
LXT5624	Britten: Spring Symphony	ROHCG	Britten	[SXL2264]
LXT5625	Corelli: Concerto Grosso 8, etc	StCO	Munchinger	[SXL2265]
LXT5626	Rossini: Overtures (Magpie, Barber, Semiramide, Tell, Ladder)	LSO	Gamba	[SXL2266]
LXT5627	Puccini: Fanciulla del West (hlts)	AdSC	Capuana Tebaldi	[SXL2267]
LXT5628	Rimsky Korsakov: Scheherazade	OSR	Ansermet	[SXL2268]
LXT5629	Tchaikovsky: Romeo & Juliet ov, Strauss,R: Don Juan	VPO	Karajan	[SXL2269]
LXT5630	Mozart: Eine Kleine Nachtmusik, Musical Joke, etc	StCO	Munchinger	[SXL2270]
LXT5631	Recital (Rossini, Donizetti, Mozart, Bellini)	VPO	Quadri Sciutti	[SXL2271]

LXT5632	Mozart: Haffner Serenade K250	VPO	Munchinger	[SXL2272]
LXT5633	Ravel: Daphnis & Chloe, Alborada del Gracioso, Tombeau, etc	OSR	Ansermet	[SXL2273]
LXT5634	Bizet: Symphony in C, Jeux D'Enfants, etc	OSR	Ansermet	[SXL2275]
LXT5638	Mahler: Symphony 4	Ccgbw	Solti Stahlman	[SXL2276]
LXT5639	Stravinsky: Les Noces, Symphony of Psalms	OSR	Ansermet	[SXL2277]
LXT5640	Franck: Piano Quintet	Vienna Philharmonic Quartet		[SXL2278]
LXT5641	Tchaikovsky: Violin Conc/Dvorak Violin Conc	LSO	Sargent Ricci	[SXL2279]
LXT5642	Offenbach: Gaite Parisienne, Gounod: Faust	ROHCG	Solti	[SXL2280]
LXT5643-4	Mascagni: Cavalleria Rusticana, Operatic recital	AdSC	Serafin Simionato	[SXL2281-2]
LXT5645	Beethoven: Symphony 9	VPO	Kleiber Gueden etc	
LXT5647	Haydn: Symphonies 83, 100	VPO	Munchinger	[SXL2284]
LXT5648	Tchaikovsky: Scenes from Swan Lake	Ccgbw	Fistoulari	[SXL2285]
LXT5649	Mozart: Quartets K499, K589	Vienna Philharmonic Qt		[SXL2286]
LXT5650	Debussy: Images, Ravel: Pavane, Stravinsky	OSR	Ansermet	[SXL2287]
LXT5651	"1001 Nights" (Johann Strauss, Josef Strauss, Ziehrer)	VPO	Boskovsky	[SXL2288]
LXT5652	Dvorak: Symphony 9	VPO	Kertesz	[SXL2289]
LXT5653	Mozart: Divertimenti K136, K334	Vienna Octet		[SXL2290]
LXT5654	Franck: Symphony, Le Chasseur Maudit	OSR	Ansermet	[SXL2291]
LXT5655	Prokofiev: Classical Symphony, Borodin, Glinka	OSR	Ansermet	[SXL2292]
LXT5656	Encores (Bach, Beethoven, Brahms, Liszt, Chopin, Mozart, etc)		Katchen	[SXL2293]
LXT5657	Xmas with Leontyne Price	VPO	Karajan Price	[SXL2294]
LXT5658	"Operetta Evergreens" (Lehar, Kalman, Strauss, Stolz, etc)		Gueden	[SXL2295]
LXT5659	Falla: Three Cornered Hat	OSR	Ansermet	[SXL2296]
LXT5660	Brahms: Clarinet Quintet, Wagner: Adagio	Vienna Octet		[SXL2297]
LXT5661	Britten: Cello Sonata, Debussy: Cello Sonata, etc, Schumann	Rostropovich Britten		[SXL2298]
LXT5662	Hymns from Norway	Flagstad	Fotland (organ)	
LXT5663	The Art of Oda Slobodskaya	LSO	Fistoulari	[SXL2299]
LXT5664-5	Bach,JS: Orchestral Suites	StCO	Munchinger	[SXL2300-1]
LXT5666	Handel: Water Music, Fireworks Music	LSO	Szell	[SXL2302]
LXT5667	Faure: Pelleas & Melisande, Debussy	OSR	Ansermet	[SXL2303]
LXT5668	"On the Wings of Song"	ROHCG	Downes Resnik	[SXL2304]
LXT5669	Holst: The Planets	VPO	Karajan	[SXL2305]
LXT5671-2	Prokofiev: Romeo & Juliet, Cinderella	OSR	Ansermet	[SXL2306-7]
LXT5673	Tchaikovsky: Nutcracker, Grieg Peer Gynt	VPO	Karajan	[SXL2308]
LXT5674	Britten: Peter Grimes (hlts)	ROHCG	Britten Pears	[SXL2309]
LXT5675	Schumann: Dichterliebe	Waechter	Brendel	[SXL2310]
LXT5676	Frank Martin: Concerto for 7 wind Instruments etc	OSR	Ansermet	[SXL2311]
LXT5677	Debussy: Nocturnes, Faun Prelude	LSO	Monteux	[SXL2312]
LXT5682	Herold/Lanchberry: La Fille Mal Gardee	ROHCG	Lanchberry	[SXL2313]
LXT5683	Otello (hlts)	VPO	Karajan	[SXL2314]
LXT5684	Donizetti: Lucia di Lammermoor (hlts)	AdSC	Pritchard	[SXL2315]
LXT5685	Handel: Messiah (hlts)	LSO	Boult	[SXL2316]

Note that most LXT6xxx have not been listed because they have exactly the same numbers as the corresponding stereo SXL records. However, there are a small number with no corresponding stereo. These include the set LXT6277-80 which was one of several series issued to celebrate the 125th anniversary of the VPO. The other sets (SXL6282-4 for example) were issued in stereo.

LXT6014	Beethoven: Diabelli Variations		Backhaus	
LXT6126	Recital	Maggie Teyte (soprano)		
LXT6277	Beethoven: Symphony 9	VPO	Kleiber	[LXT2725-6]
LXT6278	Mahler: Das Lied von der Erde	VPO	Walter Ferrier	[LXT2721-2]
LXT6279	Bruckner: Symphony 4	VPO	Knappertsbusch	[LXT5065-6]

LXT6280	Mozart: Symphonies 34, 38	VPO	Bohm	[LXT5111]
LXT6907	Pergolesi: Stabat Mater	Boyd Neel Orch Ferrier		[1946 78s]
SXL6934	Song Recital (Brahms, Bach, Gruber, etc)	Various	Ferrier	

Decca LX (10")

At the same time as Decca released the 12" LP (LXT series) in June 1950, they issued a 10" series (prefix LX). LX labels are identical with LXT labels (i.e. orange with gold lettering). All the surviving LX issues were deleted from the catalogue in December 1958.

LX3001	Mendelssohn: Violin Concerto	LPO	Van Beinum Campoli
LX3002	Bach,JS: Suite 3	StCO	Munchinger
LX3003	Prokofiev: Peter and the Wolf	LPO	Malko Frank Phillips
LX3004	Mendelssohn: Symphony 4	Turin SO	Rossi
LX3005	Operatic recital (Verdi, Gounod, Leoncavallo, Thomas)	NSO	Erede Giuseppe Valdengo (bar)
LX3006	Bach,JS: Cantata 11 ("Praise our God")	Jacques Orch Jacques Ferrier	
LX3007	Bach,JS: Cantata 67 ("Hold in Affection Jesus Christ")	Jacques Orch Jacques Ferrier	
LX3008	Operatic and Lieder recital	New SO	Braithwaite Ellabelle Davis (sop)
LX3009	Haydn: Symphony 101	OSR	Ansermet
LX3010	Mozart: Symphony 41	LSO	Krips
LX3011	Haydn: Symphony 99	LSO	Royalton Kisch
LX3012	Schubert: Symphony 8	LSO	Krips
LX3013	Dukas, Chabrier, Glinka	PCO	Jorda
LX3014	Grieg: Holberg Suite, etc	Boyd Neel Orchestra	
LX3016	Bloch: Schelomo	LPO	Bloch Nelsova
LX3017	Bach,JS: Two Motets for Double Choir	Cantata Singers Jacques	
LX3018	Haydn: Symphony 103	LPO	Solti
LX3019	Italian Song Recital	Kingsway SO Erede Valdengo (bar)	
LX3020	Tosti: Seven Songs	Kingsway SO Erede Valdengo (bar)	
LX3021	Operatic Recital (Wagner, Strauss)	Zurich Tonhalle Knappertsbusch Reining	
LX3022	Mozart: Symphony 40	LPO	Kleiber
LX3023	Elgar: Cello Concerto	LPO	Van Beinum Anthony Pini
LX3024	Handel: Concerti Grossi 3, 4	Boyd Neel Orchestra	
LX3025	Holst: St Pauls Suite Grace Williams: Welsh Nursery Tunes	Boyd Neel Orchestra LSO	Mansel Thomas
LX3026	Beethoven: String Quartet op 95	Griller String Quartet	
LX3027	Handel: Concerti Grossi 1, 2	Boyd Neel Orchestra	
LX3028	Vivaldi: Concertos op 25/2, op 25/4	London CO Bernard Sabatini (viola)	
LX3029	Bach,JS: Brandenburg Concertos 2,3	StCO	Munchinger
LX3030-1	Mozart: Requiem K626	Vienna Hofmusikkapelle Krips	
LX3032	Brahms: Six Piano Pieces op 118		Kempff
LX3033	Brahms: Three Intermezzi op 117		Kempff
LX3034	Wagner: Rienzi Ov, Siegfried Forest Murmurs	VPO	Knappertsbusch Lechleitner (tenor)
LX3035	Chopin: Piano Concerto 2	LSO	Ansermet Ballon
LX3036	Wagner: Parsifal (hlts)	VPO	Knappertsbusch Treptow (tenor)
LX3037	Opera recital (Delibes, Rossini, Verdi)	New SO	Blareau Mado Robin (sop)
LX3038	Bliss: String Quartet 2	Griller String Quartet	
LX3040	Folk Song recital	Ferrier	Spurr (piano)
LX3041	Operatic recital (Verdi, Rossini, Bellini, Mussorgsky)	OSR	Erede Raphael Arié (bass)
LX3042	Music of the 20th century (Bloch, Barber, Copland)	Boyd Neel Orch Bloch (piano) Nelsova (cello)	
LX3043	Bach,JS: Suite 2	StCO	Munchinger
LX3044	Chopin: Ballade 1, Etude 3, Mazurkas 17,20,24		Backhaus
LX3045	Stravinsky: Firebird Suite	OSR	Ansermet
LX3046	Byrd: Mass for Four Voices	Fleet Street Choir Lawrence	

LX3047	Stravinsky: Symphony of Psalms	LPO	Ansermet
LX3048	Barber: Cello Concerto	New SO	Barber Nelsova
LX3049	Barber: Medea op 23	New SO	Barber
LX3050	Barber: Symphony 2	New SO	Barber
LX3051	Lieder recital (Brahms, Wolf)	Danco	Agosti
LX3052	Debussy: Song Cycles	Danco	Agosti
LX3053	Beethoven: Symphony 8	PCO	Munch
LX3054	Arias (Mozart, Strauss)	LSO	Krips Hollweg (sop)
LX3055	Handel: Concerti Grossi op 6/5-6	Boyd Neel Orchestra	
LX3056	Franck: Violin Sonata in Amaj	Lola Bobesco Jacques Genty	
LX3057	Faure: Violin Sonata in Amaj Op 13	Lola Bobesco Jacques Genty	
LX3058	Puccini: Opera Highlights	OSR	Erede Noli (sop) Campora (ten)
LX3059	Schubert: Fantasy in Cmaj (Wanderer)		Curzon
LX3060	Byrd: Mass for Five Voices	Fleet Street Choir Lawrence	
LX3061	Mozart: Serenade K525, Divertimento K136	StCO	Munchinger
LX3062	Liszt: Piano Sonata in Bmin		Magaloff
LX3063	Famous Overtures (Gluck, Cimarosa)	LSO	Royalton Kisch
LX3064	St-Saens: Piano Concerto 2	LPO	Martinon Lympany
LX3065	"Xmas Eve in Vienna"	VSO & Chorus Rossmayer	
LX3066	Rawsthorne: Piano Concerto 2	LSO	Sargent Curzon
LX3067	Operatic Recital (Verdi, Mozart)	VPO	Krauss Gueden
LX3068	Operatic Recital (Lehar, J Strauss)	Vienna SO Loibner Gueden Friedrich	
LX3069	Bach,JS: Suite 3 for Cello		Mainardi
LX3070	Piano Recital (Bach, Schubert, Beethoven, Liszt)		Ellen Ballon
LX3071	Operetta Recital (Milloecker, Lehar, Kalman)	Vienna SO Loibner Gueden	
LX3072	Debussy, Stravinsky, Ravel, Prokofiev	OSR	Ansermet
LX3073	Scarlatti: Sonatas		Kathleen Long
LX3074	Schumann: Carnaval op 9		Magaloff
LX3075	Villa-Lobos: Piano Works		Ellen Ballon
LX3076	Chopin: Waltzes, Mazurkas, Polonaises		Magaloff
LX3077	Song Cycles (Ravel, Falla)	Souzay	Bonneau (piano)
LX3078	Brahms: Handel Vns & Fugue op 24		Katchen
LX3079	Chopin Recital (Ballade op 47, Scherzo op 39, Fantaisie op 49)		Katchen
LX3080	Recital (Ravel, Faure, Auber, etc)	Irma Kolassi Bonneau (piano)	
LX3081	Handel: Concerti Grossi op 6/7-8	Boyd Neel Orchestra	
LX3082	Schubert: Symphony 5	Ccgbw	Van Beinum
LX3083	Beethoven: Piano Concerto 2	VPO	Krauss Backhaus
LX3084	Beethoven: Symphony 1	VPO	Schuricht
LX3086	Wiren: Serenade, Larsson: Pastoral Suite	Stockholm Radio Westerburg	
LX3087	Mozart: String Quartet K159, Haydn: String Quartet op 3/5	Griller Quartet	
LX3088	Rubbra: String Quartet op 73	Griller Quartet	
LX3091	Chopin: Etudes (selection from op 10 & op 25)		Backhaus
LX3093	Messager: Deux Pigeons, Chabrier	Opera Comique Orch Blareau	
LX3094	Operatic Arias (Verdi, Puccini)	AdSC	Erede Del Monaco
LX3095	Mozart: Opera Recital	Erede/Maag Fernando Corena (bass)	
LX3096	Handel: Fireworks, Berlioz: Damnation of Faust (hlts)	Ccgbw	Van Beinum
LX3097	Debussy: Danses, Ravel: Intro for Flute, Harp, Clarinet, String Qt	Amsterdam Chamber Music Soc Van Beinum	
LX3098	Songs of the British Isles	Ferrier	Phyllis Spurr (piano)
LX3099	Handel: Concerti Grossi Op 6/9-10	Boyd Neel Orchestra	
LX3100	Vivaldi: Bassoon Concerto, Marcello: Oboe Concerto	OSR	Ansermet Soloists
LX3101	Nielsen: Helios Overture op 17, Schultz: Serenade for Strings	DSRO	Tuxen
LX3102	Gabrielli, Telemann	StCO	Munchinger
LX3103	Mozart: Exsultate Jubilate, Operatic Arias	VPO	Erede Gueden
LX3104	Schubert: Recital	Souzay	Bonneau (piano)
LX3105	Mozart: Divertimento K247	Vienna Octet	
LX3106	Vivaldi: Sonata in Cmin, Rameau: 3 pieces	Trio di Trieste	

LX3107	Schumann: Liederkreis op 39	Danco	Agosti (piano)
LX3108	"This is my Vienna" (Viennese Songs)	Orch	Kurt Adler Gueden
LX3109	Italian Operatic Recital	OSR	Erede Protti (bar) Corena (bass)
LX3110	Lieder recital (Mozart, Strauss)	Danco	Agosti (piano)
LX3111	Faure: La Bonne Chanson Op 61	Danco	Agosti (piano)
LX3112	"Classical Arias" (Mozart, Scarlatti, Gluck, Lully, Rameau)	PCO	Cornman Souzay
LX3113	Recital of 17th & 18th Century Music	Danco	Agosti (piano)
LX3114	Donizetti: Lucia di Lammermoor, Thomas: Hamlet (hlts)	PCO	Blareau Mado Robin (sop)
LX3115	Paganini: Caprices 13 , 20, Dohnanyi	Campoli	G.Malcolm (piano)
LX3116	Elizalde: Violin Concerto	LSO	Poulet Ferras
LX3117	Xmas Songs	Vienna SO	Rossmayer Gueden
LX3118-21	Gregorian Chant vol 2	Monks of Abbey of St Pierre de Solesmes	
LX3122	Viennese "Heurigen" Songs	Schrammel Quartet Patzak (tenor)	
LX3124	Handel: Concerti Grossi Op 6/11-12	Boyd Neel Orchestra	
LX3125	Grieg: Lyric Suite, Reesen: Himmerland	DSRO	Tuxen/Reesen
LX3126	Verdi: Un Ballo in Maschera (hlts in German)	Carla Martinis Helge Roswaenge	
LX3127	Operatic Recital (Verdi, Puccini, Giordano)	AdSC	Erede Poggi (tenor)
LX3128	Bizet: Symphony in Cmaj	OSR	Ansermet
LX3129	SELMER demonstration disc - The Clarinet vol 1	Paris Clarinet Sextet	
LX3130	SELMER demonstration disc - The Saxophone vol 1	Paris Saxophone Quartet	
LX3131	SELMER demonstration disc - The Trombone vol 1	Paris Trombone Quartet	
LX3132	SELMER demonstration disc - The Trumpet vol 1		
LX3133	Song Recital (Stanford & V Williams)	Ferrier	Stone (piano)
LX3134	Brahms: 2 Rhapsodies Op 79, 3 Pieces Op 117		Kempff
LX3135	SELMER demonstration disc - The Saxophone vol 2	Paris Saxophone Quartet	
LX3136	SELMER demonstration disc - The Clarinet vol 2	Paris Clarinet Sextet	
LX3137	Tartini: "Devil's Trill" Sonata	Campoli	G.Malcolm (piano)
LX3138	SELMER demonstration disc - The Clarinet vol 3	Paris Clarinet Sextet	
LX3139	The Clarinet vol 4: Milhaud: Clarinet Sonatina, Honegger	U&J Delacluse	
LX3140	SELMER demonstration disc - The Saxophone vol 3	Paris Saxophone Quartet	
LX3142	SELMER demonstration disc - The Saxophone vol 4	Paris Saxophone Quartet	
LX3143	SELMER demonstration disc - The French Horn	Paris Horn Quartet	
LX3145	SELMER demonstration disc - The Trombone vol 2	Paris Trombone Quartet	
LX3146	Martin: Violin Concerto	OSR	Ansermet Schneiderhan
LX3147	SELMER demonstration disc - The Clarinet vol 5	Paris Clarinet Sextet	
LX3148	Fornerod, Gagnebin	Orch de Chambre de Lausanne Desarzens	
LX3149	Faure: 5 Verlaine Songs, Ravel: Histoires Naturelles	Souzay	Bonneau (piano)
LX3150	Chausson: Poeme de L'Amour et de La Mer	LPO	de Froment Kolassi
LX3151	Falla: El Amor Brujo	OSR	Ansermet de Gabarain (mezzo)
LX3152	Bach,JS: Concerto for Harpsichord & Strings	Ansbach Bach Festival Richter	
LX3153	Milhaud: Creation du Monde, Respighi: Fountains	OSR	Erede
LX3154	Schubert: Lieder Recital	Souzay	Bonneau

Decca LW (10")

Decca launched their 10" Medium Play (LW series) in July 1953 to contain medium length pieces of music complete on one side. These are predominantly reissues of material which had previously been included in earlier LXT or LX issues. The labels are black with gold lettering.

By 1960 the LW series was superceded by the 7" CEP series, the SEC stereo 7", and the new 10" mono LP BR series. However, many survived until the series was deleted in its entirety from October 1967.

Cat #	Work	Orchestra	Conductor/Artist
LW5001	Mozart: Overtures Don Giovanni, Magic Flute	LSO	Krips
LW5002	Weber: Overtures Euryanthe, Oberon	VPO	Bohm
LW5003	Suppe: Overtures Light Cavalry, Morning Noon&Night in Vienna	LPO	Solti
LW5004	Suppe: Overtures Pique Dame, Poet & Peasant	LPO	Solti
LW5005	Strauss: Overtures Die Zigeunerbaron, Fledermaus	VPO	Krauss
LW5006	Rossini: Ov Italian in Algiers, Donizetti: Ov Don Pasquale	New SO	Erede
LW5007	Herold: Overture Zampa, Adam: Overture: Si J'Etais Roi	LPO	Martinon
LW5008	Ovs: Rossini: Barber of Seville, Nicolai: Merry Wives of Windsor	OSR	Olof
LW5009	Strauss,J: Waltzes	LSO	Krips
LW5010	Thomas: Ov Mignon, Ponchielli: Dance of the Hours	PCO	Fistoulari
LW5011	Strauss,J: Waltzes	NatSO	Krips
LW5012	Strauss,J: Waltzes	NatSO	Krips
LW5013	Gounod: Faust (Jewel Song, etc),Verdi: Aida	OSR Erede Tebaldi	
LW5014	Berlioz: Ovs Corsaire, Benvenuto Cellini	PCO	Munch
LW5015	Beethoven: Overtures Coriolan, Egmont	LPO	Van Beinum
LW5016	Beethoven: Overtures: Leonora 3, Consecration of the House	LPO	Van Beinum
LW5017	Rossini: Ov Gazza Ladra, Scala di Seta	Cgbw	Van Beinum
LW5018	Beethoven: Overtures Prometheus, Fidelio	LPO	Van Beinum
LW5019	Strauss,Joseph: Overtures	VPO	Krauss
LW5020	Strauss,J: Waltzes (Vienna Woods, Morgenblätter)	VPO	Krauss
LW5021	Mozart: Overtures Abduction from Seraglio, The Impressario	LSO	Krips
LW5022	Gluck: Overtures Alceste, Iphegenie in Aulis	LSO	Royalton Kisch
LW5023	Boieldieu: Ovs Caliph of Baghdad, La Dame Blanche	LPO	Martinon
LW5024	Sullivan: Overtures Mikado, Pinafore	SO	Isidore Godfrey
LW5025	Humperdinck: Hansel & Gretel, Strauss,R: Rosenkavalier Waltzes	LPO	Collins
LW5026	Chopin: Ballade 1, Mazurkas 17,20,24		Backhaus
LW5027	Offenbach: Ovs Orpheus in the Underworld, La Belle Helene	LPO	Martinon
LW5028	Massenet: Ov Phedre, St-Saens: Ov La Princesse Jaune	Opera Comique	Wolff
LW5029	Strauss,R: Scenes from Arabella	VPO	Moralt Della Casa Gueden
LW5030	St-Saens: Danse Macabre, Le Rouet D'Omphale	OSR	Ansermet
LW5031	Debussy: Faune Prelude, Ravel: Alborada	OSR	Ansermet
LW5032	Weber: Ovs Peter Schmoll, Preciosa	VPO	Bohm
LW5033	Chabrier: Marche Joyeuse, Ravel: Pavane	OSR	Ansermet
LW5034	Delibes: La Source, Sibelius: Valse Triste, etc	OSR	Olof
LW5035	Bizet: Carmen Duets	Michaeau	Juyol de Luca
LW5036	Delius: Paradise Garden, First Cuckoo	LSO	Collins
LW5037	Moussorgsky: Songs and Dances of Death	Rehfuss (bar)	Haeusslein (piano)
LW5038	Wagner: Mastersingers Preludes to act 1 & 3	VPO	Knappertsbusch
LW5039	Rossini: Semiramide, William Tell Ovs	Ccgbw	Van Beinum
LW5040	Verdi: Ovs Nabucco, Sicilian Vespers	NewSO	Erede
LW5041	Brahms: Academic Festival Ov, Tragic Ov	Ccgbw	Van Beinum
LW5042	Berlioz: Ov Benvenuto Cellini, Lalo: Ov Le Roi D'Ys	Opera Comique	Wolff
LW5043	Brahms: Rhapsodies op 79 nos 1 & 2		Kempff

LW5044	Puccini: La Boheme, Madama Butterfly (hlts)	AdSC	Erede Tebaldi
LW5045	Verdi: Aida (Nile Scene)	AdSC	Erede Tebaldi Del Monaco
LW5046	Mendelssohn: Ov Midsummer Nts Drm, Schubert: Ov Rosamunde	Cgbw	Van Beinum
LW5047	Elgar: Intro & Allegro, Serenade in E op 20	New SO	Collins
LW5048	Dvorak: Slavonic Dances 1,2,3,16	Hamburg Radio SO	Schmidt-Isserstedt
LW5049	Jones: The Geisha (hlts), Stolz: White Horse Inn (hlts)	Berlin Opera	
LW5050	Arias from Tchaikovsky: Queen of Spades, Verdi: Un Ballo	Vienna Opera Moralt Welitsch	
LW5051	Nielsen: Chaconne op 32, Liszt: Liebestraume 3, Paganini/Liszt/Busoni: La Campanella		Ellegaard (piano)
LW5052	Strauss,J: Five Favourite Polkas	VPO	Krauss
LW5053	Strauss,Joseph: Five Polkas	VPO	Krauss
LW5054	Lehar : Merry Widow Ov etc	Tonhalle Zurich	Lehar
LW5055	Turina: Procesion Del Rocio, Albeniz: Iberia (El Puerto&Triana)	PCO	Jorda
LW5056	Strauss,R: 4 Last Songs	VPO	Bohm Della Casa
LW5057	Walton:Coronation March (Orb&Sceptre), Bax:Coronation March	LSO	Sargent
LW5058	Elgar: Pomp & Circumstance Marches 1 & 4	LSO	Sargent
LW5059	German: 3 Dances from Henry 8, 3 Dances from Nell Gwyn	NewSO	Olof
LW5060	Borodin: Steppes of Central Asia, Moussorgsky: Bare Mt	PCO	Ansermet
LW5061	Arias from Russian Opera (Glinka, Tchaikovsky, Borodin, etc)	PCO	Erede Arie (bass)
LW5062	Viktoria und Ihr Husar: Hochzeitsnacht in Paradies	Grosses OperettenOrch	Lampertz
LW5064	Verdi: Aida, Macbeth, Traviata, Luisa Miller (hlts)	AdSC	Erede Del Monaco
LW5065	Recital (Verdi, Puccini, etc)	AdSC	Erede Tebaldi
LW5066	Brahms: Hungarian Dances 1,2,3,5,6,7,10	Hamburg RSO	Schmidt-Isserstedt
LW5067	Moussorgsky: Boris Godunov, Rubinstein: The Demon	PCO	Erede Arie (bass)
LW5068	Shostakovich: Sonata in Dmin op 40	Brabec (cello)	Holetschek (piano)
LW5069	Franck: Psyché	Cgbw	Van Beinum
LW5070	Britten: A Ceremony of Carols	Copenhagen Boys Choir Britten	
LW5071	Lehar: Ovs: Gypsy Love, Land of Smiles	Zurich Tonhalle	Lehar
LW5072	Recital of Arias	LSO	Sargent Ferrier
LW5073	Liszt: Deux Legendes		Kempff
LW5074	Massenet: Le Cid Ballet Music	LSO	Irving
LW5075	Scottish Country Dances	Angus Fichet's Scots Dance Band	
LW5076	Recital of Handel Arias	LPO	Boult Ferrier
LW5077	Handel: Violin Sonatas 4, 6	Campoli	Malcolm
LW5078	Recital of French Songs (Debussy and Ravel)	PCO	Lindenburg Souzay
LW5079	Verdi: Don Carlos, Moussorgsky: Boris Godunov	Arie (bass)	
LW5080	Verdi: Aida (closing duets)	AdSC	Erede Tebaldi Del Monaco
LW5081	Villa-Lobos: Piano Music		Ellen Ballon (piano)
LW5082	Wagner: Mastersingers (Sachs' monologues)	VPO	Knappertsbusch Schoeffler
LW5083	Recital of Bach arias (Matthew Passion, Bmin Mass, etc)	LPO	Boult Ferrier
LW5084	Minkus: Don Quichotte, Weber-Berlioz: Spectre de la Rose	New SO	Fistoulari
LW5085	St Saens: Introduction & Capriccioso, Havanaise	LSO	Fistoulari Campoli
LW5086	Meyerbeer: Les Patineurs	LSO	Irving
LW5087	Recital of Russian Songs (Moussorgsky, Glinka, etc)	Arie (bass)	Parry (piano)
LW5088	Khachaturian: Masquerade Suite	PCO	Blareau
LW5089	Schumann: Frauenliebe und Leben Op 42	Ferrier	Newmark (piano)
LW5090	Light Opera hlts	Zurich Tonhalle	Reinshagen
LW5091	"Recital of Old French Airs"	Souzay	Bonneau (piano)
LW5092	Brahms: Paganini Variations		Charles Rosen (piano)
LW5093	Operatic Recital (Leoncavallo, Ponchielli, Verdi)	AdSC	Erede Del Monaco
LW5094	Brahms : 4 Serious Songs	Ferrier	Newmark (piano)
LW5095	Bach,JS: Toccata & Fugues in Gmin, Dmin		Demessieux (organ)
LW5096	Prokofiev: Symphony 1 ("Classical")	OSR	Ansermet
LW5097	Gounod: Six Songs	Souzay	Bonneau (piano)
LW5098	Recital (Schubert, Schumann)	Ferrier	Spurr (piano)
LW5101	Wagner: Mastersingers (hlts)	VPO	Knappertsbusch Schoeffler

Cat. No.	Title	Performer(s)
LW5102	"Songs of England"	Vyvyan Lush (piano)
LW5103	Wagner: Mastersingers (hlts)	VPO Knappertsbusch Gueden etc
LW5104	Recital of Russian Songs	LSO Fistoulari Arie (bass)
LW5105	Sibelius: Swan of Tuonela, Lemminkainen's Return	DSRO Jensen
LW5106	Wagner: Flying Dutchman Overture, Ride of the Valkyries	VPO Knappertsbusch
LW5107	Walton: Facade Suites 1/2	LSO Irving
LW5108	Schubert: Impromptus op 142/3-4	Curzon (piano)
LW5109	Brahms: Waltzes op 39	Weisz (piano)
LW5110	Tchaikovsky: Nutcracker Suite	PCO Fistoulari
LW5111	Operatic Recital (Bellini, Verdi, etc)	Chors & Orch Narducci Penno (tenor)
LW5112	Cimarosa: Il Maestro di Capella	Musicali di Milano Amaducci Corena
LW5113	Svendsen: Festival Polonaise op 12, etc	DSRO Tuxen
LW5114	Liszt: Hungarian Rhapsody 4, Tchaikovsky: Marche Slave	DSRO Tuxen
LW5115	"The Immortal Works of Ketelbey"	NewSO Robinson
LW5116	Liszt: Polonaises 1, 2	Katin (piano)
LW5117	Sullivan: Ov Di Ballo, Sibelius: Finlandia	Grenadier Guards band
LW5118	Operatic Recital (Mascagni, Leoncavallo)	AdSC Erede Del Monaco
LW5119	Mendelssohn: Capriccio Brillant, Rondo Brillant	LPO Martinon Katin
LW5120	"The Immortal Works of Ketelbey" vol 2	NewSO Robinson
LW5121	Operatic Recital (Catalani, Giordano, Puccini)	AdSC Ghione Del Monaco
LW5122	Britten: Folk Songs	Pears Britten (piano)
LW5123	Mahler: 3 Ruckert Songs	VPO Walter Ferrier
LW5124	Grieg: Suite Sigurd Jorsalfar op 56	Cincinatti SO Johnson
LW5125	Berlioz: Ovs Benvenuto Cellini, Beatrice&Benedict	OSR Denzler
LW5126	Operetta Recital	Vienna Op Schonherr Gueden
LW5127	Piano Recital (Ravel, Debussy, Gagnebin, Marescotti)	Morel (piano)
LW5128	Song Recital (Bellini, Gounod)	Danco Agosti (piano)
LW5129	Greek Folk Songs	Irma Kolassi Collard (piano)
LW5130	Ravel: Tombeau de Couperin	OSR Ansermet
LW5132	Nielsen: Maskarade (hlts)	DSRO Jensen
LW5133	Operetta Recital (Strauss, Kreisler, Lehar, etc)	Vienna State Op Schonherr Gueden
LW5134	Liszt: Rigoletto, Paraphrase de Concert, Hungarian Rhapsody 2	Katin
LW5135	Schubert: Impromptus op 142/1-2	Curzon
LW5136	Liszt: Mephisto Waltz, Tone Poem Prometheus	PCO Munchinger
LW5139	Operatic Recital (Rossini, Verdi, Bellini)	AdSC Ghione Simionato
LW5140	"The Immortal Works of Ketelbey" vol 3	NewSO Robinson
LW5141	Grieg: Elegiac Melodies op 34, Sibelius: Finlandia	DSRO Tuxen
LW5142	Recital of Italian and Spanish Music	Spagnolo (piano)
LW5143	Popular Spanish Songs	Kolassi Collard (piano)
LW5144	Gluck: Ov Alceste, Schumann: Ov Manfred	OSR Munchinger
LW5145	Debussy: Fêtes Galantes - 1st series	Danco Agosti (piano)
LW5146	Brahms: Deutsche Volkslieder, Dvorak: Gypsy Songs op 55	Lichtegg (tenor)
LW5147	Handel: Ovs Alcina, Berenice	Boyd Neel Orch
LW5148	Verdi: Operatic Recital (Don Carlos, Nabucco, Ernani)	AdSC Erede Siepi
LW5149	Warlock: Capriol Suite, Ireland: Minuet	Boyd Neel Orch
LW5150	Liszt: Hungarian Rhapsody 2, Massenet: Werther Prelude	PCO Wolff
LW5151	V Williams: Old King Cole Suite	LPO Boult
LW5154	Auber: Ovs Masaniello, Fra Diavolo	PCO Wolff
LW5155	Dukas: Sorcerer's Apprentice, Honegger: Pacific 231	PCO Ansermet
LW5156	Chopin: Ballades 1-4	Gulda
LW5157	Bach-Walton: The Wise Virgins	LPO Boult
LW5159	Italian Song Recital	Orch cond Nicelli Poggi (tenor)
LW5160	Liszt: Hungarian Rhapsody 12, Balakirev: Islamey	Katchen
LW5161	Debussy: Songs	Irma Kolassi Collard (piano)
LW5162	Wolf: Michelangelo Lieder	Rehfuss (bar) Haeusslein (piano)
LW5163	Britten: A Simple Symphony op 4	NSOL Goossens

LW5164	Beethoven: Ovs Leonora 1, Leonora 2	VPO	Krauss
LW5165	Beethoven: Ovs Leonora 3, Fidelio	VPO	Krauss
LW5166	Arnold: English Dances	LPO	Boult
LW5167	Auber: Ovs The Bronze Horse, The Crown Diamonds	PCO	Wolff
LW5168	Italian Song Recital	Orch cond Nicelli	Del Monaco
LW5169	Operatic Recital (Verdi, Meyerbeer, etc)	AdSC	Erede Siepi (bass)
LW5170	Bach: Chromatic Fantasia & Fugue in Dmin, Italian Concerto		George Malcolm
LW5171	"Famous Gypsy Melodies" vol 1		Kocze Antal and his Orchestra
LW5172	Sullivan: Ovs Pirates of Penzance, Iolanthe	NewSO	Isidore Godfrey
LW5173	Delius: Song of Summer, Summer Night on the River	LSO	Collins
LW5174	Elgar: 3 Bavarian Dances, Chanson de Matin, Chanson de Nuit	LPO	Boult
LW5175	Holst: Perfect Fool Suite, Butterworth: Shropshire Lad	LPO	Boult
LW5176	Berlioz: Ov Carnaval Romain, Damnation of Faust (hlts)	Ccgbw	Van Beinum
LW5177	Harp Recital (Handel, Lully, Buxtehude)		Henrik Boye (harp)
LW5178	Operatic Recital (Verdi, Puccini)	AdSC	Erede Gueden
LW5179	Granados: Goyescas Part 2		Magaloff
LW5180	Violin Recital	Campoli	Gritton (piano)
LW5183	Bizet: Carmen (choruses)	Opera Comique	Wolff
LW5184	Verdi: Aida (choruses)	AdSC	Erede
LW5185	"Famous Gypsy Melodies" vol 2		Kocze Antal and his Orchestra
LW5186	Verdi: Otello (Duets from Acts 1 & 3)	AdSC	Erede Tebaldi Del Monaco
LW5187	Debussy: Children's Corner Suite		Spagnolo (piano)
LW5190	Chopin: Four Impromptus		Magaloff (piano)
LW5191	Italian Song Recital	Orch cond Nicelli	Corena (bar)
LW5192	Falla: 7 Popular Songs, Ravel: Don Quichotte	Estanislao (bar)	Salquin (piano)
LW5193	Mendelssohn: Overtures Fingal's Cave, Ruy Blas	VPO	Schuricht
LW5194	Faure: Nocturnes 2,5,7,8		Kathleen Long (piano)
LW5195	Walton: Ovs Scapino, Portsmouth Point	LPO	Boult
LW5196	Vivaldi (arr D'Indy): Cello Sonata, Couperin: Three Pieces	StCO	Munchinger Fournier
LW5198	Verdi: Otello, Puccini: Manon lescaut (hlts)	AdSC	Molinari-Pradelli Tebaldi
LW5199	Verdi: Otello (hlts)	AdSC	Erede Del Monaco
LW5200	Verdi: La Traviata (hlts)	AdSC	Molinari-Pradelli Tebaldi
LW5201	Chausson Songs (Nanny, Le Charme, Le Colibri, etc)	Souzay	Bonneau (piano)
LW5203	Massenet: Manon (duets)	Opera Comique	Wolff Micheau (sop) De Luca (ten)
LW5204	Massenet: Manon (hlts)	Opera Comique	Wolff Micheau (sop) De Luca (ten)
LW5206	Verdi: Rigoletto (hlts)	AdSC	Erede Del Monaco
LW5207	Rossini: Ovs Barber of Seville, Italian Girl in Algiers	LPO	Solti
LW5208	Verdi: The Lady and the Fool, Ballet	NewSO	Irving
LW5209	Sibelius: Karelia Suite, Pelleas & Melisande (hlts)	LSO	Collins
LW5210	Aria Recital (Verdi: Traviata, Puccini: Manon Lescaut)	AdSC	Molinari-Pradelli Tebaldi
LW5211	Brahms: Rhapsodies Op 79/1, Op 79/2		Kempff
LW5212	Recital: Beethoven Bagatelles and Handel		Kempff
LW5213	Janacek: Sinfonietta	VPO	Kubelik
LW5214	Recital of Welsh Songs	Thomas	Hanneman (piano)
LW5215	Recital of Negro Spirituals		Gloria Davy (sop)
LW5216	Falla: Nights in the Gardens of Spain	NSO	Jorda Curzon
LW5217	"Homage to Kreisler"		Campoli
LW5218	"Homage to Kreisler" vol 2		Campoli
LW5220	Eight Marches		Vienna Police Band Neusser
LW5222	Recital of Welsh Songs vol 2	Thomas	Hanneman (piano)
LW5223	Rossini: Ovs Cenerentola, Siege of Corinth	LSO	Gamba
LW5224	Operetta Favourites No 2 (Lehar, Zeller, etc)	Orch cond Reinshagen	Lichtegg (ten)
LW5225	Recital (Blow the Wind Southerly, Messiah, Mahler)		Ferrier
LW5226	Sullivan: Ovs Gondoliers, Patience, Ruddigore	NewSO	Isidore Godfrey
LW5227	Sullivan: Ovs Yeoman of the Guard, Princess Ida, Sorcerer	NewSO	Isidore Godfrey
LW5228	Puccini: Love Duets (Madama Butterfly, Tosca)	AdSC	Erede Tebaldi Campora

LW5229	Song Recital	Danco	Agosti (piano)
LW5230	Operatic Recital (Puccini, Verdi, Boito, Mascagni, etc)	AdSC	Erede Campora
LW5231	Operatic Recital (Catalani, Refice, Cilea)	AdSC	Erede Tebaldi
LW5232	Song Recital (Schubert, Beethoven, Brahms, etc)	Maran (ten)	Newton (piano)
LW5233	V Williams: On Wenlock Edge	Maran (ten)	Newton (piano)
LW5234	Orch Concert (Falla, Chabrier, Moussorgsky, Debussy)	OSR	Ansermet
LW5235	Schubert: Lieder Recital	Rehfuss (bar)	Martin (piano)
LW5237	Beethoven: Sacred Songs	Strienz (bar)	Corajod (organ)
LW5238	Bellini: Arias from Puritani, Sonnambula	LPO	Fistoulari Robin (sop)
LW5239	Song Recital	LPO	Fistoulari Robin (sop)
LW5240	Operatic Recital (Mozart, Rossini, Mascagni)	AdSC	Erede Tebaldi
LW5241	"20th Century English Songs"	Pears	Britten
LW5242	Recital of Encores vol 2		Campoli
LW5243	"Elizabethan Lute Songs"	Pears	Bream
LW5244	Britten: Peter Grimes (4 Sea Interludes)	Ccgbw	Van Beinum
LW5245	"Italian Arie Antiche" (vocal recital)	Irma Kolassi	Bonneau (piano)
LW5246	Ravel: Cinq Mélodies Populaires, Chansons Madécasses	Kolassi	Bonneau
LW5247	Mozart: Concert Arias	LPO	Maag Vyvyan (sop)
LW5248	Traditional Songs	Proctor (alto)	Redshaw (piano)
LW5250	Serbian Songs	Choir of Yugoslav Army cond Krstich	
LW5251	Music for 2 Pianos (Tchaikovsky, Borodin)	Rawicz	Landauer
LW5253	Mozart: Arias from Figaro, Giovanni	VPO	Kleiber/Krips Siepi
LW5254	Lieder Recital (Brahms 49 German Folksongs, Wolf Ital Songbook)	Delman (sop)	Newton (piano)
LW5255	Gounod: Mireille (hlts)	PCO	Erede Robin (sop)
LW5256	Kodaly: Hary Janos Suite	LPO	Solti
LW5257	Schubert: Symphony 8 (Unfinished)	VPO	Bohm
LW5258	Mendelssohn: Symphony 4	LSO	Krips
LW5259	Beethoven: Symphony 8	VPO	Bohm
LW5260	Mozart: Piano Concerto K449	LPO	Gulda
LW5261	Mozart: Clarinet Concerto K622	LSO	Collins de Peyer
LW5262	Mozart: Symphony 35 (Haffner)	LPO	Van Beinum
LW5263	Handel (arr Harty): Water Music	LPO	Van Beinum
LW5264	Haydn: Symphony 94	Ccgbw	Van Beinum
LW5265	Mozart: Symphony 39	LSO	Krips
LW5267	Debussy: La Mer	OSR	Ansermet
LW5269	Brahms: Haydn Variations	Ccgbw	Van Beinum
LW5271	Operatic Recital (Puccini, Ponchielli, Giordano)	AdSC	Previtali Labo (ten)
LW5272	Mozart: Violin Concerto K216	StCO	Munchinger Ferras
LW5273	Haydn: Symphony 104	LSO	Krips
LW5274	Tchaikovsky: Suite 3 (Variations)	PCO	Schuricht
LW5275	Borodin: Symphony 2	OSR	Ansermet
LW5276	Rimsky-Korsakov: Golden Cockerel Suite	OSR	Ansermet
LW5277	V-Williams: The Wasps Suite	LPO	Boult
LW5278	Debussy: Suite Bergamasque		Gulda (piano)
LW5279	Villa-Lobos: Bachianas Brasileiras 4		Ballon (piano)
LW5280	Haydn: Symphony 88	VPO	Munchinger
LW5281	Mozart: Symphony 29	OSR	Maag
LW5282	Ibert: Divertissement	PCO	Desormiere
LW5283	Debussy: Nocturnes	OSR	Ansermet
LW5284	Tchaikovsky: Sleeping Beauty Suite	PCO	Desormiere
LW5287	Mozart: Symphony 40	LSO	Krips
LW5288	Haydn: Symphony 102	LPO	Solti
LW5289	Tchaikovsky: Swan Lake (hlts)	LSO	Fistoulari
LW5290	Bruch: Violin Concerto Op 44	LSO	Fistoulari Elman
LW5293	Haydn: Symphony 92	LSO	Krips
LW5294	Mozart: Piano Concerto K414	Aldeburgh	Britten

LW5295	Mendelssohn: Midsummer Nights Dream Incidental Music	Ccgbw	Van Beinum
LW5296	Prokofiev: Love of Three Oranges Suite	LPO	Boult
LW5297	Orch Showpieces in HiFi (Sullivan, Grainger, etc)	NewSO	Collins
LW5298	Tchaikovsky: Sleeping Beauty (hlts)	PCO	Fistoulari
LW5299	Mozart: Symphony 34 K338	VPO	Bohm
LW5300	Britten: A Charm of Lullabies, Purcell: Music for a While	Bowden (alto)	Gellhorn (piano)
LW5301	Mozart: Symphony 25 K183	LSO	Solti
LW5302	Wagner: Wesendonck Lieder	VPO	Knappertsbusch Flagstad
LW5303	Schumann: Symphony 3	PCO	Schuricht
LW5304	Rimsky-Korsakov: May Night, Russian Easter Festival	OSR	Ansermet
LW5305	Massenet: Scènes Pittoresques	PCO	Wolff
LW5306	Sarasate: Zigeunerweisen, Wieniawski: Légende op 17	LSO	Gamba Campoli
LW5315	Mozart: Symphony 33	Cgbw	Van Beinum
LW5316	Mozart: Symphony 38	VPO	Bohm
LW5317	Haydn: Symphony 96	Cgbw	Van Beinum
LW5318	Grieg: Holberg Suite op 40	StCO	Munchinger
LW5319	Berlioz: Damnation of Faust (hlts)	LSO	Fistoulari Kolassi
LW5320	Wagner: Gotterdammerung (Rhine Journey, Funeral Music)	VPO	Knappertsbusch
LW5321	Berlioz: Ovs King Lear, Corsair	PCO	Wolff
LW5323	Tchaikovsky: Rococo Variations	OSR	Ansermet Gendron
LW5325	Ponchielli: Dance of the Hours, Mascagni, etc	LSO	Gamba
LW5326	Rimsky-Korsakov: Antar Symphonic Suite	OSR	Ansermet
LW5327	Mozart: Symphony 31, Marriage of Figaro Ov	LSO	Krips
LW5328	Schubert: Symphony 3 D200	Cincinatti SO	Johnson
LW5329	Liadov: Baba-Yaga, Kikimora, etc	OSR	Ansermet
LW5332	Dvorak: Serenade for Strings op 22	IPO	Kubelik
LW5334	Haydn: Scena di Berenice, St Cecilia Mass (hlts)	Haydn Orch	Newstone Vyvyan
LW5335	Operatic Recital (Gluck, Mascagni, Verdi, Debussy, Dvorak)	LSO	Fistoulari Borkh (sop)
LW5336	Strauss,R: Der Rosenkavalier (hlts)	VPO	Kleiber Gueden Jurinac
LW5337	Schumann: Piano Concerto op 54	LSO	Krips Kempff
LW5338	Tchaikovsky: Eugene Onegin (hlts)	Belgrade Opera	Danon
LW5339	Liszt: Piano Concerto 1	LSO	Fistoulari Kempff
LW5340	Schubert: Rosamunde (Overture, Entracte, Ballet in G)	Ccgbw	Van Beinum
LW5342	Handel: Messiah (choruses)	LPO	Boult
LW5343	Mozart: Magic Flute (hlts)	VPO	Bohm Gueden Simoneau
LW5344	Paganini: Violin Concerto 1 op 6	LSO	Collins Ricci
LW5346	Liszt: Piano Concerto 2	LPO	Argenta Katchen
LW5347	Chopin: Les Sylphides	PCO	Maag
LW5348	Mozart: Les Petits Riens - Ballet	StCO	Munchinger
LW5349	Bartok: Music for Strings Percussion and Celesta	OSR	Ansermet
LW5350	Grieg: Piano Concerto op 16	LSO	Fistoulari Curzon
LW5352	Bruch: Violin Concerto 1	LSO	Gamba Ricci
LW5353	Song Recital	Ferrier	Stone (piano)
LW5354	Noel Coward: London Morning	LPO	Corbett

Decca BR (10")

The Decca 10" mono BR series was launched in late 1959 initially under the title "Immortal Masterpieces". As the series was enlarged other titles were used, e.g. "Favourite Ballet Music" and "Artists Portrait Series".

The label is bright blue with silver lettering. Although a few of the BR issues were new recordings they were generally reissues of material from LXT, LX, and LK originals. From 1961 some BRs were reissued in stereo with the prefix SWL. The entire BR/SWL series was deleted from the catalogue from October 1967.

BR3001	Beethoven: Piano Concerto 1		VPO	Schmidt-Isserstedt Backhaus
BR3002	Ravel: Bolero, la Valse		PCO	Ansermet
BR3003	Rossini: Ovs Tell, Tancredi, Cenerentola, Siege of Corinth		LSO	Gamba
BR3004	Mendelssohn: Symphony 4		IPO	Solti
BR3005	Bizet: L'Arlesienne Suite		OSR	Ansermet
BR3006	Grieg: Peer Gynt Suite		LSO	Fjeldstad
BR3007	Bach,JS: Brandenburg Concertos 3, 5		StCO	Munchinger
BR3008	Mozart: Piano Concerto K537		NewSO	Collins Gulda
BR3009	Falla: El Amor Brujo		OSR	Ansermet de Gabarain (mezzo)
BR3010	Beethoven: Piano Sonatas 8, 14			Backhaus
BR3011	Tchaikovsky: Swan Lake (hlts)		OSR	Ansermet
BR3012	Tchaikovsky: Nutcracker Suite (hlts)		OSR	Ansermet
BR3013	Delibes: Coppelia (hlts)		OSR	Ansermet
BR3014	Rossini-Respighi: La Boutique Fantasque		IPO	Solti
BR3015	Meyerbeer: les Patineurs (hlts), Massenet: Le Cid (hlts)		IPO	Martinon
BR3016	Adam: Giselle (hlts)		PCO	Martinon
BR3017	Gretry: Ballet Suite, Gluck: Ballet Suite 1		NewSO	Irving
BR3018	Mozart: Piano Concerto K595		VPO	Bohm Backhaus
BR3019	Haydn: Symphony 101		VPO	Munchinger
BR3020	Beethoven: Ovs Egmont, Coriolan, Leonora 3		VPO	Munchinger
BR3021	Strauss,R: Salome (hlts)		VPO	Krauss Goltz Patzak
BR3022	Puccini: La Fanciulla del West (hlts)		AdSC	Capuana Tebaldi Del Monaco
BR3023	Puccini: Madama Butterfly (hlts)		AdSC	Serafin Tebaldi Bergonzi
BR3024	Verdi: Il Trovatore (hlts)		Geneva	Erede Simionato Del Monaco
BR3025	Mozart: Don Giovanni (hlts)		VPO	Krips Gueden Della Casa
BR3026	Mozart: Marriage of Figaro (hlts)		VPO	Kleiber Gueden Della Casa
BR3027	Gounod: Romeo et Juliette (hlts)		PCO	Erede Micheau Rehfuss
BR3028	Ponchielli: La Gioconda (hlts)		Florence	Gavazzeni Simionato
BR3029	Tchaikovsky: Sleeping Beauty (hlts)		OSR	Ansermet
BR3030	Debussy: Faune Prelude, Dukas: Poeme danse: La Peri		OSR	Ansermet
BR3031	Mahler: Kindertotenlieder		VPO	Boult Flagstad
BR3032	Chopin: Piano Works			Kempff
BR3033	Strauss,J: Der Zigeunerbaron (hlts)		VPO	Krauss Patzak
BR3034	Lehar: Der Zarewitsch (hlts)		Zurich Tonhalle	Reinshagen Della Casa
BR3035	Lehar: Giuditta (hlts)		Vienna Op	Moralt Gueden
BR3037	Haydn: Trumpet Concerto, Mozart: Flute Concerto K314		OSR	Ansermet Longinotti Pepin
BR3038	Beethoven: Piano Concerto 3		VPO	Schmidt-Isserstedt Backhaus
BR3039	Grieg: Sigurd Jorsalfar Suite,		LSO	Fjeldstad
	Holberg Suite		StCO	Munchinger
BR3040	Wagner: Gotterdammerung (hlts)		Norwegian	Fjeldstad Flagstad Svanholm
BR3041	Debussy: La Boite a Joujoux, Danse		OSR	Ansermet
BR3042	Tchaikovsky: Piano Concerto 1		VPO	Solti Curzon
BR3043	Waltzes and Polkas by the Strauss Family		VPO	Knappertsbusch/Krips

BR3044	Waltzes and Polkas by the Strauss Family	VPO	Boskovsky
BR3045	Waltzes and Polkas by the Strauss Family	VPO	Boskovsky
BR3046	Ballet Waltzes (Swan Lake,Sleeping Beauty,Nutcracker,Coppelia)	OSR	Ansermet
BR3047	Liszt: Chopin, Weber, Khachaturian	PCO	Munchinger Wolff
BR3048	Schumann: Piano Concerto in Amin	VPO	Wand Backhaus
BR3049	Schumann: Le Carnaval	OSR	Ansermet
BR3050	Mozart: Symphony 41	IPO	Krips
BR3051	Schubert: Symphony 5	IPO	Solti
BR3052	Folk Song Recital	Ferrier	Spurr (piano)
BR3053	Operatic Recital (Tchaikovsky, Verdi, Lehar, etc)	Vienna State	Moralt Welitsch
BR3054	Giordano: Andrea Chenier (hlts)	AdSC	Gavazzeni Tebaldi Del Monaco
BR3055	Sullivan: The Mikado (hlts)	NewSO	Isidore Godfrey
BR3056	Sullivan: Pirates of Penzance (hlts)	D'Oyly Carte	Isidore Godfrey
BR3057	Mozart: Clarinet Concerto K622	LSO	Maag De Peyer
BR3058	Beethoven: Symphony 8, Egmont Ov	OSR	Ansermet
BR3059	Song Recital (Strauss, Wolf, Grieg, Sibelius)	LSO	Fjeldstad Flagstad
BR3060	Delibes: Sylvia Ballet,	OSR	Ansermet
	La Source (hlts)	PCO	Maag
BR3061	Puccini: La Boheme (hlts)	AdSC	Serafin Bergonzi Tebaldi
BR3062	Operatic Recital (Beethoven, Offenbach, J Strauss)	VPO	Patzak (tenor)
BR3063	Concert (Wagner, Brahms, J Strauss)	VPO	Knappertsbusch
BR3064	Operatic and Song Recital	LSO	Gibson Berganza
BR3065	Piano Recital (Bach,Handel,Liszt,Beethoven,Chopin)		Kempff
BR3066	Song Recital (Schubert and British Songs)	Pears	Bream Britten
BR3067	Tchaikovsky: Serenade for Strings op 48	IPO	Solti
BR3068	Sibelius: Symphony 5	LSO	Collins
BR3069	Mozart: Piano Concerto K450	StCO	Munchinger Kempff
BR3070	Beethoven: Grosse Fuge op 133, Leonora Ov 2	OSR	Ansermet
BR3071	Bizet: Symphony in C	OSR	Ansermet
BR3072	Haydn: Symphony 45	Aldeburgh Fest Orch	Britten
BR3073	Beethoven: Piano Concerto 2	VPO	Schmidt-Isserstedt Backhaus
BR3074	Prokofiev: Lt Kije	PCO	Boult
	Stravinsky: Renard	OSR	Ansermet
BR3075	Bach,JS: Organ Works		Karl Richter
BR3076	Liszt: Les Preludes, The Huns	OSR	Argenta/Ansermet
BR3078	Concert (Weber, Rimsky-Korsakov, Bizet, Tchaikovsky, Debussy)	OSR	Ansermet
BR3079	Britten: Nocturne	LSO strings	Pears
BR3080	Moussorgsky: Pictures at an Exhibition	OSR	Ansermet
BR3081	Bach,JS: Brandenburg Concertos 2, 4	StCO	Munchinger
BR3082	Mozart: 6 Dances K509,	LSO	Maag
	Divertimento K251	StCO	Munchinger
BR3083	Rodrigo: Guitar Concerto, etc	NOS	Argenta Yepes
BR3084	Donizetti: L'Elisir d'amore (hlts)	Florence	Molinari-Pradelli Gueden
BR3085	Mozart: Cosi fan Tutte (hlts)	VPO	Bohm Della Casa
BR3086	Mendelssohn: Midsummer Nights Dream (hlts)	LSO	Maag
BR3087	Puccini: Turandot (hlts)	AdSC	Erede Tebaldi Del Monaco
BR3088	Rossini: Barber of Seville (hlts)	Florence	Erede Simionato
BR3089	Wagner: Mastersingers (final scene)	VPO	Knappertsbusch Schoeffler
BR3090	Schubert: Rosamunde (hlts)	OSR	Ansermet
BR3091	Puccini: Tosca (hlts)	AdSC	Molinari-Pradelli Tebaldi
BR3092	Verdi: Otello (hlts)	AdSC	Erede Tebaldi Del Monaco
BR3093	Ravel: Mother Goose Suite, Alborada del Gracioso	OSR	Ansermet
BR3095	Boito: Mefistofele (hlts)	AdSC	Serafin Tebaldi Del Monaco
BR3096	Handel: Organ Concertos 13, 16	Richter CO	Karl Richter (organ)
BR3097	"Carnegie Hall Encores" (Schubert,Schumann,Liszt,Brahms, etc)		Backhaus
BR3098	Corelli: Concerto Grosso 8, Mozart: Eine Kleine Nachtmusik	StCO	Munchinger

BR3099	Albeniz: Iberia	OSR	Ansermet
BR3100	Strauss,R: Capriccio (closing scene), 4 Last Songs	VPO	Bohm/Hollreiser Della Casa
BR3101	Schumann: Symphony 1	LSO	Krips
BR3102	Mozart: Horn Concertos 2, 4	LSO	Maag Tuckwell
BR3104	Grieg: Piano Concerto in Amin	LSO	Fjeldstad Curzon
BR3105	Smetana: Ma Vlast (hlts)	VPO	Kubelik
BR3107	Beethoven: Piano Sonatas 15 (Pastoral), 26 (Les Adieux)		Backhaus
BR3108	Prokofiev: Peter and the Wolf	LSO	Henderson Lillie (narrator)
BR3109	Bizet: Carmen Suite (hlts)	OSR	Ansermet
BR3110	Tchaikovsky: Violin Concerto	LSO	Sargent Ricci
BR3112	Operatic Recital (Mozart,Verdi,Meyerbeer,Donizetti,etc)	Various orch/cond	Sutherland

The BR 85xx series was issued from October 1962 at the same time as corresponding stereo SWL discs with parallel numbering. The label was identical with the earlier BR3xxx series. All discs (mono and stereo) were deleted from the catalogue in October 1967.

BR8500	Beethoven: Piano Sonatas Op 109, Op 111		Backhaus
BR8501	Verdi: Arias from Aida and Otello	VPO	Karajan Tebaldi
BR8502	Stravinsky: Petrushka	IPO	Maazel
BR8503	Britten: Cello Sonata, Debussy: Cello Sonata	Rostropovich	Britten
BR8504	Debussy: Images	OSR	Ansermet
BR8505	Rimsky-Korsakov: Snow Maiden Suite	OSR	Ansermet
	Rachmaninov: Paganini Variations	LPO	Boult Katchen
BR8506	Verdi: Arias (La Traviata, Rigoletto, Ernani, etc)	ROHCG	Molinari-Pradelli Sutherland
BR8507	Haydn: Canzonettes, Britten: 6 Holderlin Fragments	Britten	Pears
BR8508	Handel: Messiah (choruses)	LSO	Boult
BR8519	Mozart: Sinfonia Concertante K364	MPO	Kondrashin D&I Oistrakh
BR8521	Chopin: Piano Concerto 2	LSO	Zinman Ashkenazy

Decca ACL
"Ace of Clubs"

The Ace of Clubs series, Decca's first reduced price LPs and mainly reissues of LXT and LX originals was introduced in June 1958 and issues continued until 1969 by which time Decca had introduced the stereo Ace of Diamonds series and the Eclipse label. The majority of ACL issues had been withdrawn by 1973.

Label: The label is dark green with silver lettering with the Ace of Clubs logo in the upper half.

ACL 1	Beethoven: Symphony 5		PCO	Schuricht	[LXT2513]
ACL 2	Beethoven: Symphony 6		LPO	Kleiber	[LXT2587]
ACL 3	Tchaikovsky: Symphony 5		Hamburg RSO	Schmidt-Isserstedt	[LXT2758]
ACL 4	Mendelssohn: Violin Concerto		LPO	Van Beinum Campoli	[LX3001]
ACL 5	Beethoven: Violin Concerto		LPO	Boult Ricci	[LXT2750]
ACL 6	Rachmaninov: Piano Concerto 2		LSO	Fistoulari Katchen	[LXT2595]
ACL 7	Rossini-Respighi: La Boutique Fantasque		LSO	Ansermet	[LXT2555]
ACL 8	Chopin: Les Sylphides, Tchaikovsky: Sleeping Beauty		PCO	Desormiere	[LXT2868/2610]
ACL 9	Bizet: L'Arlesienne Suites, Carmen		LPO	Van Beinum	[LXT2510]
ACL 10	Tchaikovsky: Overtures 1812, Hamlet		LPO	Boult	[LXT2696]
ACL 11	Tchaikovsky: Romeo & Juliet Ov,		LPO	Van Beinum	[LXT2531]
	Capriccio Italien		PCO	Schuricht	[LXT2761]
ACL 12	"Music from Spain" (Falla,Granados,Turina,Albeniz)		PCO	Jorda	[LXT2521]
ACL 13	Franck: Symphony, Symphonic Variations		PCO	Munch E.Joyce	[LXT2692]
ACL 14	Brahms: Symphony 3		VPO	Bohm	[LXT2843]
ACL 15	Rossini: Overtures Tell, Magpie, Silken Ladder, etc		Ccgbw	Van Beinum	[LXT2733]
ACL 16	Strauss,R: Till Eulenspiegel, Don Juan		VPO	Krauss	[LXT2549]
ACL 17	Brahms: Violin Concerto		VPO	Schuricht Ferras	[LXT2949]
ACL 18	Dvorak: New World Symphony		NSOL	Jorda	[LXT2608]
ACL 19	Handel: Water Music		Boyd Neel Orchestra		[LXT2988]
ACL 20	Tchaikovsky: Symphony 6		PCO	Munch	[LXT2544]
ACL 21	Rachmaninov: Piano Concerto 3		LSO	Collins Lympany	[LXT2701]
ACL 22	Wagner: Tannhauser, Dutchman, Ride of the Valkyries		VPO	Knappertsbusch	[LXT2822]
ACL 23	Dvorak: Slavonic Dances, Brahms: Hungarian Dances		Hamburg SO	Schmidt-Isserstedt	[LXT2814]
ACL 24	Strauss,J: "A Night in Vienna"		VPO	Krauss	[LXT2634]
ACL 25	Tchaikovsky: Violin Concerto		LPO	Boult Elman	[LXT2970]
ACL 26	Holst: The Planets		LSO	Sargent	[LXT2871]
ACL 27	Berlioz: Symphonie Fantastique		Ccgbw	Van Beinum	[LXT2642]
ACL 28	Weber: Overtures Euryanthe, Oberon, Preciosa, Peter Schmoll		VPO	Bohm	[LXT2633]
ACL 29	Bach,JS: Suites 2 & 3		StCO	Munchinger	
	[LX3043/3002]				
ACL 30	Britten: Young Person's Guide		Cgbw	Van Beinum	[LXT2886]
	Prokofiev: Peter & The Wolf		LPO	Malko Philips	[LX3003]
ACL 31	Stravinsky: Petrushka		OSR	Ansermet	[LXT2502]
ACL 32	Schubert: The Trout Quintet		Vienna Octet	Panhoffer	[LXT2533]
ACL 33	Mendelssohn: Overtures (Ruy Blas, Fingal's Cave,				
	Calm Sea & Prosperous Voyage, Fair Melusina)		VPO	Schuricht	[LXT2961]
ACL 34	Sibelius: Symphony 2		LSO	Collins	[LXT2815]
ACL 35	Beethoven: Symphony 3		VPO	Kleiber	[original]
ACL 36	Beethoven: Piano Concerto 4		VPO	Krauss Backhaus	[LXT2629]
ACL 37	St-Saens: Danse Macabre, Chabrier: Espana, Marche Joyeuse,				
	Ravel: Pavane		OSR	Ansermet	[LXT2760]
ACL 38	Bizet: Carmen (hlts)		PCO	Wolff	[LXT2615-7]

Catalog	Work	Orchestra	Conductor	Original
ACL 39	Mozart: Requiem in Dmin	Vienna Hofmusikkapelle	Krips	[LX3030-1]
ACL 40	Tchaikovsky: Nutcracker Suites 1 & 2	PCO	Fistoulari	[LXT2611]
ACL 41	Haydn: Symphony 94,	Cgbw	Van Beinum	[LXT2686]
	Symphony 100	LPO	Krips	[LXT2683]
ACL 42	Khachaturian: Piano Concerto	LPO	Fistoulari Lympany	[LXT2767]
ACL 43	Rimsky-Korsakov: Le Coq D'Or Suite, Capriccio Espagnol	OSR	Ansermet	[LXT2769]
ACL 44	Brahms: Acad Fest Ov, Tragic Ov, Haydn Variations	Ccgbw	Van Beinum	[LXT2778]
ACL 45	Ballet Excerpts (Swan Lake, Don Quixote, Sleeping Beauty, etc)	LSO/PCO	Fistoulari	[original]
ACL 46	Dvorak: Symphony 8	Ccgbw	Szell	[LXT2641]
ACL 47	Mozart: Clarinet Quintet	Italian Qt	De Bavier	[LXT2698]
ACL 48	Mussorgsky-Ravel: Pictures at an Exhibition, Ravel: la Valse	PCO	Ansermet	[LXT2896]
ACL 49	"A Night in Vienna" vol 2	VPO	Krauss	[LXT2645]
ACL 50	Brahms: Symphony 2	LPO	Furtwangler	[LXT2586]
ACL 51	Chabrier: Suite Pastorale, Bizet: Jeux D'Enfants	PCO	Lindenburg	[LXT2860]
ACL 52	Bach,JS: Cantatas	Jacques Orch	Jacques Ferrier	[LX3006-7]
ACL 53	Ravel: Daphnis & Chloe	OSR	Ansermet	[LXT2775]
ACL 54	Grieg: Peer Gynt Suites 1 & 2	LPO	Cameron	[LK4008]
ACL 55	Elgar: Enigma Vns, Suite from the Dramatic Music of Purcell	LSO	Sargent	[LXT2786]
ACL 56	Works for Trumpet & Orch (Haydn, Vivaldi, Purcell)	Unicorn Orch	Dickson Voisin Ghitalla	
ACL 57	Beethoven: Symphony 7	Ccgbw	Kleiber	[LXT2547]
ACL 58	Liszt: Piano Concertos 1, 2	LSO	Fistoulari Kempff	[LXT5025]
ACL 59-61	Puccini: Madame Butterfly	AdSC	Erede Tebaldi	[LXT2638-40]
ACL 62	Meyerbeer: Les Patineurs, Massenet: Le Cid	LSO	Irving	[LXT2746]
ACL 63	Tchaikovsky: Piano Concerto 1, Liszt: Hungarian Fantasia	LSO	Gamba Katchen	[LXT5164]
ACL 64	Bruch: Violin Concerto 1	LSO	R-Kisch Campoli	[LXT2596]
	St-Saens: Havanaise, Intro & Rondo Capriccioso	LSO	Fistoulari Campoli	[LW5085]
ACL 65	Rachmaninov: Paganini Vns, Dohnanyi: Nursery Song Vns	LPO	Boult Katchen	[LXT2862]
ACL 66	Mozart: Symphony 35 (Haffner),	LPO	Van Beinum	[LXT2534]
	Symphony 40	LPO	Kleiber	[LX3022]
ACL 67	Handel: Messiah (hlts)	ZIM	Thompson Stone	[Kapp]
ACL 68-9	Bach,JS: Brandenburg Concertos	StCO	Munchinger	[LXT5198-9]
ACL 70	Schubert: Symphony 9	Ccgbw	Krips	[LXT2719]
ACL 71	Brahms: Symphony 1	Ccgbw	Van Beinum	[LXT2675]
ACL 72	Sibelius: Symphony 5, Karelia Suite	DSRO	Tuxen	[LXT2744]
ACL 73	Strauss,J: Die Fledermaus (hlts)	VPO	Krauss Gueden	[LXT2550-1]
ACL 74	Delibes: Coppelia	PCO	Desormiere	[LM4501]
ACL 75	Kodaly: Hary Janos Suite, Dances of Galanta	LPO	Solti	[LXT5059/2771]
ACL 76	Sibelius: En Saga, Tapiola	Ccgbw	Van Beinum	[LXT2776]
ACL 77	Beethoven: Symphony 9	OSR	Ansermet	[SXL2274]
ACL 78	Stravinsky: Firebird Suite, Ravel: Rapsodie Espagnole	OSR	Ansermet	[LX3045/LXT2637]
ACL 79	Adam: Giselle Ballet Music	Paris Opera	Blareau	[LXT2844]
ACL 80	"Strauss Concert" (Waltzes and Polkas)	VPO	Krauss	[LXT2755]
ACL 81	"Famous French Overtures" (Zampa, White Lady, etc)	LPO	Martinon	[LXT2606]
ACL 82	Prokofiev: Symphony 5	DSRO	Tuxen	[LXT2764]
ACL 83	Berlioz: Overtures Corsaire, King Lear, Francs-Juges, etc	PCO	Wolff	[LXT5162]
ACL 84	Beethoven: Piano Concerto 1, Moonlight Sonata	VPO	Bohm Gulda	[LXT2627]
ACL 85	Schubert: Rosamunde (Incidental Music),			
	Mendelssohn: Midsummer Nights Dream	Ccgbw	Van Beinum	[LXT2770]
ACL 86	Schubert: Symphony 8, Beethoven: Symphony 8	VPO	Bohm	[LXT2998/2824]
ACL 87	Suppe: Overture (Poet&Peasant, Pique Dame, Light Cavalry, etc)	LPO	Solti	[LXT2589]
ACL 88	Mozart: Posthorn Serenade K320	OSR	Maag	[LXT2671]
ACL 89	Tchaikovsky: Suite 3,	PCO	Schuricht	[LXT2761]
	Francesca da Rimini	PCO	Jorda	[LXT2531]
ACL 90	Mendelssohn: Symphony 4	LSO	Krips	[LXT2887]
	Haydn: Symphony 104	LPO	Krips	[LXT2683]
ACL 91	Vivaldi: The Four Seasons	StCO	Munchinger	[LXT2600]

ACL 92	Dvorak: Cello Concerto	LSO	Krips Nelsova	[LXT2727]
ACL 93	Sullivan: Overtures (Gondoliers, Pinafore, Mikado, Pirates, etc)	New SO	Godfrey	
ACL 94	St-Saens: Piano Concerto 2	LPO	Martinon Lympany	[LX3064]
	Chopin: Piano Concerto 1	LPO	Boult Gulda	[LXT2925]
ACL 95	Beethoven: Symphony 4	LPO	Solti	[LXT2564]
ACL 96	Mozart: Serenade K525, Divertimento K136	StCO	Munchinger	[LX3061]
ACL 97	Beethoven: Overtures Egmont, Coriolan, Leonora 3, Fidelio, Prometheus, Consecration of the House	LPO	Beinum	[LW5015,6,8]
ACL 98	Beethoven: Piano Concerto 5	VPO	Krauss Backhaus	[LXT2839]
ACL 99	"Vienna Philharmonic Pops"	VPO	Krauss	[LXT2913]
ACL100-1	Tchaikovsky: Swan Lake (abridged)	LSO	Fistoulari Campoli	[LXT2681-2]
ACL102	Falla: Nights in the Gardens of Spain	LSO	Jorda Curzon	[LXT2621]
	Grieg: Piano Concerto	LSO	Fistoulari Curzon	[LXT2657]
ACL103	Brahms: Symphony 3	Ccgbw	Szell	[LXT2676]
ACL104	Offenbach: Overtures (Orpheus, Belle Helene, Bluebeard, etc)	LPO	Martinon	[LXT2590]
ACL105	Mozart: Divertimento 17 in D K334	Vienna Octet		[LXT2542]
ACL106	Debussy: La Mer, Nocturnes	OSR	Ansermet	[LXT2632/2637]
ACL107	Mozart: Symphony 33	Ccgbw	Van Beinum	[LXT2686]
	Haydn: Symphony 103	LPO	Solti	[LX3018]
ACL108	"Showpieces for Orch" (Ponchielli, Mascagni, Sullivan, etc)	LSO	Gamba	[LXT5325]
ACL109-11	Bach,JS: St Matthew Passion	Jacques Orch	Jacques Ferrier	[from 78s]
ACL112	Gounod: Faust, Ponchielli: Gioconda, Thomas: Mignon (hlts)	PCO	Fistoulari	[LK4018]
ACL113	Arnold: English Dances 1-8, Bax: Tintagel, Elgar, Holst, etc	LPO	Boult	[LXT5015]
ACL114	Liszt: Hungarian Rhapsodies 2,4	PCO	Wolff	
	Tchaikovsky: Marche Slave, Sibelius:Finlandia [LW5150/5114/5141]	DSRO	Tuxen	
ACL115	Schubert: Symphony 6	LSO	Krips	[LXT2585]
ACL116	Beethoven: Symphony 2,	VPO	Schuricht	[LXT2724]
	Overture Leonora 2	VPO	Krauss	[LW5164]
ACL117	Wagner: Tristan & Isolde hlts, Gotterdammerung hlts	PCO	Schuricht	[LXT5026]
ACL118-20	Handel: Messiah	LPO	Boult Vyvyan	[LXT2921-4]
ACL121-2	Puccini: La Boheme	AdSC	Erede Tebaldi	[LXT2622-3]
ACL123	Prokofiev: Classical Symphony, Glinka, Borodin, Mussorgsky	OSR	Ansermet	[LXT2833]
ACL124	Lalo: Symphonie Espagnole	LPO	Van Beinum Campoli	[LXT2801]
	Falla: Love the Magician	LPO	Collins Campoli	[LXT2518]
ACL125	Beethoven: Archduke Trio	Trio di Trieste		[LXT2717]
ACL126	Dvorak: Symphony 2	Hamburg SO	Schmidt-Isserstedt	[LXT2807]
ACL127	Tchaikovsky: Symphony 4	OSR	Denzler	[original]
ACL128	Mozart: Symphonies 31 (Paris), 40	LSO	Krips	[LXT2689/2819]
ACL129	Tchaikovsky: Symphony 6	OSR	Ansermet	[LXT5306]
ACL130	Puccini: Madama Butterfly (hlts)	AdSC	Erede Tebaldi	[LXT2638-40]
ACL131	Elgar: Introduction & Allegro for Strings, Serenade for Strings, Delius: Brigg Fair, On Hearing the First Cuckoo in Spring	LSO	Collins	[LXT2699/2788]
ACL132	Brahms: Symphony 4	LSO	Krips	[LXT5368]
ACL133-4	Tchaikovsky: Sleeping Beauty (abridged)	PCO	Fistoulari	[LXT2762-3]
ACL135	Haydn: Symphony 92, Mozart: Symphony 39	LSO	Krips	[LXT2819/2689]
ACL136	Schumann: Piano Concerto, Weber: Konzertstucke	VPO	Andreae Gulda	[LXT5280]
ACL137	Elgar:Pomp&Circumstance 1, Imperial March, Walton, Bax	LSO	Sargent	[LXT2793]
ACL138	Sibelius: 4 Legends op 22	DSRO	Jensen	[LXT2831]
ACL139-140	Rachmaninov: 24 Preludes		Lympany	[LXT2579-80]
ACL141	'Operatic Hlts for Orch'	NSOL	Erede	[LK4038]
ACL142	Auber: Overtures Bronze Horse, Crown Diamonds, Fra Diavolo	PCO	Wolff	[LXT5005]
ACL143	Mozart: Piano Concertos 13, 20	New SO	Maag Katchen	[LXT5145]
ACL144	V Williams: Greensleeves, Tallis Fantasia			[LXT2699]
	Delius: Paradise Garden, Song of Summer	LSO	Collins	[LXT2788]
ACL145-6	Strauss,J: Die Fledermaus	VPO	Krauss Gueden	[LXT2550-1]

Cat.	Work	Orch	Performer	Original
ACL147	Beethoven: Symphony 1	VPO	Schuricht	[LX3084]
	Mozart: Symphony 36	VPO	Bohm	[LXT2558]
ACL148	Beethoven: Piano Concerto 2,	VPO	Krauss Backhaus	[LX3083]
	Piano Concerto 3	VPO	Bohm Backhaus	[LXT2553]
ACL149	Mendelssohn: Symphony 3	LSO	Solti	[LXT2768]
	Verdi: Overture Force of Destiny	LPO	Solti	[LK4017]
ACL150	Strauss,J: Graduation Ball	LSO	Fistoulari	[LXT5372]
ACL151	"The Art of Erna Sack"		Erna Sack	[LM4517/4531]
ACL152	Schubert: Symphonies 4, 5	Ccgbw	Van Beinum	[LXT2779/LX3082]
ACL153	Rimsky-Korsakov: Scheherazade	PCO	Ansermet	[LXT2508]
ACL154-5	Puccini: Tosca	AdSC	Erede Tebaldi	[LXT2730-1]
ACL156	Mendelssohn: Capriccio Brilliant, Rondo Brillant,			
	Liszt: Totentanz	LPO	Martinon Katin	[LXT2932]
ACL157	Mozart: Symphonies 28, 29	OSR	Maag	[LXT2840]
ACL158	Rossini: William Tell Ballet Music, Strauss, Blue Danube Ballet	LPO	Martinon	[LXT5149]
ACL159	Prokofiev: Love of 3 Oranges, Lt Kije	LPO	Boult	[LXT5119]
ACL160	Handel: Organ Concertos op 4/1-2	OSR	Ansermet Demessieux	[LXT2759]
ACL161	Bartok: Piano Concerto 3, Prokofiev: Piano Concerto 3	OSR	Ansermet Katchen	[LXT2894]
ACL162	Handel: Water Music	LPO	Van Beinum	[LXT2792]
	Britten: 4 Sea Interludes (Peter Grimes)	Ccgbw	Van Beinum	[LXT2886]
ACL163	Puccini: Operatic Recital	AdSC	Patanè Zeani	[LXT5509]
ACL164	Coates: The Three Elizabeths Suite, Four Centuries Suite	NSOL	Coates	[LK4056]
ACL165	Tchaikovsky: Symphony 5	PCO	Solti	[LXT5241]
ACL166-7	Strauss,J: The Gypsy Baron	VPO	Krauss Patzak Loose	[LXT2612-3]
ACL168	Beethoven: Piano Concerto 4	LPO	Zecchi Haskil	
	Mozart: Piano Concerto 24	Ccgbw	Van Beinum Long	[from 78s]
ACL169	Mendelssohn: Piano Concertos 1 & 2	LSO	Collins Katin	[LXT5201]
ACL170	Sibelius: Symphony 1	LSO	Collins	[LXT2694]
ACL172-4	Verdi: Aida	AdSC	Erede	[LXT2735-7]
ACL175	"Carols for Xmas"	Westminster Abbey Choir		[LF1029-30]
ACL176	Respighi: Fountains of Rome,	OSR	Erede	[LX3153]
	Pines of Rome	AdSC	Previtali	[LXT5278]
ACL177-8	Offenbach: Tales of Hoffmann	RPO	Beecham	[LXT2582-4]
ACL179	Franck: Symphony in Dmin	VPO	Furtwangler	[LXT2905]
ACL180	Tosca (hlts)	AdSC	Erede Tebaldi	[LXT2730-1]
ACL181	Sibelius: Symphonies 3, 7	LSO	Collins	[LXT2960]
ACL182	Falla: 3 Cornered Hat, Liadov: Baba-Yaga, Kikimora	OSR	Ansermet	LXT2716/2966]
ACL183	Grieg: Piano Concerto, Litolff: Concerto Symphonique (scherzo)	LPO	Davis Katin	[original]
ACL184	Sibelius: Symphony 4, Pohjola's Daughter	LSO	Collins	[LXT2962]
ACL185	Lehar: The Merry Widow (hlts)	Zurich Tonhalle	Reinshagen	[LXT2607]
ACL186	Puccini: La Boheme (hlts)	AdSC	Erede Tebaldi	[LXT2622-3]
ACL187	Elgar: Cello Concerto,	LPO	Van Beinum Pini	[LX3023]
	Cockaigne Ov, Wand of Youth	LPO	Van Beinum	[LXT2525]
ACL188	Mahler: Symphony 1	VPO	Kubelik	[LXT2973]
ACL189	Ibert: Divertissement, Poulenc: Les Biches Ballet Suite	PCO Desormiere		[LW5282/LXT2720]
ACL190	Music for Trumpet & Orch vol 2	Voisin & Rhea (trumpets)		[original]
ACL191	Music for Trumpet & Orch vol 3	Voisin & Rhea (trumpets)		[original]
ACL192	Tchaikovsky: Rococo Vns, Schumann: Cello Concerto	OSR	Ansermet Gendron	[LXT2895]
ACL193	Verdi: Aida (hlts)	AdSC	Erede	[LXT2735-7]
ACL194	Telemann : Suite in Amin, Vivaldi : Concertos in Cmaj, Gmin	Krainis Baroque Ensemble		[original]
ACL195	Lehar: Der Graf von Luxemburg, abridged	Zurich Tonhalle	Reinshagen	[LXT2593]
ACL196	Haydn: Symphonies 96, 97	Ccgbw	Van Beinum	[LXT2847]
ACL197	Handel: Messiah (hlts)	LPO	Boult Vyvyan	[LXT2921-4]
ACL198	Rossini: Overtures William Tell, Cenerentola, Tancredi, etc	LSO	Gamba	[LXT5137]
ACL199-200	Mascagni: Cavalleria Rusticana	Orch	Ghione Nicolai	[LXT2928-9]
ACL201-2	Leoncavallo: Pagliacci	AdSC	Erede Del Monaco	[LXT5223-5]

Cat. No.	Work	Orch.	Artist	Original
ACL203-5	Verdi: Rigoletto	AdSC	Erede Gueden	[LXT5006-8]
ACL206-7	Strauss,R: Salome	VPO	Krauss Patzak Goltz	[LXT2863-4]
ACL211	Beethoven: Kreutzer Sonata, Mozart: Violin Sonata K454		Kulenkampff Solti (piano)	[1st UK issue]
ACL212	Mahler: Symphony 4	Ccgbw	Van Beinum Ritchie	[LXT2718]
ACL216	French Overtures (Berlioz, Lalo, Massenet, St-Saens)	Opera Comique	Wolff	[LXT2625]
ACL217	Liszt: Recital (Liebestraume 1-3, Hungn Rhapsodies 2,6,15, etc)		Katin	[LXT2971]
ACL218	Glazunov: The Seasons etc,	PCO	Wolff	[LXT5240]
	Bach/Walton: The Wise Virgins Ballet Suite	LPO	Boult	[LW5157]
ACL219	Scarlatti: The Good Humoured Ladies	PCO	Desormiere	[LXT2720]
	Walton: Facade Suite	LSO	Irving	[LXT2791]
ACL220-2	Mendelssohn: Elijah	LPO	Krips	[LXT5000-2]
ACL223	Haydn: Symphony 49, Mozart: Divertimento 2	LMP	Blech	[LXT2753]
ACL224	Elgar: Wand of Youth,	LPO	Van Beinum	[LXT5015]
	Walton, Butterworth	LPO	Boult	[LXT2525/5028]
ACL225	Music for French Horn&Orch (Telemann,Handel, Steinmetz,etc)	Kapp Sinfonietta	Stagliano Berv	[original]
ACL226	Mozart: Symphony 39, 4 German Dances, Weber: Symphony 1	Cologne RSO	Kleiber	[1st UK issue]
ACL227	Brahms: Piano Concerto 1	Cgbw	Van Beinum Curzon	[LXT2825]
ACL228	Sibelius: Symphony 6, Pelleas & Melisande Suite	LSO	Collins	[LXT5084]
ACL229	Britten: Variations on a theme of Frank Bridge,	Boyd Neel Orchestra		[LXT2790]
	Soirées Musicales, Matinées Musicales	NSOL	Cree	[W91075]
ACL230	Music for Trumpet and Orch vol 4	Kapp Sinfonietta	Voisin (trumpet)	[original]
ACL231	Schumann: Symphony 3, Overture Scherzo & Finale Op 52	PCO	Schuricht	[LXT2985]
ACL232-4	Verdi: La Traviata	AdSC	Molinari-Pradelli	[LXT2992-4]
ACL235	Rachmaninov: Piano Concerto 2	NSOL	Davis Katin	[original]
ACL236	Schumann: Symphony 2	PCO	Schuricht	[LXT2745]
ACL237	Schubert: Symphony 9	Cologne	Kleiber	[1st UK issue]
ACL238	Weber: Der Freischutz (hlts)	VPO	Ackermann	[LXT2597-9]
ACL239	Bliss: Colour Symphony, Intro and Allegro	LSO	Bliss	[LXT5170]
ACL240	Mozart: Clarinet Concerto, Bassoon Concerto	LSO	Collins	[LXT2990]
ACL241	Strauss,R: Ein Heldenleben	VPO	Krauss	[LXT2729]
ACL242	Bach,JS: Organ Music		Demessieux	[LXT2915]
ACL243	Alfred Piccaver 1932-41: Popular Song Recital		Piccaver	[78s]
ACL244	St-Saens: Cello Concerto 1, Lalo: Cello Concerto	LPO	Boult Nelsova	[LXT2906]
ACL245	Delius: Paris-Song of a Great City, In a Summer Garden, etc	LSO	Collins	[LXT2899]
ACL246	Bach: Organ Concerto 2, Franck: Chorales 1, 2, 3		Demessieux	[LXT5185]
ACL247-8	V-Williams: A Sea Symphony, The Wasps	LPO	Boult	[LXT2907-8]
ACL249	Strauss,R: Aus Italien	VPO	Krauss	[LXT2917]
ACL250	Brahms: Violin Sonatas Op 78, Op 100, op 108		Kulenkampff Solti	[78s]
ACL251	The Golden Age of Brass	Brass Ensemble	Voisin	[original]
ACL252	Debussy: Piano Works vol 1		Daniel Ericourt	[original]
ACL253	Debussy: Jeux, 6 Antique Epigraphs, etc	OSR	Ansermet	[LXT5454]
ACL254	Choral Recital (Purcell, Britten, Holst)	Columbia Univ Chapel Choir		[original]
ACL255	V Williams: Symphony 2, Wasps Ov, Greensleeves	Queens Hall Orch	Henry Wood	[78s]
ACL256	Brahms: Symphony 2	VPO	Schuricht	[LXT2859]
ACL257	Faure: Ballade, Francaix: Concertino	LPO	Martinon	[LXT2963]
ACL258	Tchaikovsky: Capriccio Italien, Francesca da Rimini	LSO	Collins	[LXT5186]
ACL259	Debussy: Piano Works vol 2		Ericourt	[original]
ACL260	Ravel: Tombeau de Couperin, Valses Nobles et Sentimentales	OSR	Ansermet	[LXT5633]
ACL261	Orchestral highlights from the Opera (Mascagni, Puccini, etc)	MMF	Gavazzeni	[LXT5288]
ACL264	Barber: Symphony 2, Cello Concerto [LX3050/3048]	LSO	Barber Nelsova	
ACL266	Massenet: Orch Suites 4, 7	PCO	Wolff	[LXT5100]
ACL267	Roussel: Symphonies 3, 4	OSR	Ansermet	[LXT5234]
ACL268	Operatic Duets (Puccini and Verdi)	AdSC	various Tebaldi	[various]
ACL269	Tchaikovsky: Symphony 2 ("Little Russian")	PCO	Solti	[LXT5245]

ACL270	Roussel: Petite Suite Pour Orch, Festin de L'Araignee	OSR	Ansermet	[LXT5035]
ACL271	Recorder recital	Krainis Consort		[original]
ACL272	Albeniz: Iberia, Turina: Danzas Fantasticas	PCO	Argenta	[LXT2889]
ACL273	Gluck & Gretry: Ballet Suites	NSOL	Irving	[LXT5063]
ACL274	Beethoven: Piano Sonata 26 (Les Adieux), Eroica Variations		Gulda	[LXT2594]
ACL275	Recorder recital (Telemann, Handel, Purcell, etc)		Baghuis (recorder)	[original]
ACL276	Bizet : The Pearl Fishers (hlts), Gounod : Mireille (hlts)	PCO	Erede Micheau	[LXT2789]
ACL277	Dvorak: Piano Quintet op 81	Quintetto Chigiano		[LXT2519]
ACL278	Bloch: Sacred Service	LPO	Bloch	[LXT2516]
ACL279	Nielsen: Symphony 1	DSRO	Jensen	[LXT2748]
ACL289	V Williams : Symphony 6	LPO	Boult	[LXT2911]
ACL290	V Williams : London Symphony	LPO	Boult	[LXT2693]
ACL291	V Williams : Sinfonia Antartica	LPO	Boult Ritchie	[LXT2912]
ACL292	Nielsen: Flute Concerto, Clarinet Concerto	DSRO	Woldike/Jensen	[LXT2979]
ACL293	Gluck: Orfeo ed Euridice (hlts)	Glyndebourne Stiedry Ferrier		[LXT2893/78s]
ACL303	Song Recital (Schubert, Schumann, V Williams, etc)	Marie Wilson Quartet		[78s]
ACL305	Mahler: Das Lied von der Erde	VPO	Walter	[LXT2721-2]
ACL306	Brahms: 4 Serious Songs, Rhapsody for Orch and Contralto	LPO	Krauss Ferrier	[LXT2850]
ACL307	Lieder recital (Schumann, Schubert, Wolff) [LXT2556/5324/LW5098]		Ferrier	
ACL308	Arias from St Matthew Passion, Elijah, Gluck, Handel, etc		Ferrier	[78s]
ACL309	Recital of British Folk Songs	Ferrier	Spurr (piano)	[78s]
ACL310	Aria and Song Recital (Purcell, Handel, Bridge, etc)	Ferrier	Spurr/Stone(piano)	[various]
ACL311	V Williams: Symphonies 3, 5	LPO	Boult	[LXT2787/2910]
ACL312	Elgar: Violin Concerto	LPO	Boult Campoli	[LXT5014]
ACL313	V Williams: Job, Walton: Overture Scapino	LPO	Boult	[LXT2937/5028]
ACL314	Britten: Diversions for Piano & Orch, Sinfonia da Requiem	LSO DSRO	Britten Katchen Britten	[LXT2981]
ACL315	V Williams: Symphony 4, Old King Cole Ballet Suite	LPO	Boult	[LXT2909, LW5151]
ACL316	Elgar: Falstaff, Ireland: Minuet, Warlock: Capriol Suite	LSO Boyd Neel String Orch	Collins	[LXT2940] [LW5149]
ACL317	Bliss: Violin Concerto	LPO	Bliss Campoli	[LXT5166]
ACL318	Strauss,R: 4 Last Songs Mahler: 3 Ruckert Songs	VPO VPO	Bohm Della Casa Walter Ferrier	[LW5056] [LXT2722]
ACL319	Sibelius: Symphony 5, Night Ride and Sunrise	LSO	Collins	[LXT5083]
ACL320	Brahms: Piano Concerto 2	VPO	Knappertsbusch Curzon	[LXT5434]
ACL321	Beethoven: Piano Concerto 4	VPO	Knappertsbusch Curzon	[LXT2948]
ACL322	Rachmaninov: Piano Concerto 2	LPO	Boult Curzon	[LXT5178]
ACL323	A Tribute to Ada Alsop (Handel, Bach, Boyce, Arne, etc)	Boyd Neel String Orch		[78s]
ACL1044	"The Immortal Works of Ketèlbey"	NSOL	Stanford Robinson	

Decca Brunswick

Decca Brunswick AXTL series

A series of 12" LPs introduced from January 1953 and continuing to late 1962.

Label: The label is dark maroon with silver letters with the word 'Brunswick' in script in the upper half.

AXTL1001	Mozart: Serenade K100, Cassation K63a	ZIM	Zazofsky
AXTL1002	Boyce: Symphonies 1, 2, 7, 8	ZIM	Zazofsky
AXTL1003	Boyce: Symphonies 3, 4, 5, 6	ZIM	Zazofsky
AXTL1004	Concert (Scarlatti, Tartini, Vivaldi, Albinoni)	VdiR	Fasano
AXTL1005	Guitar recital		Segovia (guitar)
AXTL1006	V Williams: Concerto for Violin and Strings,		
	Tansman: Tryptich for String Orch	ZIM	J Fuchs
AXTL1007	Mozart: Clarinet Quintet K581	Fine Arts Quartet	Kell
AXTL1008	Brahms: Quintet in Bmaj for Clarinet and Strings op 115	Fine Arts Quartet	Kell
AXTL1009	Mozart: Serenata Notturna K239,		
	Telemann: Suite in Amin for Flute & Strings	ZIM	Pappoutsakis (flute)
AXTL1010	Segovia Concert (Handel, Bach, Scarlatti, etc)		Segovia (guitar)
AXTL1011	Mozart: Trio in Eflat maj,	Kell	J Fuchs Horszowski
	Beethoven: Trio in Bflat maj Op 11	Kell	Miller Horszowski
AXTL1012	Bach,JS: Concertos 1, 5	ZIM	Foss (piano)
AXTL1013	Mozart: Serenades for Wind Instruments K375, K388	Kell Chamber Players	
AXTL1014	Schumann: Trio op 63, Schubert: Nocturne op 148	Mannes-Gimpel-Silva Trio	
AXTL1015-6	Bach,JS: 6 Sonatas for Flute & Harpsichord	Baker (flute)	Marlowe (hpsd)
AXTL1017	Grieg: Violin Sonatas 1 op 8 & 3 op 45	J Fuchs	Sheridan
AXTL1018	Mozart: Sinfonia Concertante K364	ZIM	J Fuchs L Fuchs
AXTL1019	Beethoven: Trio 8 op posth, Clara Schumann: Trio op 17	Mannes-Gimpel-Silva Trio	
AXTL1020	Vivaldi: Concertos vol 1	VdiR	Fasano
AXTL1021	Mozart: Oboe Quartet K370	Gomberg (oboe) Galimir Banat Kouguell	
	Telemann: Sonata in Cmin for oboe and Harpsichord	Gomberg (oboe) Criasson (hpsd)	
AXTL1022	Copland: The Red Pony, Thomson: Louisiana Story	Little Orch Society	Scherman
AXTL1023	Concert (Marcello, Cirri, Albinoni, Pergolesi)	VdiR	Fasano
AXTL1024-5	Beethoven: Diabelli Variations op 120, Eroica Variations op 35		Arrau
AXTL1026	Brahms: Serenade Op 11	Little Orch Society	Scherman
AXTL1027	Bach,JS: 15 3-part Inventions		Foss (piano)
AXTL1028-9	Handel: Sonatas for Flute and Harpsichord	Baker (flute)	Marlowe (hpsd)
AXTL1030	Mozart: Duo 2 in Bflat maj for Violin and Viola K424,		
	Martinu: 3 Madrigals for Violin and Viola	J Fuchs	L Fuchs
AXTL1031	Mozart: Divertimento K563	Bel Arte Trio	
AXTL1032	Xmas Music (Corelli, Vivaldi, Scarlatti, Torelli, Boccherini)	VdiR	Fasano
AXTL1033	Beethoven: Serenade for Flute, Violin and Viola,	Baker (flute) J Fuchs L Fuchs	
	Trio for Violin, Viola, Cello	J Fuchs	L Fuchs H Fuchs
AXTL1034	Liszt: Dante Symphony	LAPO	Wallenstein
AXTL1035	Music in the Night	Cincinatti SO	Cleva
AXTL1036-1041	Bach,J.S: Well Tempered Clavier Books 1 & 2		Tureck (piano)
AXTL1042	Concert (Bonporti, Cambini, Marcello, Rossini)	VdiR	Fasano
AXTL1043	Chopin: Complete Works for Piano vol 1		Arrau
AXTL1044	Chopin: Complete Works for Piano vol 2		Arrau
AXTL1045	Beethoven: Violin Sonatas op 47 (Kreutzer), op 12/1	J Fuchs	Balsam
AXTL1046	Beethoven: Violin Sonatas 2, 10	J Fuchs	Balsam
AXTL1047	Copland: Sonata for Violin&Piano, Stravinsky: Duo Concertant	J Fuchs	Balsam Smit (piano)
AXTL1048	French Renaissance Vocal Music	Vocal & Instrumental Ensemble	Boulanger

AXTL1049	Charpentier: Excerpts from Medée	Vocal & Instrumental Ensemble	Boulanger
AXTL1050	Beethoven: Violin Sonatas Op 12/3, Op 30/6	J Fuchs	Balsam
AXTL1051	Monteverdi: Madrigals	Vocal & Instrumental Ensemble	Boulanger
AXTL1052	Beethoven: Violin Sonatas 5 ("Spring"), 8	J Fuchs	Balsam
AXTL1053	Rameau: Opera Excerpts	Vocal & Instrumental Ensemble	Boulanger
AXTL1054	Prokofiev: Quintet for Oboe, Clarinet, Violin, Viola, Double Bass op 39, Swanson: Night Music	Ensemble	Mitropoulos
AXTL1055	Music of Mexico (Chávez, Moncayo)	SO of Mexico	Chávez
AXTL1056	Beethoven: Trios op 9/1, op 9/2	Bel Arte Trio	
AXTL1057	Beethoven: Violin Sonatas op 23, op 30	J Fuchs	Balsam
AXTL1058	Beethoven: Symphony 8, Mendelssohn: Symphony 5	LAPO	Wallenstein
AXTL1059	Schubert: Symphonies 4, 5	LAPO	Wallenstein
AXTL1060	Segovia recital (Villa-Lobos, Brahms, Gluck, etc)		Segovia (guitar)
AXTL1061	Vivaldi: Concertos	VdiR	Fasano
AXTL1062	Show Pieces for Orchestra vol 1 (Borodin, Enesco, etc)	LAPO	Wallenstein
AXTL1063	Show Pieces for Orchestra vol 2 (Chabrier, Smetana, Berlioz)	LAPO	Wallenstein
AXTL1064	Brahms: Symphony 1	LAPO	Wallenstein
AXTL1065	Beethoven: Symphony 3	Stadium Concerts SO of New York	Bernstein
AXTL1066	Brahms: Symphony 4	Stadium Concerts SO of New York	Bernstein
AXTL1067	Schumann: Symphony 2	Stadium Concerts SO of New York	Bernstein
AXTL1068	Tchaikovsky: Symphony 6	Stadium Concerts SO of New York	Bernstein
AXTL1069	Bach,JS: Chaconne, Sor,Mendelssohn,Villa-Lobos,Rodrigo		Segovia (guitar)
AXTL1070	Recital (Frescobaldi, Ponce, Rameau, etc)		Segovia (guitar)
AXTL1071	Mozart: Clarinet Concerto K622	ZIM	Kell (clarinet)
	Brahms: Trio op 114	Kell Miller (cello)	Horszowski (piano)
AXTL1074	Jose Greco Ballet	Orquestra Zarzuela de Madrid	Machado
AXTL1075	Arriaga: Sinfonia a gran Orquestra, etc	Orquestra Sinfonica de Madrid	Arambarri
AXTL1076	Turina: Danzas Fantasticas, Preludios 1-5, Partita in C, etc		de Larrocha (piano)
AXTL1077	Fiesta in Madrid	Orquestra Zarzuela de Madrid	Tórroba
AXTL1078	Olé! Olé!	Orquestra Zarzuela de Madrid	Tórroba
AXTL1080	Granados: Goyescas 1, 2, 3, 4, 7		de Larrocha (piano)
AXTL1081	Music for 2 Pianos (Schubert, Strauss, Rachmaninov, etc)	Vronsky	Babin
AXTL1082	Brahms: Sonatas for Violin and Piano op 78, op 100	Goldberg	Balsam (piano)
AXTL1083	Fauré: Sonata 1 op 13, Franck: Sonata in Amaj	J Fuchs	Balsam (piano)
AXTL1084	Chopin: Etudes op 10, Impromptus 1, 2		Slenczynska (piano)
AXTL1085	Chopin: Etudes op 25, Impromptus 3, 4		Slenczynska (piano)
AXTL1086	The Play of Daniel – a 12th Century Musical Drama	NY Pro Musica Greenberg	[SXA4001]
AXTL1088	Recital (Ponce, Rodrigo, etc)	Symphony of the Air Jorda	Segovia (guitar)
AXTL1089	Recital (Weiss, Torroba, Ponce, Roussel, Granados, etc)		Segovia (guitar)
AXTL1090	Recital (Sor, Rodrigo, Granados, Castelnuovo-Tedesco, etc)		Segovia (guitar)
AXTL1091	Chopin: Scherzi 1-4		Slenczynska (piano)
AXTL1092	Recital (Castelnuovo-Tedesco, Villa-Lobos, etc)		Segovia (guitar)
AXTL1093	"Virtuosi, USA" (Paganini, Wieniawski, Bach)	Virtuosi, USA Vardi	[SXA4002]
AXTL1094	Bach,JS: Harpsichord Concertos BWV 1061, 1064, 1065	Baroque CO Saidenberg	[SXA4003]
AXTL1095	Josquin des Pres: Masses and Chansons	NY Pro Musica Motet Choir Greenberg	[SXA4004]
AXTL1096	Chopin: Ballades 1-4, Liszt: 6 Chants Polonais		Slenczynska (piano)
AXTL1097	Mozart:Sinfonia Concertante K364,Adagio K261,Rondo K373	Aeterna CO J Fuchs L Fuchs	[SXA4005]
AXTL1098	Mussorgsky:Pictures at an Exhibition,Schumann:Carnaval op 9	Moiseiwitsch (piano)	[SXA4006]
AXTL1099	Instl Music from Courts of Elizabeth and James	NY Pro Musica Ensembles Greenberg	[SXA4007]

Decca Brunswick AXA series

After AXTL1099 the numbering changes to a new series AXA45xx, but each of these has a stereo equivalent, SXA45xx, with the exception of the small number that follow, which were issued in mono only.

AXA4502	Vivaldi: Concertos	VdiR	Fasano
AXA4504	Recital (Couperin, Haydn, Ponce, Torróba, Aguirre, etc)		Segovia (guitar)
AXA4505	Vivaldi: Concertos	VdiR	Fasano
AXA4507	Concert (Moór, Bartok, Vivaldi, Jongen)	NY Philharmonic Cello Quartet	
AXA4508	Recital for 2 Pianos (Chopin, Schubert, Liszt, Milhaud)	Vronsky	Babin
AXA4512	Recital (Sor, Ponce, Albeniz, Granados, etc)		Segovia (guitar)
AXA4519	Recital (Chopin, Debussy, Liszt)		Novaes (piano)

Decca Brunswick AXL series

A series of 10" LPs introduced Jan 1953 and completed by 1955.

AXL2001	Hindemith: The 4 Temperaments	ZIM	Foss (piano)
AXL2002	Mozart: Clarinet Concerto K622	ZIM	Kell
AXL2003	Beethoven: Romances op 40, op 50	Little Orch Society Scherman	Fuchs (violin)
AXL2004	Beethoven: Serenade op 8	J Fuchs	L Fuchs Rose (cello)
AXL2005	Hindemith: Kammermusik op 24, Stravinsky: Suites 1, 2	Little Orch Society Scherman	
AXL2006	Copland: Our Town, V Thomson: Plow That Broke the Plains	Little Orch Society Scherman	
AXL2007	Italian Art Songs	de Luca (bar) Cimara (piano)	
AXL2008	Dohnanyi: Suite in F#min op 19	LAPO	Wallenstein
AXL2009	V Thomson: 10 Etudes for Piano		Schapiro (piano)
AXL2010	Tchaikovsky: Favourites	Camerata and Orch J Fuchs (violin)	
AXL2011	Brahms: Trio for clarinet, cello, piano op 114	Kell	Miller Horszowski
AXL2012	Tchaikovsky: Waltzes	LAPO	Wallenstein
AXL2014	Offenbach: Overtures	LAPO	Wallenstein
AXL2015	Foote: Night Piece for Flute and String Quartet, Griffes: Poem for Flute and Orchestra	Chamber Orch Saidenberg Baker (flute)	
AXL2016	Concert of Light Classical Music	Camerata and Orch Kell (clarinet)	
AXL2017	Violin Recital (Dvorak, Ravel, Benjamin, Godowsky, etc)	Heifetz	Kaye (piano)

Ace of Diamonds Grand Opera Series (GOM)

Decca introduced this series in 1966 with the prefixes GOM (mono) and GOS (stereo). They are reissues of complete operas originally issued mainly on the LXT and SXL labels.

Label: The label is identical with the Ace of Diamonds label, i.e. white with black lettering, but with the legend "Grand Opera Series" in the upper half.

The mono and stereo issues had identical numbers but with the appropriate prefix. Most of the earlier numbered sets were issued only in mono, and the later ones only in stereo. In many cases mono and stereo versions were issued simultaneously.

This handbook lists those sets which were issued only in mono (GOM). The companion stereo handbook lists those sets that were issued in stereo (GOS). The majority of the mono issues were deleted from August 1971, though a few survived into the 1980s.

GOM504-8	Wagner: Parsifal	Bayreuth	Knappertsbusch	[LXT2651-6]
GOM512-5	Strauss,R: Der Rosenkavalier	VPO	Kleiber	[LXT2954-7]
GOM516-8	Verdi: Aida	AdSC	Erede	[LXT2735-7]
GOM519-21	Verdi: Rigoletto	AdSC	Erede	[LXT5006-8]
GOM522-4	Verdi: La Traviata	AdSC	Molinari-Pradelli	[LXT2992-4]
GOM528-30	Puccini: Madama Butterfly	AdSC	Erede	[LXT2638-40]
GOM531-2	Puccini: La Boheme	AdSC	Erede	[LXT2622-3]
GOM533-4	Puccini: Tosca	AdSC	Erede	[LXT2730-1]
GOM535-9	Wagner: The Mastersingers	VPO	Knappertsbusch	[LXT2659-64]
GOM546-8	Debussy: Pelleas and Melisande	OSR	Ansermet	[LXT2711-4]
GOM549-50	Strauss,R: Salome	VPO	Krauss	[LXT2863-4]
GOM560-1	Britten: Turn of the Screw	English Opera Group	Britten	[LXT5038-9]
GOM579-80	Wagner: Gotterdammerung (hlts)	Norwegian	Fjeldstad	[LXT5205-10]

Lyrita

The List: This list is believed to be complete for all mono Lyritas.

The Lyrita 'Recorded Edition' was launched by Richard Itter in October 1959. With one single exception the recordings concentrated on British music, most of which had never previously been recorded.

Label: The mono label has the same appearance as the stereo label but is green rather than blue.

RCS 1	Number not used		
RCS 2	Jacob: Piano Sonata, Div fpr Solo Cello, Elegy for Cello & Piano	Hooton (cello)	Loveridge/Parry (piano)
RCS 3	Moeran: Piano Music		Loveridge
RCS 4			
RCS 5	Tippett: Piano Sonata, Hamilton: Piano Sonata op 13		Kitchin
RCS 6	Bax: Legend – Sonata, Sonatina in Dmaj	Hooton (cello)	Parry (piano)
RCS 7	Bax: Cello Sonata in Eflat min: Folk Tale	Hooton (cello)	Parry (piano)
RCS 8			
RCS 9	Berkeley: Piano Sonata op 20, 6 Preludes op 23, Concert Studies, etc		Horsley
RCS 10	Bax: Piano Sonata 1, A Hill Tune, Water Music, etc		Loveridge
RCS 11	Bax: Piano Sonata 2, Dream in Exile, Paean, etc		Loveridge
RCS 12	Bax: Piano Sonata 3, Winter Waters, etc		Loveridge
RCS 13	Wordsworth: Piano Sonata op 13, Ballade op 41, Cheesecombe St op 27		Kitchin
RCS 14			
RCS 15	Ireland: Piano Music (London Pieces, Greenways Suite, Sonattina, etc)		Rowlands
RCS 16	Alwyn: Piano Music (Fantasy Waltzes 1-11, Sonata alla Toccata		Randall
RCS 17	Bowen: Piano Music (10 Preludes from op 102, Partita op 157, etc)		Bowen
RCS 18	White: Piano Music (Sonatas 1, 4, 5, 9)		Kingsley
RCS 19	Reizenstein: Piano Music (Sonata op 19, Legend op 24)		Reizenstein
RCS 20	Benjamin: Piano Music (Pastorale, Arioso & Finale, Scherzino, Siciliana, etc)		Crowson
RCS 21			
RCS 22	Recital of Brazilian Piano Music (Villa-Lobos, etc)		Powell
RCS 23	Ireland: Piano Music (Sarnia, For Remembrance, Ballade, Aubade, etc)		Rowlands
RCS 24	Ireland: Piano Music (Piano Sonata, Towing Path, Rhapsody, etc)		Rowlands
RCS 25			
RCS 26	Bax: Piano Sonata 4, A Romance, Burlesque, Gopak, etc		Loveridge
RCS 27	Hoddinott: Piano Music (Piano Sonatas 1, 2, etc)		Tryon
RCS 28	Ireland: Piano Music (Decorations, 2 Pieces, Preludes, Summer Evening, etc)		Rowlands
RCS 29	Ireland: Piano Music (Columbine, Sea Idyll, Merry Andrew, etc)		Rowlands

For further copies of this book and of its companion "Audiophile Record Collector's Handbook" please go to:

www.cranmorepublications.co.uk

www.ingramcontent.com/pod-product-compliance
Lightning Source LLC
LaVergne TN
LVHW061342060426
835512LV00016B/2634

9781907962592